PN Review 230

VOLUME 42: NUMBER 6

Editorial

THE ARTS COUNCIL has a new website. It urges clients to 'Tell your story! Spread the word on Twitter – because #culturematters.' On 1 June a sad story, not website fodder, reached its climax. The Poetry Book Society, established as a book club in 1953 by T. S. Eliot and colleagues to 'propagate the art of poetry' by supporting readers and encouraging the sale of poetry books, went into liquidation. Literature, always the poor cousin when it comes to funding, is poorer for the loss. How is it that more than six decades of important work for poetry can be allowed to fail, in an age lavish in various forms of public subsidy for the ever-broader category of activities described as *the arts*?

In recent times the Poetry Book Society published a quarterly Bulletin, made selections and recommendations of new books of poetry, pamphlets and translation, spearheaded the Next Generation initiatives, and administered the annual T. S. Eliot Poetry Prize. It lost Arts Council funding in 2011, occasioning protests and a letter of support signed by a hundred poets. The poet laureate described the cut as 'disgraceful'. That same year Faber and Faber secured public funding to publish poetry. A former Faber director, Desmond Clarke, also a former chair of the board at the Poetry Book Society, remarked: 'As a commercially profitable publisher, Faber is more than capable of investing in a small number of poets each year. The reality is that Faber has made enormous amounts of money by publishing poetry, and out of the royalties of Cats which has provided it with many millions over the years.'

The Arts Council found ways of assisting the Poetry Book Society without restoring regular funding, and the operation, with aid from individual benefactors, survived, its pulse slowing, for a further five years.

The announcement of its closure was up-beat. The T. S. Eliot Foundation will assume responsibility for the T. S. Eliot Poetry Prize, and Inpress will take over the book club functions (including the Bulletin) with transitional funding. Inpress is a not-for-profit organization set up in 2002 with Arts Council support to help sell and market the products of small and medium-sized independent poetry and literary publishers.

The Poetry Book Society, underfunded and vocational like most significant operations in the poetry world, achieved important cultural results with three dedicated employees. The benefits it brought to poetry were considerable. It had authority, a history and cultural clout, things that do not appear on balance sheets or tick the key indicator boxes in application forms. All the same, book and pamphlet publishers will miss it; poets and readers will miss it.

Twenty years ago, the *PN Review* 111 'Editorial' memorialized the magazine's destructive scrape with history:

On 15 June the Corn Exchange from which *PN Review* has been edited for a quarter of a century sustained severe bomb damage. No one seems clear, even now, how severe that damage is. Like other buildings in the heart of Manchester ours was sealed off. Writing now, a month and a half after that Saturday, we have been given only the briefest access to our premises. In a half hour's supervised visit, wearing hard hats and sturdy shoes and wading through rubble and a century's pigeon-droppings, we recovered a bagful of records.

Though in due course we will recover other materials, much is lost: contributors' submissions, records, review books, the main stock of back issues of the magazine, and our only complete run of *PN Review* and *Poetry Nation*. Although *PNR* 110 appeared very nearly on time, and a week after the blast we were beginning to deal with editorial and production matters once more, the events inevitably affect our programme and plans.

Poets submitting work can get used to the geological editorial pace of certain journals. In this case,

Some correspondents, contributors and would-be contributors will wait in vain for a reply from us: their letters and submissions lie buried. Rain falls through the broken roof and blows in where windows and outer wall were. Pigeons who used to look in at us now nest among the papers and look out. We'd planned changes in the magazine, but nothing quite so radical as this.

We reflected on the then continuing uncertainty of the situation: what *had* happened, and what *would* happen. 'There is, too, anger at the perpetrators,' the editorial said, 'and anger that the dislocation is so soon forgotten. This is not Canary Wharf – nor Belfast; just the English provinces, and the North West at that. After a couple of weeks of waiting, of gathering true and false information, most of us began reluctantly to realise that the Corn Exchange was over. A chapter had closed in brutal uncertainty. The quest for permanent accommodation began. And this is perhaps the most troubling step: projecting a future, starting again with so much that once provided the dynamic of growth and change out of reach in the ruins.' The bombers, incidentally, were never found, though their identities are said to be known.

To end the editorial, a happier note was found. It is heartening to remember some elements of aftermath. After all, 'there is the wider fabric of any venture of this sort: writers, readers, subscribers and supporters – the Arts Council, the City Council, one's proprietor, the Rylands Library, the Department of English at the University, the students who work with us, our competitors (Bloodaxe in particular, who took up a collection on our behalf), and our well-wishers. That is the unrendable fabric, the true ground of an enterprise such as this.'

When, later that year at the Frankfurt Book Fair, I saw Gerry Adams with his army of publicists and body-guards striding by our modest stand to the launch of his latest book, *Before the Dawn: An Autobiography*, my positive feelings abated. 'My overwhelming personal political priority for some years,' his 'Foreword', written in February of 1996, begins, 'has been to advance the peace strategy of Sinn Féin, the party I am proud to represent.'

News & Notes

Professor Citizen

At the end of May, Claudia Rankine was elevated to the post of Frederick Iseman Professor of Poetry at Yale. Her duties there commence in the autumn. Before the multi-award-winning *Citizen: an American Lyric* her poetry collections include *Don't Let Me Be Lonely: An American Lyric* (2004) – that 'American Lyric' epithet again! – and *Nothing in Nature is Private* (1994). Langdon Hammer, chair of the Department of English at Yale, said, 'She has helped Americans think about race and identity in productively fresh, pointed, complex, and disorienting ways. She is also an innovative, intellectually challenging teacher, involved not only in poetry but in film, theater, and visual art...'

Professor Ireland

On 3 June Irish president Michael D. Higgins announced that Eiléan Ní Chuilleanáin is the new Ireland Professor of Poetry, following in the wake of Paula Meehan in the three-year term. Starting in October, the Cork-born poet will be the seventh Ireland Professor, a post set up in 1998 after Seamus Heaney was awarded the Nobel Prize for Literature 'to honour other Irish poets'. The *Irish Times* in a warm citation said, 'She moves at ease between Irish and European landscapes, between the material and the spiritual realms, unifying them by the force of her compelling imagination.' She helped found and edit *Cyphers*. She received the Patrick Kavanagh Award for *Acts and Monuments* (1966). Later books include *The Girl Who Married a Reindeer* (2001); *Selected Poems* (2009); and *The Sun-fish* (2010), which won the International Griffin Poetry Prize. Her most recent book is *The Boys of Bluehill* (2015). She is an Emeritus Fellow of Trinity College Dublin where she taught from 1966 until her retirement as Professor of English in 2011.

Previous Professors are John Montague, Nuala Ni Dhomhnaill, Paul Durcan, Michael Longley and Harry Clifton.

Pulitzer 2016

This year's Pulitzer Prize for poetry was awarded to the Armenian-American Peter Balakian for *Ozone Journal* (University of Chicago Press): 'Poems that bear witness to the old losses and tragedies that undergird a global age of danger and uncertainty,' says the citation. The title poem, a sequence, is built out of the experience of excavating the bones of Armenian genocide victims in the Syrian desert in 2008, with a crew of television journalists. The poem's speaker – close to the voice of Balakian's own experience – moves between personal and historical memory. Balakian is a Professor of Humanities at Colgate University where he heads the creative writing programme. Shortlisted with *Ozone Journal* were *Alive: New and Selected Poems* by Elizabeth Willis (NYRB) and *Four-Legged Girl* by Diane Seuss (Graywolf Press).

Trying to Un-White-Out

On 11 May the Ruth Lily Poetry Prize was awarded by the Poetry Foundation to Ed Roberson for 'outstanding lifetime achievement'. Commenting on the $100,000 prize, Don Share, editor of *Poetry*, declared: 'In both language and in life (his studies have taken him to Alaska, South America, Africa and Bermuda), Ed Roberson is an explorer. Working at a healthy remove from the precincts of professional critics and tastemakers, but admired deeply by them, Roberson's ten books of poetry take readers, as they have taken the poet himself, to every corner of the vivid labyrinth of life.' Michael Palmer has called Roberson 'one of the most deeply innovative and critically acute voices of our time'. He is a writer unsettling the language. 'Words and phrases in [his] experimental poetry actively resist parsing, using instead what Mackey has called "double-jointed syntax" to explore and bend themes of race, history, and culture. "I'm not creating a new language. I'm just trying to un-White-Out the one we've got," said Roberson in a 2006 interview with *Chicago Postmodern Poetry*.'

'At Least 50% of My Body Is Made of Books'

La voz de Galicia reported on 24 May the death of 'a fundamental figure in revitalizing Galician poetry, publisher of the first book of poems in Galician after the Spanish Civil War, Sabino Torres Ferrer.' He 'was half-composed of books' not only as an editor (though he was active in this field) but also as a journalist, a writer and, of course, a reader. Born in 1924 in Pontevedra, he died aged ninety-two in Madrid, having edited the work of major Galician poets, many of them active in resistance to Franco. His first major publication was distributed without the permission of the censors in 1949. He repeated the deed some years later, though the second time the edition was confiscated and he was heavily fined. Like Whitman, he was a man who wore his hat as he pleased, indoors or out.

Dreaming on aTrain

Michael S. Harper, described by the *New York Times* (10 May) as a 'poet with a jazz pulse', has died at the age of seventy-eight. Well loved as a writer and teacher, he was innovative in the sounds his poems made (his first book, in 1970, was entitled *Dear John, Dear Coltrane*) and thematically inventive, another heir of Whitman with an open sense of personal and Black history, but with elements shared between the American races. 'My poems are rhythmic rather than metric,' he wrote, 'the pulse is jazz; the tradition generally oral; my major influences musical; my debts, mostly to the musicians who taught me to see about experience, pain and love, and who made it artful and archetypal.' History is key to his imagination and to the embrace of his poetry: *History is Your Own Heartbeat* (1971) was the title of his second book. His use of notable lives and his sense of kinship proved useful to other writers. It is no surprise to learn that one of his teachers was Christopher Isherwood. He was a professor of literature at Brown University and in 2008 received the Frost Medal for Lifetime Achievement. In 2002 Arc published his poems in Britain. His poem 'Here Where Coltrane Is' ends,

Dreaming on a train from New York
to Philly, you hand out six
notes which become an anthem
to our memories of you:
oak, birch, maple,
apple, cocoa, rubber.
For this reason Martin is dead;
for this reason Malcolm is dead;
for this reason Coltrane is dead;
in the eyes of my first son are the browns
of these men and their music.

'What Moves Me Is Ironies'

Aged ninety-four, Daniel Berrigan, the legendary Jesuit priest, peace activist, poet and teacher, has died. He will be remembered for his active resistance to the wars in Indo China and for his always public witness, most notably as one of the celebrated or notorious (depending on one's point of view) Catonsville Nine, who used napalm to destroy draft files in 1968, issuing a statement: 'We confront the Roman Catholic Church, other Christian bodies, and the synagogues of America with their silence and cowardice in the face of our country's crimes. We are convinced that the religious bureaucracy in this country is racist, is an accomplice in this war, and is hostile to the poor.' Later protests garnered publicity and prison sentences and had consequences for the American conscience. His poems live in their

historical moments. 'Time in its turning/lipped the clay lightly, taught it words/remembered for gentleness when a face recedes/to its stone image in an honored place.'

Janet Fisher: An Old Friend

Janet Fisher died on 11 April. She had been long active in the world of poetry, for the last twenty years in Huddersfield. She wrote four books of poems and was a co-founder of The Poetry Business. Her Quaker funeral was conducted at the burial ground at High Flatts Meeting House, near Birdsedge. It was followed by a commemoration of Janet's life. It would have been nice if her poem 'Canon' (*PN Review* 171, 2006) had suggested the music for the event.

A Brief Resurrection

General Pinochet has not been cleared of the murder, by poison, of the Chilean Nobel Prize-winning poet Pablo Neruda in 1973. But the poet, exhumed, examined over a period of three years, and now reburied at his former home in Isla Negra, facing the Pacific (as most of Chile does) could provide no proof of guilt. The mystery will persist.

Drift

In *PNR* 229 Rowland Bagnall's poem 'Drift' was headed with an unattributed epigraph. The lines are from David Morley's poem 'Skeleton Bride': 'This happened to me and it didn't happen to me / or I spied it when I only heard it or found it / when it was given me through a greater grief.'

Letters

DEAR SIR,

In 'Charles Tomlinson at Bristol' (*PN Review* 229) C. K. Stead initiates one of the 'critical conversations poetry constantly requires those of us who are serious about it to have'. The one he introduces here concerns the poetry (and personality) of Charles Tomlinson (1927–2015). Essentially, according to Stead's memoir, when the two knew each other in the late fifties, he found Tomlinson's poetry problematic. Even today, while admitting their difference in temperament and conceding some talent to Tomlinson, Stead continues to 'run up against what seems to me a wall of abstraction and effete discourse'.

The primary reason I disagree with Stead's judgment is that where he sees effeteness, I see vitality.

The difference may be one of focus. Mine is not on Tomlinson as an explorer of abstract ideas, but on his persuasive rendition of the beauty and perils in nature (especially of landscape and the spirit of place). To me, Tomlinson is the poet of 'the commonplace miraculous' – as he calls it 'Bread and Stone' – and the implicit tragedy lies in our all-devouring urban sprawl:

It was a language of water, light and air
   I sought – to speak myself free of a world
Whose stoic lethargy seemed the one reply
   To horizons and to streets that blocked them back
In a monotone fume, a bloom of grey.
                                              'The Marl Pits'

At the time Stead knew Tomlinson he felt, in the latter's poetry, 'a kind of *dis*engagment' in the lines 'as if the words had been chosen with immense care, but with a faint feeling of distaste'. So Tomlinson's *Seeing is Believing* (1958), for example, displayed for Stead 'a sharp visual perception driving a keen intelligence' but was 'a little precious, a little gutless'. I question that. To me the poems have vigour. Any weakness is, in fact, the necessary consequence of the poet's enormous ambition. As Tomlinson explains in 'Winter Encounters' our confrontations with nature:

though of moment in themselves,
Serve rather to articulate the sense
    That having met one meets with more
Than the words can witness.

The senses are the source of the collection's vitality, satisfying in any number of images where observation has a surreal, often humorous cast. In 'Oxen: Ploughing at Fiesole' the animals are hardly burdened by their 'matchwood yoke' which looks like 'The debris of captivity / Still clinging there' from a fresh escape. 'The Mediterranean' describes a 'country of grapes / Where the architecture / Plays musical interludes'. So Tomlinson writes of the wine stopper in 'Variant on a Scrap of Conversation': 'Its head (cut into facets) / An eye for the cubist.' Or in 'Civilities of Lamplight' where a man walks the darkness while his light 'Hollows the hedge-bound track, a sealed / Furrow on dark, closing behind him.'

Again and again Tomlinson arrests the fluidity of seeing momentarily, his poems light-filled, like the artists he loves and learns from, Vermeer for instance:

White earthenware,
A salver, stippled at its lip by light,
    The light itself, diffused and indiscriminate
On face and floor, usher us in,
    The guests of objects

'At Delft'

I take these examples from the early part of this painterly collection and yet already, as reader, I have been amply rewarded. Tomlinson rarely intrudes. This is not to everyone's taste, but it was to his American masters. The clarity of his phrasing, his imaginative skills and observational detail remind one of Tomlinson's acknowledged masters: Pound, Stevens and Moore. Their influence in his poetics matches his tendency to mute 'the gust of personality'. As he recounts in *Some Americans: A Personal Record* (1981) a consideration of the example of Poe and Hart Crane drew him toward his 'own basic theme':

one does not need to go beyond sense experience to some mythic union, that the 'I' can only be responsible in relationship and not by dissolving itself away into ecstasy or the Oversoul.

Despite his fidelity to American models, Tomlinson explained in *Some Americans*, 'if through them the tonality sounded American, the tradition of the work went back to Coleridge's conversation poems'. Nevertheless America recognised him at a time when England did not. William Carlos Williams'

'measure' became another influence, translated into the idiom of Queen's English, and the poetry of George Oppen and Louis Zukovsky.

Tomlinson's vision was remarkably consistent over fifty years, though his stance was not always that of the effaced observer. Camaraderie, conversation and the glow of history are also characteristic. 'The Return', for instance – for me Charles Tomlinson's finest verse letter, a form he handled superbly – is an elegy for the wife of an old friend and fellow poet. In the poem, the two men take the roads of thirty years before and remember the conversations the three of them had, as well as other voices from those hills, for 'We cannot climb these slopes without our dead.'

To me Tomlinson's 'engagement' stems from his self-appointed mission, romantically expressed in the poem 'In a Cambridge Garden' (which takes the form of a second conversation with Octavio Paz):

I thought
That I could teach my countrymen to see
    The changing English light, like water
That drips off a gunwhale driving through the sea,
    Showing the way the whole world
Dipping through space and cloud and sun,
    Surges across the day as it travels on
Turning.

Unlike C. K. Stead, I never met Charles Tomlinson and would not question the account of Tomlinson's off-putting manner in 1957, his 'depleted energy' that might be illness or affectation, but I can record that I did correspond with the poet on three occasions in his last few years and, despite his increasing blindness, found him full of energy and encouragement. As for evaluating the worth of the poetry, 'there are no right answers, no final solutions', C. K. Stead reminds us. Of course he is right about that – thank goodness.

TONY ROBERTS

DEAR SIR,

There appears to be a curious mistake in Claire Crowther's otherwise excellent article on syllabics: three seconds to pronounce a syllable? More like 0.3 of a second. Thirty seconds to pronounce a ten-syllable line? More like three seconds.

ANTHONY RUDOLF

Thanks, Anthony Rudolph, you are right. The decimal point slipped. I am thus outed as a near-innumerate and it is curious, as you say, because why would such as I chain myself to a strictly number-controlled line? Another argument for the perversity of syllabics, perhaps?

CLAIRE CROWTHER

Out of Bounds

VAHNI CAPILDEO

THE ANTONINE WALL, built in the second century on the orders of the Emperor Antoninus Pius, stretched from the Forth to the Clyde in Scotland. Much of the construction was turf. The defensive capacity was therefore different from a wall like Hadrian's. Still, it must have been at the least an interruption for locals to encounter the Antonine life in full swing, even when or if there were no active hostilities. Oiled Romans might have been scraping themselves with strigils. Others might have been gambling; yet others soaking, chilling or steaming under the eyes of a curvaceous stone Fortuna. What would the person surprised by them – herder, laundress, domestic traveller following one of those lightly landmarked, muscle-remembered paths which do not require built lines and look like nothing to people who do not walk them, so do not know them – have noticed first? The interruption of the view? The light winking from the mica in sandstone? The noise?

The babble would have been a not entirely Latinate Babel. The Romans who worked at the Wall were a varied lot; archers, horsemen, consumers who were an attractive market for skilled workers and foreign traders; connected to Thuringia, Scythia, Arabia. They left behind a great many North African cooking vessels. In the Hunterian Museum, you can see a seal of the kind likely to have been used by a high-ranking man on his letters home; where was that home? Where were these 'Romans' from? How much of the Romano-Celtic design on stone and other items indicated forced labour, how much artistic exchange or human fusion? It became possible to see the Wall as a boundary as well as a limit; an imposition leading to creation, not just conflict; a place of mixing at every level.

When the *Out of Bounds* team contacted me about becoming their first 'poet on tour' (a position now held by Kayo Chingonyi), I knew that an Antonine Wall site would have to be on any project map I had a hand in. The concept of *Out of Bounds* had become known to me in its early instantiation as an anthology from Bloodaxe, edited by Jackie Kay, James Procter, and Gemma Robinson. The anthology's byline, 'British Black & Asian Poets', somewhat belied the contents, as did the back cover's promise of an 'alternative A to Z of the nation'. The wonderful Introduction, while not denying the realities of 'alienation, unbelonging and dislocation', refuses the kind of loss that becomes a litany. The scores of poems included here do not sing a blueprint blues. Rather, they evidence 'rich and manifold attachments to place, region, city and landscape'. The editors admit that they are discontented with imposing a collective 'Black and Asian' identity except in so far as this gives a force to questioning the 'easy and singular'.

To compile is not to freeze or canonise. The editors present the anthology's contents as on the move, a 'transnational trek' between Scotland, England, Wales, global communities and empire. Compass points and large regions provide one ordering mechanism.

However, this is happily complicated again, like marked but unnamed footpaths on an Ordnance Survey map: poets have drawn their inspiration from, in and against a range of places, featuring for example both in 'Scotland' and in 'South' sections. Like the body language of Shakespeare's Cressida, who spoke even with her foot, all the elements of the peritext are eloquent. The biographies at the back of the book dazzle with filaments of connexion that do not necessarily register directly in the poetic texts on offer, but are part of the texture of the *Out of Bounds* project, the poetic re-imagination of place. There are gems such as the precise botanical detail of blazing montbretia in a poem by Maggie Harris (Guyanese, with ties to Kent) daydreaming in her Welsh garden about a past visit to Ireland. What shines here is the freedom of memory and imagination to dance together, in expansive and tiny movements too often distrusted or misunderstood by those who prefer their poems nailed down in anecdote and identity-card form.

The 2015–16, AHRC-funded phase of *Out of Bounds* consists of a series of events across the British Isles, programmed by the poets on tour; workshops with six schools in Scotland and the North of England; and an active online presence, including the @OoBPoetry Twitter feed. Sound recordings will be archived by the British Library. Project partners include the Scottish Poetry Library, Bloodaxe Books, and Cultureword (Manchester). Material generated from these activities and happenings – some public, some experimental or ephemeral – will inform new digital tools, including a literal clickable 'poetic map' of Britain.

When speaking as 'the Out of Bounds poet', it was interesting to find who did and didn't 'get it'. A woman with whom I had points in common – a chance meeting in an airport, a chance trip into different parts of the same tropical forest – reached for the adjective 'controversial' on hearing my starry-eyed spiel about place poetry most naturally registering diversity, transitions and new psychogeographic loves. Someone else decided that the project was about promoting non-white poets, and that there was no point hosting us in areas where there were few people from 'that demographic' – apparently there was nothing culturally relatable or transferable in the meetings and makings of wanderers, which somewhat contradicts one traditional role found cross-culturally allotted to wordsmiths.

In the lead-up to the Antonine Wall event which I had programmed at the remains of the bath-house in Bearsden, near Glasgow, I began to doubt myself. Did I like this imperial construction so much because the cookware and some inscriptions suggested that black people might have been here, too? Was I falling into the way of wanting to make claims based on skin colour and length of time? Arriving with the digital guy, one of the anthology editors, and the Glasgow-Zimbabwean poet Tawona Sithole, to find poet Sally Evans of the excellent Kings Bookshop

Callander sitting and chatting on the quartz-studded gravel with a younger writer who describes herself as from a part of Scotland 'where the planes don't fly', a great sense of simplicity brought peace to me.

Now was curious about then, here invited elsewhere, no two accents or sets of languages the same: the discontinuities were the continuity, and for one non-escapist interval, there was something to make.

Letter from Wales

Sam Adams

As part of its quatercentenary salute to Shakespeare, the National Museum of Wales in Cardiff invited Michael Bogdanov to speak on 'The Welsh in Shakespeare'. His visit drew a large audience to the museum's Reardon Smith Lecture Theatre, attracted by his fame as a multi-award-winning theatre director and his subject. His list of credits for theatre productions – plays, opera, musicals, and in film and television, is of such staggering length, and in so many venues worldwide, you marvel at his creative energy and how he finds time to sleep. With a lot of experience in various media behind him, mostly in Ireland, where he had graduated from Trinity College, Dublin, he joined the RSC in 1970 as assistant director on a production that transformed the presentation of Shakespeare on stage, Peter Brook's *A Midsummer Night's Dream*. (I saw it on tour at the New Theatre, Cardiff, and it remains the most exciting, most memorable, theatrical experience of my life.) He has been a disciple of Brook, dedicating himself, he says, to making Shakespeare politically relevant to people today, and viewing each directorial challenge as 'like reading a detective story, piecing clues together, never taking anything for granted, ignoring received opinion'.

Throughout his international career Michael Bogdanov has maintained a connection with Wales, including a lengthy commitment, 2003–2009, as artistic director of the Wales Theatre Company, which had its home in Swansea. The location was a fitting choice for one born just down the road in Neath, to a Welsh mother and a Jewish father whose own boyhood was spent in pre-Revolutionary Russia. And here he was on another visit, picking up the trail and following the clues to the Welsh in Shakespeare, at a brisk pace that pressed the audience to an eager canter to keep up.

It comes as a surprise to learn that some of our neighbours over the Dyke think the Tudors were English. They were of course Welsh, Henry VII being the grandson of Owain ap Maredudd ap Tudur of Penmynydd, Anglesey, who was the second husband of Catherine de Valois, widow of Henry V. At his majority, Henry VI, Catherine's son by that earlier marriage, ensured that his stepfather and half-brothers, Edmund and Jasper, were afforded rank and protection. Edmund was married to Margaret Beaufort and their son, Henry, took the crown from Richard III. The Welsh who had supported him at Bosworth followed him to London. They found places in the law, at court and in parliament; hence, to be Welsh was not a handicap to the able and ambitious in the reign of Elizabeth I. The queen's greatly-esteemed Secretary of State and Lord Treasurer, William Cecil, Lord Burghley, took pains to establish his Welsh pedigree.

In Act IV of Beaumont and Fletcher's *The Pilgrim*, a 'Welsh Madman' enters calling, 'Give me some ceeze and onions, give me some wash-brew' and is dismissed as 'a mountaineer, a man of goatland'. Knowing of their influence at court, no matter what his feelings towards them were, Shakespeare was politically astute enough not to give offence gratuitously in his portrayal of the Welsh. (That the Chamberlain's men were accused of sympathy with the Essex faction, though they escaped censure or worse, demonstrates the hairsbreadth hazards of the time.) The evidence of the plays suggests an altogether warmer appreciation of the Welsh. He viewed them, as all men, with amusement perhaps for harmless foibles, but also with respect and even affection. It may have counted that he had a Welsh grandmother, Alys Griffin, but there were also fellow actors who, by their names, were Welsh – Augustine Phillips (a shareholder in the Globe), Robert Goughe and John Rice. Textual evidence supports the thesis. It is rare in Shakespeare that a nation speaks in its own language, but in *Henry IV Part 1*, a sequence of stage directions (frequently overlooked in modern productions) demands actors speak Welsh: 'Glendower speakes to her in Welsh, and she answeres him in the same'; 'The Lady speakes in Welsh'; The Lady speakes againe in Welsh'; 'Heere the Lady sings a Welsh song'. They tell us that the company also had a Welsh-speaking boy actor.

At the grammar school in Stratford, Shakespeare probably had a teacher of Latin from Wales, Thomas Jenkins, who may well have been the prototype of Sir (not of the knightly sort) Hugh Evans in *The Merry Wives of Windsor*. A good deal of support is given to the suggestion that Fluellen in *Henry V*, the most expansive and memorable of Shakespeare's Welsh, is modelled on Sir Roger Williams, from Penrhos in Monmouthshire, 'an obstreperous and opinionated' warrior in the Protestant cause and expert in the conduct of warfare. Their tricks of speech, in the pronunciation of English words, or the use of a noun for verb or adjective ('can you affection the 'oman?', as Sir Hugh asks), and stock phrases, such as Fluellen's 'look you' were incorporated into the repertoire of comic stage Welsh and may linger still in vulgar performance. But Shakespeare is not laughing at his characters, to whom he gave humanity and even just a hint of noble virtue along with un-English eccentricity. In *Henry V*, the king sets his seal on this amalgam in addressing Fluellen: 'For I am Welsh, you know, good countryman.' Glendower's brand of high-flown magic realism, in *Henry IV Part 1*, is pitted against the threatening, plain bluntness of Hotspur, and it is the latter who retracts his truculence.

And then there are the plays set in a British past, *King Lear* and, particularly, *Cymbeline*, in which scenes are set in Wales, and more specifically, the great natural harbour of Milford Haven. Had Shakespeare ever been there? Had he even once visited Wales? It seems unlikely, but he had read his histories and had a circle of Welsh acquaintance ever ready to supply local colour. In any case, it is all one, he might have said, for there is no England in *Cymbeline*; Rome, yes, but no England. The 'Great Britain' project was just beginning. To Shakespeare and his contemporaries Britain and British meant Wales and the Welsh language. All this is pretty well known. A splendid book, referenced by Michael Bogdanov, *Shakespeare and the Welsh* by Frederick J. Harries, first published in 1919, is an exhaustive study of the subject, and though fresh nuances have emerged from close textual study, little that is new has been added to it since.

John Crichton Stuart, third Marquess of Bute, 1847–1900, who in a sixteen-year-long partnership with the architect William Burges continued his family's restoration of Cardiff Castle and created Castell Coch, the Victorian gothic masterpiece overlooking the Taff gorge, gave to the people of Cardiff Bute Park and Sophia Gardens, and Cathays Park, where broad avenues are lined with grand Edwardian civic buildings – including the National Museum. Such munificence! – albeit from a man at the very top of the Victorian 'rich list' with an income said to have been £300,000 a year. It seems churlish to regret on this Shakespearean occasion that he did not also give the city the recently authenticated First Folio from his library at Mount Stuart House on the Isle of Bute.

From the Journals of R. F. Langley

THE POET R. F. LANGLEY (1938–2011) was also, privately, a prolific prose writer. Extracts from his journals, which he began in 1969, first appeared in *PN Review* in 2002. The notes to Langley's *Complete Poems*, edited by Jeremy Noel-Tod, cite a number of unpublished journal entries that directly informed the writing of his verse.

August 1981, Westhall, Bohun aisle

No-one comes. Tractor noises make a continuous background, and a cock crows. Children speak in the hidden garden to the south. Sparrows chirp. By sitting still and unfocusing the eyes the whole space somehow speaks out, rises, tautens, opens, accepts the third dimension, stops being a record in bits of things you know, and facts of definition or memory. The ranks of poppy heads move out into stiffness and root there; the two roofs link and spread over, the walls draw up and round. Corners meet. Each poppy head has a double ghost on the south wall, the two images overlapping in a darker central clot. No edges – a perfect blur. The row of eight along the white wall, absolutely still and soundless. Because I touched a hung lamp, to straighten its chimney, I suddenly realise how long their chains up to the roof are – how impossible to stop it moving, though I try. A quarter of an hour later, watching rigidly, I see it is still twisting and just moving, where one of its angled chains crosses the edge of a window embrasure, so the vertical division, from darker inner wall to brighter side of the window recess, is a vertical, close to the sloping chain – you see the long thin triangle of light grow way up, then shrink. So now the total immobility of the other six lamps amazes. The untouched. The long pull of constant gravity.

But, within this undisturbed hold – a shuffling. Beyond each window the sunny trees, billowing. Within, the blazing lights cast through panes onto plaster. Sheaved with fine cracks in multiple directions like crushed crystal, the print of old glass, set in the thick, angled, furry shadows of mullion bars; the leaves make shiftings, switch on or off the blobs of gold, or alter them swiftly. Over the north door, far brighter than the dried-out red stain of Christopher and the horned Moses, the brilliant little local flames flicker ferociously – noiseless frenzy. Below, in the grid of the beamed door, solid stillness. A bee hums somewhere for some time. A 1752 edition of Elizabethan sermons and the Thirty-nine Articles is left, with nineteenth-century Bible and Psalms, at the back. 'Keep the church sweet and clean.' Sweet in its filth, this one embodies the hush of immobility played into by the living golden-white tongues. I watch one poppy head with sun on its ear and shoulder. It rules the aisle, touched with a quality. Over a minute the light on its head goes smoothly out, young gold to old silver, wet to dry, shine to dust... then that on its shoulder, so that now it joins the others and space unifies in even clarity of secondary luminousness. Things detach themselves into simultaneity...

Letter from Beirut

Norbert Hirschhorn

IN THE FRONT GARDEN of the beautiful Sursock mansion, now housing an elegant Beirut art museum, stands a sandstone sculpture of two women: one veiled, one unveiled – Muslim and Christian. Mothers, perhaps widows, they are seated, arms extended but not touching, meeting over the space meant to represent an urn for human ashes. The work is by Lebanese artist Youssef el Howayek (1883–1962), who had been commissioned to create a monument commemorating the 1916 hanging of nearly three dozen Arabs, Muslim and Christian alike – intellectuals, journalists, and poets – seeking to be free of their ruthless Ottoman Turkish overlords.

The monument, unveiled in 1930, stood facing the sea in front of Beirut's mercantile and government districts, an area still known as 'Martyrs' Square'. Howayek meant as well to honour the unity of two Arab religions bonded in mutual grief. From the beginning, however, strident Lebanese nationalists called for its removal, describing the work as a 'servile and weeping monument'. And so in 1951 it was hidden away in the Sursock mansion, to be replaced by a newer work that 'neither weeps nor bows'. In 1960, the replacement in bronze was unveiled, sculpted by the Italian Marino Mazzacurati (1907–1969). It could stand in any country: a heroic ensemble of two wounded men looking up at a triumphant female figure carrying a torch, and guiding another male figure. Ironically, during the Lebanese Civil War (1975–1990), the statue was badly shot up and the standing man 'lost' his left arm. The fragments of the statue were uncovered in the debris of the war's destruction and reassembled. What it now commemorates is debatable: heroic men dying for their sectarian beliefs? Deaths of thousands of civilians caught up in a senseless, protracted war? Irony is in the eye of the beholder, but Mazzacurati's work certainly holds nothing of the tenderness of the Howayek piece, where reconciliation resides. Instead, as the Roman senator Tacitus (56–117) bitterly concluded, 'To plunder, butcher, steal, these things they misname empire; they make a desolation and they call it peace.'

The same warlords who prosecuted the fifteen-year Lebanese Civil War (120,000 deaths, 20,000 missing, countless traumas) now rule their various religious fiefdoms and have selfishly blocked all political, social and economic progress for over two years – no president elected, an unconstitutional parliament, a paralysed cabinet headed by an emasculated Prime Minister; and a powerful non-state armed force now fighting for the regime in Syria. For several months uncollected garbage piled up in the streets, the valleys and woods. Water and electricity are rationed in a land where neither should be scarce. Corruption, yes. When civil society protesters took to the downtown streets near Parliament and the Prime Minister's offices last year under the banner of the 'You Stink' movement, the security forces closed off large nearby sections home to upscale restaurants and shops that were built to demonstrate Lebanon's recovery from the Civil War. Many now display dusty 'for rent' signs. The struggling economy hasn't helped either as western nations and Arab Gulf states warn their citizens not to visit Lebanon. We find this peculiar as each Saturday morning in the same area we and hundreds of others enjoy shopping at the organic farmers' market.

Over eighty years ago the renowned Lebanese poet Kahlil Gibran warned presciently: 'Pity the nation that is full of beliefs and empty of religion. [...] Pity the nation whose statesman is a fox, whose philosopher is a juggler, and whose art is the art of patching and mimicking. [...] Pity the nation divided into fragments, each fragment deeming itself a nation.'

There is no war now in Lebanon, although the occasional car bomb and assassination remind us of its potential. In the region lies military mayhem: Syria, Yemen, Libya, Gaza, Iraq. The greatest number of refugees since World War II flee for safety; well over a million Syrians and Iraqis have come to Lebanon, nearly one-third of the native population. Syrian beggars, mainly women and small children, sit on sidewalks. If and when the wars end, someone will surely commission heroic statues.

Nevertheless, we live a good life, albeit in a privileged bubble. We have many dear friends, go out to concerts, plays and art galleries, browse bookshops, attend poetry readings, eat well at restaurants, walk along the sea-side corniche where traditionally-dressed people share space with young moderns, fishermen line the railings, while joggers and bicyclists manoeuvre around us. To the east we view the high mountain range that runs down the spine of the country – snow-covered in winter – and to the west, glorious sunsets. Fishing boats, swimmers, the patrolling German destroyer (UN-mandated after the 2006 Israeli war with Hezbollah), and container ships heading to the port, make up the panorama of lives going on normally.

We live in an old 1960s building near the campus of the American University of Beirut, one of the few green spaces in the whole city, but off limits to the general public. Our lane is called 'California Street'. From our north-facing balcony and rooms we have views of the Mediterranean Sea, broken by expensive high-rise condominiums in which few of their owners actually live. From the south we look over to the new Saudi Arabian embassy, a Jeddah-like cream-coloured tower decorated with wooden *mashrabiyya* window covers, with fountains and gardens behind thick walls, overseen by video cameras. The ambassador, staff and their families are housed there.

The lane is blockaded to traffic at both ends, and pedestrians are meant to walk along a narrow defile off the street. Security is provided by three different Lebanese armed forces: At one end is the army, a gaggle of young men often lounging, smoking, their rifles held loosely, smart-phones at the ready, and guarding a cannon-armed personnel carrier that would take some time to mobilise. At the other end is a special contingent of police in blue camouflage uniforms whom we call the 'blue meanies'. They grunt when greeted. Before our building entrance are the Interior Ministry's ISF, the Internal Security Force, in grey and white camouflage. Knowing the usual meaning of 'internal security' in this part of the world, you might think these would be the most frightening, but in fact they are the friendliest, responding to our regular greetings of the day. They address my wife as Professor and me as Uncle. One of the armed men brought me a jar of honey from his village in the south. One welcome benefit of the barricades and security is that we no longer fear SUVs coming at us in both

directions at top speed. A tribe of cats has proliferated.

Next to our building lies a twisted pomegranate tree, a remnant of an orchard that used to cover our lane and the condo building plots. It straggles up against a concrete wall, limbs misshapen, bearing a surprising number of fruits each summer. In front of one neighbouring high-rise are gardenia bushes from whose overhanging branches I pluck flowers each spring to bring as gifts to my wife.

I thank Professor Walid Sadek of the American University of Beirut for his insightful essay on the Sursock sculptures, 'Pensive Monument'.

Master of Two Worlds

Andrew Latimer

YOU CAN IMAGINE the anticipation: Hyam Plutzik, a thirty-year-old American-Belarusian farmhand, secretary, journalist and, most successfully, poet, licks the back of an envelope containing a seventy-two-page letter, which had taken him seven months to construct, in which he expounds upon the previous seven years of his life's experiences since leaving Yale in 'disgrace' – complete with poetic extracts, mystical fibrillations and a varied, if not a little deflating, curriculum vitae. And who was the addressee of this epistolary magnum opus? None other than his old Yale professor, Odell Shepard.

More than just any old university professor, Shepard was the type of professor that has in a way come to define the golden age of American academia of the 1940s and '50s – learnéd, without being overly scholarly, politically motivated (I mean a genuinely politically active citizen, not in the way that many university professors think of themselves as 'political' now) and first and foremost a teacher of first-class calibre. In fact, Plutzik described Shepard as 'one of the great teachers of our time [...] an upholder of dignity against system and mechanism'. Shepard won the Pulitzer Prize for Biography in 1938 for his *Pedlar's Progress: The Life of Bronson Alcott*.

And what was Shepard's reply to his long-estranged student's unexpected intrusion? A guarded two-page answer – never actually posted – full of the paternal restraint appropriate to a teacher not wishing to encourage his pupil further. Shepard's response is almost beautiful in its curtness and is the absolute antithesis of Plutzik's letter: the haiku to Plutzik's jeremiad. All of which begs the question, what on earth possessed Hyam Plutzik, on turning thirty – seven years out of college and during a time of international chaos – to write this seventy-two-page letter to an old teacher who remembered him dispassionately, if at all?

Guilt, would be my first suggestion. Woody Allen, reflecting on his own experience of 'Jewish guilt',

once joked: 'When we played softball, I'd steal second base, feel guilty and go back.' Plutzik, the son of Jewish immigrants from Belarus (who spoke only Yiddish, Hebrew and Russian until the age of seven), is clearly haunted by this kind of guilt, which I am told is different to Catholic guilt because, whereas the Catholic resigns himself to a form of eternal naughtiness, the Jew always feels that he should be doing better – or in the words of the Angeleno Rabbi Mordecai Finley, 'I just always feel like I'm fucking up absolutely everything.' Not unrelated to this notion of Jewish guilt, in Plutzik's letter there is a more pertinent streak of a guilt almost as terrifying and persuasive: academic guilt.

Intellectually curious and poetically accomplished (he won the Yale Poetry Award twice), Plutzik's approach to learning was more heuristic than ordinary academic practice allowed. He secured a scholarship from Trinity College only to leave Yale 'as meek as whipped dog', before finishing his studies – the president of Trinity referred to him as 'a disgrace'. Cast out onto the streets of New York as an idealistic but, ultimately, shy young man – 'If there is one outstanding element in my character it is that I am slow in making friends' – Plutzik winds up working for, amongst others, the *Brooklyn Eagle* – Walt Whitman's old haunt. But, as he finds out, much has changed since Whitman was there one hundred years before – the shock of the city overwhelms his delicate sensibility:

I love my fellow men to be sure – as individuals. But humanity *en masse* is a monstrous thing, particularly if it is pressed together so tightly that the individuals in it lose their human dignity. And to a poet such humanity is absolutely devastating.

One is reminded of a young Thom Eliot encountering 'the dead' of early twentieth-century London.

Throughout his metropolitan interregnum – for Plutzik is a pastoralist at heart – one is aware of his constant struggle with what was, and to some extent still is, an inevitability for the young and intellectually stimulated youth: the academic career. He is disgusted by it – 'I hated graduate work and thought it a waste of time'. But his disgust is all the more insidious because he knows that he is well suited to the career. Whenever he is engaged in the unacademic – loafing through New York, pretending to be a secretary, getting 'scoops' for low-brow publications – Plutzik's sense of guilt, sometimes an altogether more Calvinist-damnation version of it, is palpable:

as I wandered in the city, seeing the sordidness, the evil and the pain, there came to me the feeling that somehow we were astray [... that] this was some lost path, a shadowy street that moved farther and farther away from the light and from which one could not turn back. Was it our bestial ancestors?

'In New York,' hypothesises Plutzik, 'it is utterly impossible to talk oneself – with dignity.' And it is whilst in pursuit of such dignity that he eventually finds himself with 'a chance to get out into the sun and to exude some wholesome sweat', on a family-run farm in Cornwall, Connecticut.

Manual labour, perhaps unexpectedly, revives Plutzik's respect for, firstly, his fellow man and, consequently, books – 'I was discovering that books were not spectres at all, but friends; that, indeed, I was a bookman at heart.' At Purple Rim Farm, Plutzik kills a woodchuck that had been pestering the crops. The unexpected violence of this act grips him, leading to a metaphysical tremble, the kind that readers of Plutzik's poetry will be so familiar with, and which forms the stock for his first long poetic meditation 'Death at *The Purple Rim*' (1941):

And I heard in the tall grass an agonized threshing,
The groan of an articulate throat, the rattle
Of death that had come through my hand. And my breath
    shortened.

The editors of *Letter from a Young Poet* were wise to make the connection in their title between Plutzik's letter and the correspondence that took place much earlier between the young Franz Xaver Kappus and Rainer Maria Rilke, later entitled *Letters to a Young Poet* (1929). There is much common ground: Plutzik, like Kappus, is concerned about his direction in life, and the conversation in both takes place between an older, literary man and his 'apprentice'. But whereas in the Rilke-Kappus correspondence it is the elder, more experienced writer's letters that fascinate us, here it is the younger poet's thoughts and life experiences voiced almost in soliloquy that have us turning page after page as though it were a detective thriller.

And, in a sense, it is – a piece of detective writing. Everything is probed for evidence, every facet and each fat roll of life is checked. The unravelling of adolescent sensibilities, the sense of pride one gets from cashing a pay cheque, a literary analysis of *Hamlet* is inextricably bound up in Plutzik's metaphysical examination of life – his paranoid awareness – in a way that approaches the plot of a Borges, or even a Pynchon, fiction (although the effect of his writing is very different from either). Plutzik leaps beautifully from the mundane to the mystical:

The things most people take for granted I do not take for granted. The realm of sense, on whose existence my neighbors seem to rely implicitly, I know is a film as thin as a dragon-fly's wing.

Plutzik's grasp of the physical is part of, not distinct from, his purchase on the metaphysical:

I try to express in words the world of the mystic: a curved world like the [subway] tunnel itself, where everything is driven back like the material forces of light and sound, and the mind too is frustrated as it searches for an egress.

At the end of the 'tunnel', the movement of the mind towards light and truth, there is the suggestion that, ultimately, experience must lie beyond the compass of the linguistic, or as Rilke once advised the young Kappus: 'most experiences are unsayable, they happen in a space that no word has ever entered'. Plutzik, like Rilke, was a mystic.

Thom Gunn knighted Plutzik 'the master of two worlds, the natural and the supernatural'; Ted Hughes referred to his *Collected Poems* (ed. Anthony Hecht) as a 'sacred book'; both included him in their anthology *Five American Poets* (Faber, 1963). Neither Gunn nor Hughes, however, had read Plutzik's long letter to Odell Shepard. Yet their combined assessment of Plutzik – as a mystic go-between, between this world and another – is confirmed and strengthened by the (re-)appearance of this important and fascinating letter. Its publication will do much to convince another generation of readers of Hyam Plutzik's rare and extraordinary gift.

Plutzik finally posted his letter on 11 December 1941 – the US had entered the war just three days earlier. He joined up in 1942 and was stationed in Norfolk (UK). Here, Plutzik gathered up the experiences that would later form the content for his war poems: 'Bomber Base', 'The Airfield at Shipdham' and 'The Airman Who Flew Over Shakespeare's England'. In spite of the context of his time in England, I like to think that he enjoyed what the country had to offer him: Shakespeare's land. Plutzik was a great Shakespearean. One only has to read his long poem *Horatio* (1961), a sequel to *Hamlet*, to see that Plutzik, perhaps more than any other twentieth-century poet, convincingly integrated Shakespearean free verse with the modern poetic idiom. Perhaps, even, than Gunn.

At the air base in Shipdham, Norfolk, while 'beasts with guts of metal groan[ed] on the line', Plutzik sighted a lark – a rare glimpse of High Romanticism in a time of war. 'It is too late', wrote Plutzik 'to praise its song'. Thanks to the Watkinson Library at Trinity College and the great work being done by his literary estate, it is not too late to praise Hyam Plutzik, nor should it ever be.

Hyam Plutzik's *Letter from a Young Poet* is published by Watkinson, Trinity College / Books & Books Press (2016), $15.95

Rough Notes for One or Two Undelivered Lectures on T. S. Eliot's *Dante* (1)

Frank Kuppner

1. We begin with the memorable claim which, if true, is surely one of the very greatest of the Great Oracle's very many great thoughts. To wit: 'It is a test (a positive test, I do not assert that it is always valid negatively), that genuine poetry can communicate before it is understood.'

2. Meaning, I suppose – (one tries one's best) – (even if I hardly dare assert it) – that, while 'genuine poetry can communicate before it is understood', the mere fact that some gorgeous effusion or other does *not* communicate before it is understood doesn't in itself necessarily establish that this effusion might not be genuine poetry too. (Which would leave it as being what? *Fake* poetry perhaps? (Anyway, presumably not the sort of listless and inauthentic versifying which is understood even before it communicates[?]))

3. Is it not, however, the case that, taken literally and without further elaboration, the idea that 'genuine poetry' (or any other sort of utterance, for that matter) can communicate before it is understood, is simply *wrong*? If the content is not being understood (I assume there is a content, I admit) then what can be being communicated? Not the content, self-evidently. So ... *something else* perhaps? It's actually communicating something other than (some part of) its own content? (No easy trick, one might think.) (Yes. What else, exactly?) (Or even inexactly?) And what could understanding realistically amount to, if not to a grasp or appreciation of [at least some of] the actual content?

4. Indeed, doesn't the very fact that something is being communicated at all itself show that (this) something is also being understood? Or are we meant to accept that the effecting of any alteration whatsoever in the recipient is already a form of communication? (Perhaps a conveying of the sense that there is *something* here worth persevering with – something which might well lead to eventual understanding? (Even when this proves not to be the case? (Through whose fault? The reader's? The author's? Both? Neither? (No, no, no. That wasn't what I *meant*! (If anything.) You're intuiting it all wrong!]

5. Obviously, something complex may [be] communicate[d] *in part* before we have understood *all* of it. (If we ever do. (And one could hardly understand all of it at once anyway, *d'un seul coup.*)) Yes. While this starter may be intriguing enough to persuade us it will be a rewarding experience to continue with the attempt to understand, till we have worked out [at least some of] the rest of what it might have to offer us.

6. Or perhaps I understand exactly what you mean, even though I would be very hard-put to verbalise it?

7. But of course genuine poetry can communicate before it is *completely* understood. (After all, how much of anything [even moderately complex] is ever understood *completely* anyway?)

8. Take, for instance – since Dante so often does at least *mention* love – a less than transparent phrase like 'I think I love you'. Does this halting avowal not communicate, even if it's not entirely understood? (Or, indeed, is not entirely understandable? (In fact, might the not-being-understood here – or, at the very least, the not being immediately quite understandable – not itself be said to be a certain part of what is being communicated by the utterance? (Hmm... one way or another, I dare say.))

9. How, indeed, does one ever reach *full* understanding? (Though, with religious poetry there does perhaps seem to be a particular difficulty. 'It is possible, and sometimes necessary, to argue that full understanding must identify itself with full belief.' Well, yes: if something really is necessary then it is no doubt just as well it should also be possible – and I dare say the somewhat evasive 'argue' here means something more like 'insist' – or, at the very least, 'clearly state'. (Which seems to leave us with the suggestion that genuine religious poetry, however well it communicates, cannot fully be understood except by fully assenting to the content?))

10. (What? One realises one fully understands the content by deciding that one entirely agrees with it? Or is it that one really completely agrees with the content by completely understanding it? Hmm. Which comes first? (Or do the agreement and the understanding somehow arrive simultaneously?) (For how can one ever quite rule out the possibility of miracles?)

11. Or might one not conceivably misunderstand the content – which one would presumably have completely agreed with if one had fully understood it? (As if one could never fully agree with content with which one has, to some extent at least, misunderstood! (This sort of fankle, like agreement through miscomprehension, presumably happens absolutely *all the time*.))

12. Indeed: might one not even have here another glimpse of the committed enthusiast's criticism-annihilating dream – that to disagree with my own view of the matter *ipso facto* shows that you have not understood it fully, properly, at all...

13. Yes. The Master does rather seem to be swaying elegantly all over the sacred place. Harder to hit the bullseye on a moving target, perhaps? (Or perhaps all Great Art hints at the existence of the Impossible?)

14. What? Communicating in order to be *understood*? Oh dear, no: nothing so vulgar as that. Communicating, perhaps, in order to be taken to be working at an altitude rather too high for the likes of you to reach. (Oh – all too probably...) Perhaps too elevated for just about *anyone* to reach. Communicating – which here evidently means something like: exciting by the virtuoso use of linguistic effects – in order to suggest that we (or some of us at least) (and your distinguished author certainly) have soared well beyond the limits of mere terrestrial understandings. (Which last, insofar as we actually understand anything at all, *never in fact happens*.) (Since absolutely everything we do is merely human.) (Yes. Be it never so subtle, delusional, trite, uncommunicative or advanced.)

The Plenty of Nothing

Ian Patterson

i.m. Jenny Diski, 1947–2016

Pale duty stamps about in plenty of nothing
    like the night when you know everything to time
when each step is beaten off when the rack might add
    more glory and I would watch the stars
not kin nor proof to rule the sphere to know
    by clothes and tea how to cut lino out of them

Now see who has the little boat of love and wave
    adrift more salt at its best splash scornful enough
away on your right to curve well in some hope then
    plunging like blame, my hat tossed up and bent
and lost wires lurid if there ever was one at hand
    to walk with me out of my mind's eye always apt

Old china caught to seize as springless nature seeps up
    and wells at stake to risk another fire
in a forest of beasts where silent stories end in a beer
    or in dark lists above the clause that starts to die
left to review by me my kindest cut scabbed as a free
    local disguise made naked to suffer for doing just that

You can give it up for hope's always a bit of web to ignore
    sound into the relief fire bad as you wish for
this lack of a figure in the grip of method on the screen
    to burst out of acid to be like last at the spindle instant
as a gripping vertigo flash vacuum leaves spores in place
    of humanism for us when this frolic unveils payment

End tricky time to get enough pink forms to reconcile
    two worlds of the mind to say the least at work
safe hands on what we know to move abroad like autumn
    leaves the trees revealed at last as a mouthpiece for language
a copy to taste such stress detail at times of less art chat tangled
    to a dead tune in sharp clothes in a space of her own

Make one palp by another hand leaves another letter fail to
    earth what it says out walking on skin debris from two
true stories in matters as if we lavish its fine tip on lungs of art
    to put a stop to his tread or peg out between ruts

in thin sheen as that eye that glass jar screwed cold and dark in pots
      too out all the same with a stump eyed from the window

After midnight it was a baffle or a very good copy in song style
      stapled deep with a mist full of blood for free detritus
flooding slides in capital sequence to watch them drive stout posts
      bleak to look at into the dark ground the black lightless fen
all about the aims of the front bound in like a literary theory
      snarled in rough cuts to earn a living to repudiate

The hoover fades beneath a lethal march off this page
      to another partiality from the air against his masks
to form him now in terror forays or shape him in dumps
      in flame run half afraid on a floor of damp glass a lip
at fault speaking idle threads down to the bona fide dress
      shirt in hand over fist spooning into his face

So would you care to remain here and be consumed
      round the neck as the only route downward like a load
of light verse enduring through barrage and fancy filaments
      twittering in the ceanothus of invention parcels
air bent into aesthetic shapes of this mercy or that or broken
      right apart eaten away starved crushed old mad blind and stamped on

Later level force embraces anybody if that's true and I agree
      with you out of my hands to where the cities are to play power
splashed out in a witness sense, a complex merit one class say
      or ever becoming a kind of work out loud burning
it from one end to the other just because of skin declaring decay
      that might be a view from nowhere but a day in the country

What was made by us is hanging about covered in ribbons and birdshit
      and aprons all set on this time of night for any other way through
tangles of a seedy mind to hold nothing touched or even true
      to the same life just a door step away from a sheepish mouth
munching a sliver of something carmine and ludicrously
      pastoral as fishpaste or cracks full of dust or an entire bowl

Don't nod or scramble so ruefully for dupes or lying for the poor
      furtive moon-blush army come again try the view alone
odour of almonds am here am you we're a monstrous pair of crows
      doubting summer's purchase a blush in a garden of gleams
sow seeds by the aunt clair path sow the wind in the tender cedar
      rush light charm above the door dilapidated its charm raddled

And see off a dumb tally over a long night's counting till the sun
      glides the new sand sole account crowned legendary and lost
a film a few saw sheepishly on a blank promise to be better after it
      gilded inside to do as we go into the barrier on a face opens
the book of wishes and glides illegible as badgers in a complex pattern
      buried a bad label a gesture or tab shawl they'd like to escape from

Ignore o secure relief fluid at your age one exists or leaves and will
      dissolve by final flux over you unaided inflicted and not once more
be ever one we hear so much and weep at windows in lost sentences
      ignored in the forests. The words on one level condemn us to death
of the use of them as we must simply know the part in the whole
      devoted to a singular being without being which there's nothing left.

Two Poems

JULITH JEDAMUS

Lai's Alterations

We set aside old grievances and drive to the
tailor's: Lai's Alterations for Men and Women,
though Lai and his father are the only men in
this one-room shop where fans flutter the garment bags
and Lai's sparse hair. He kneels to mark the hem for a
maid of honour as the bride admires her purple
crêpe du chine. Female chatter drowns the hum of high
rotors and Lai's voice: melodious, deferent.

The line grows longer. My mother and I hold our
limp slack-waisted skirts, in need of new elastic
and Lai's expertise. He serves my mother first; I
look away as she lifts her blouse to help him with
his measurements, but not before I see those pale
rolls of flesh... I flash back to nineteen seventy-
three, when she basked on the lawn in her bikini
and the war ended for us, if not for Lai – not

quite. Two years later the tanks rolled in and I left
my home town as Lai would leave his: Saigon, the name
scorched onto our minds just as his father's iron
would burn this crêpe du chine if he weren't careful –
but he's always careful. Even today, as Lai's wife
lies speechless in Swedish Hospital in Denver
(for she suffered, we overhear, a stroke in this
shop on Monday morning, though she's just forty-two,

born the year my mother bought her green bikini)
everything's running smoothly: the fans, the irons,
Lai's alterations. 'Can you have my daughter's skirt
by Friday?' my mother asks. 'She's flying back to
London that night.' 'I'll try,' Lai says. 'We're so sorry,'
I tell him lamely as he hands me the ticket
and a business card with a man's suit fluttering
in the top right-hand corner, as if it were blown

by a giant fan – or a hurricane. When we
come back the following week both skirts are ready.
Lai's wife, we hear, is speaking haltingly in her
room at Swedish Hospital, and eating fried rice.
'Try it on,' Lai urges me. Though I dread the whole
performance, I slip behind the yellow curtain
and emerge, the parody of a butterfly...
I stand as he tweaks and smooths. 'It's perfect,' I lie.

When did I remember Baudelaire's 'Les Bijoux'?
As I flew over Ontario and admired
the lights below, or as I looked out at the Thames
and polished up my faux alexandrines? We wore
no jewels for him, nor were our poses novel.
We didn't know his heart, or care to please him. No
low sonorities beguiled him. Only the whir
of fans stirred him, subtle as our condescensions.

Watching My Mother Read
The Man with Night Sweats

She sits in her tufted chair
by the open window where,
nine stories below, the creek
burst its banks two years ago
and drowned, with amazing speed,
a young couple unprepared
for disasters of any
magnitude. A shiny cane

rests by her side; she leans her
chin on her hand as she skims
the poems, pausing when an
image strikes her, or a word.
Expressions travel across
her face; her papery skin
rustles as leaves are disturbed
by breezes – or gusts of rain.

A frown (of concentration?
disapproval?) melts away,
or turns fearful. Was I wrong
to show them to her? I thought
it was safe. She has a gay
friend from Austin; she irons
his shirts; he teaches her to
text and tweet, gives her a high

five before he drives off in
his battered Mustang, tells her
'sweet' when she gets something right.
Lamplight casts her doubts in low
relief. She looks up, smiles, says,
'All those rhymes! I hadn't thought
there would be so many.' Then
we move to safer topics:

syllabics, George Herbert's 'Prayer'.
She's understood. No sense in
dwelling on them: the awkward
poses, the desperation,
their outrage, and his, the hard
partings... Nearly ten. Nine floors
down, the creek sings. A coal train's
whistle moans out on the plains.

Conversations with Poetry Micro-Publishers

LUKE ALLAN

3: Partus Press

Based between Reykjavik, Iceland and Manchester, England, Partus Press is an independent publisher that specialises in fostering and promoting the work of emerging writers, chiefly poets. Under the guidance of founding director Valgerður Thorodds, the press publishes small editions in Icelandic and English.

a Partus poet helping to bind books

LUKE ALLAN: *I first came across Partus in 2015 at a poetry event in London where you were reading. By then the press had been going for a few years in Reykjavik. Can you tell me where the press came from, how it got going, and what those early stages were like? I'm interested to hear about any early publishing models too.*

VALGERÐUR THORODDS: Partus grew out of a poetry chapbook series called *Meðgönguljóð*, the first book of which was published spring 2012. There were three of us in the beginning who conceived and directed the series, which was at that time published by another, very-'micro' publisher. The idea was to make slim, hand-sewn chapbooks that were beautifully made but could be bought relatively cheaply, for the price of a cup of coffee, in fact. The name *Meðgönguljóð* is a play on words: *meðganga* literally means 'pregnancy' but also, if you break it apart, 'take away'. A bit ridiculous, but it helpfully suggested both those ideas of nurture and portability. We were looking to disrupt the somewhat formal attitude people had at the time towards poetry in Iceland.

These ideas of nurture and development seem pretty central to the press. Can you describe the mentoring process that Partus authors go through?

The mentoring apparatus we've set up is central to what we do. With the poetry series, the idea is that after we accept a manuscript, we pair the poet with a more established author who helps them to prepare the work for publication. After being paired, the poet and editor meet anywhere between five and ten times to work on the manuscript, taking anywhere from three to nine months.

At the other end of this process, not only have the poems been scrutinised by someone with extensive expertise in the genre, but the poet has had ample time to digest what he or she is doing or trying to do with the manuscript. It really is a transformative experience for the poets, I think, many of whom have never had anyone to talk to about their work before, much less to comb through their manuscript. Our emphasis on in-depth editing has really become our niche.

Unlike here in the UK, where poets publishing their first selections of poems as chapbooks is standard fare, there is almost no tradition of chapbook-publishing in Iceland. When we were starting out with our series, most of the poetry books being sold in stores were around a hundred pages long and cost about twenty pounds – which is a publishing model that just doesn't make sense for younger authors. There are also very few literary magazines in Iceland (only two, in fact).

So, not surprisingly, when we were starting out, the bigger publishers hadn't touched a first collection by a poet under thirty for about ten years. The whole scene was a bit stagnant.

Kári Tulinius and I, two of the initial three people involved with the chapbook series, had both spent a lot of time in the US, so we were familiar with the concept of zines (another form that was pretty much non-existent in Iceland at the time) and this was our earliest publishing model. No one in the group seemed aware, however, of the tradition of chapbooks over here in the UK. So we pretty much reinvented the wheel in Iceland.

It wasn't until 2014 that Partus Press, as it exists now, came about. By then we had broken off from the small publisher we were originally under and I had become the *de facto* publisher, overseeing more or less everything. I had a lot of ideas about what I wanted to do with the press beyond publishing this one poetry chapbook series, so Kári and I agreed that he would take over as the head editor of the poetry series, and I would be director of Partus, a kind of umbrella for all sorts of other things which I had in the works, including similar series in different genres.

So there's you – the Publisher – and Kari, the Poetry Editor. And then there's the various mentors. Is that the long and the short of it?

Well, I also have other editors who oversee our different series. The 'emerging poets' series has three editors, in fact, our short-story series has three, and two editors are currently working on putting together an essay series. But, as you say, we outsource the bulk of the editing work to established writers who mentor our authors. That said, the majority of the busywork usually falls on me personally. I'm the glue, if you like. This includes getting the books

typeset, commissioning covers, hosting events, distributing books, coordinating promotional work, general art direction, website design, and so on.

What's your set-up, then? What equipment, materials, and outsourced labour goes into a Partus book?

My different apartments in Reykjavík over the years have served as hubs for the press up to now. This is where we do the sewing, where the books are stored, where I host a lot of meetings. I find I work best from home, with all my papers and books around me. The kind of equipment I have in-house is pretty lightweight: thread, awls, cutting boards, and so forth. In the beginning we did a lot of things ourselves that I've since chosen to outsource, saving hours of work. For example, we used to collate and fold every single sheet of paper ourselves; now the printer does that for us. A lot of little things like that have changed since the beginning. When we started out we made a point of doing most of this handiwork ourselves, thinking it would save us money. But the effort is often not worth the pennies saved. Sometimes you think you're being clever when in fact you're just being busy. And these little things add up quickly. So I've been going through all our practices trying to iron out the kinks, to make the whole operation sustainable, and to reduce the number of insubstantial but time-consuming tasks. Publishing is supposed to be about big ideas, in the end.

What's the most challenging or demanding thing about running a poetry micro-press?

The main challenge is not having a budget for anything most of the time. Both in terms of not being able to pay people for their work, as well as not being able to realise ideas or opportunities that

VT's desk, photo by Sophie Butcher & Martin Diegelman

present themselves because of financial constraints. There are so many things I would like to do, and I know so many talented people who I'd love to employ to help me do them. Alas, it will probably be a few more years before anyone gets a salary.

What about the other side of publishing, the non-book side made of events, digital media, and so on?

I think a lot of the success of the press is tied to the quality of our events, yes. For one, they're important as a way of giving our authors a platform to practise reading in public, something a lot of them simply haven't done before. But events are also a crucial way to get in contact with the poets and authors we might want to publish in the future. The environment has to go both ways for this to work – we can't function without interest and without a crowd; neither can we function without more voices coming forward and wanting to take part in what we're doing. I'm very careful to tailor our events to this point. We want to be a phenomenon that people hanker to be a part of – we want to matter to people.

How does your work for Partus tie in with your individual practice as a poet, and your other curatorial work?

My grandfather is always reminding me not to end up on 'the wrong side of the desk', so to speak. And it definitely is a struggle, prioritising one's own work when one spends all day promoting others'. But I think in general there is a kind of symbiotic relation-ship between my personal interests and efforts in poetry and curating and the activity of the press. Partus is an outlet for a lot of my creative impulses. I really like making things happen. And I like seeing things done well. The publishing of a book is a kind of curation in itself, it involves coordinating work in different artistic fields, from performance to visual art and, of course, literature. To me it's a kind of holistic artistic practice, being a publisher. And it satisfies me deeply. But I do have to watch out that it doesn't stamp out my own practice. That's the threat.

Tell me about a recent Partus title.

We just published the fourteenth, fifteenth, and sixteenth titles in the 'emerging poets' series this April. One of those books is by a poet named Elías Portela (although he goes by Elías Knörr in Iceland). He was born in Galicia but moved to Iceland a few years ago and now writes poetry in Icelandic. One of the things I am proudest of with regard to my press is the diversity of voices that we publish, not only in terms of gender, background and age, but also in terms of style. Elias's approach to language is so novel, especially when he writes in Icelandic, which is a very formal language with strict habits of usage. He knows all the rules but manipulates them in such surprising, refreshing ways. I think Icelandic needs a bit of that, a bit of shaking up.

What next?

The ball keeps rolling – our poetry and short story series will publish again this summer and fall, and then we've got a new translation series in the works and may even publish a couple of full-length collections of poetry as well as our first novels this fall. So it will be a big year. But I also very much have my eyes on the UK at the moment, I'm thinking of importing this mentorship model for poetry-pub-lishing. I've had the pleasure of collaborating with a few contemporary British poets in recent years and it's been quite eye-opening. I'm very taken with the literary scene over here. I think it's safe to say the UK will have a role to play in the future of Partus – so watch out for that.

With and Without

NICOLAS JACOBS

---

1. Magnolia

From fruit to flower, they can take thirty years;
by the time you have learnt how best they germinate –
the scarlet seeds sown soon as ripe, left out
to face, unprotected, the winter's worst
and break, unexpectedly, in spring – it may be
too late: who, after all, has those years left
to watch? This, jib as one may, I tell myself,

is where one is: no more than a spectator,
whose efforts and long patience can claim no part

in the trees with the smooth grey branches, just
beginning to crust with lichen, as each twig
erupts into goblets, into flexible stars
blushed pink, flushed purple, seagull-white against
the slaty lour or blue of the April sky:

spectator, above all, on those serene days
of petals floating, when it is very still, down
irregularly to earth – listen! – with a barely
audible flop, soft as the sound of a red
admiral's wings opening and closing on ivy
blossom one warm October afternoon –
or even two winter lovers touching, once.

2. Ashwood

So was it that, was that the difference
that made the difference? I had always
sharply resented the loss itself that,

beside the incorrigible crudity
of what resulted, made sure that when
I would give myself entire to her

or her, she would each time be left,
even if unbeknown to herself,
short-changed. And when, of all women,

you welcomed me in, so that at last
I became what I was always meant
to be, and where I was meant to be,

I resented again that I could not feel
you in fullness as I was meant to do,
as your unflawed body deserved;

but worse, once cheated, that another
enjoyed not only whom I had lost,
but what I could never know: doubled

envy, doubled resentment, salted
both wounds. So, now that they say you
could, after all, have felt the difference,

and that the difference itself might
have made the difference, so that he
was at once irresistible, and I

banished for the very shortcoming
I was, am still, most diminished by:
that is most galling of all. And only

now, when it appears that all that
no longer matters, and indeed little
else beside, am I free to ask if this

is true; and still I hardly dare – as
I dared not, when I could, ask you,
afterwards, 'Does it make a difference...?'

3. Prelude

Passing brightness of five sharps
after as many flats: blown sun

skittering on wet stone, sycamore
leaves blown inside out: promise

of more rain, but no matter. Try
to lay hands on the melody:

as well pursue a dissolving piece
of soap round the bath. Once a bolter,

always a bolter: forgiveness is
in order while there is time, while

there is still time. Memories of
her *bananes flambées*, flame many

waters cannot quench: the eluding
music dances over the mind,

recalls (but then who could forget?)
her vertical configuration of

crisped hair, the faultless corrugations
inside. Time blots all, the usurping

ideology admits few or no
grounds for distinguishing between

a prelude by Bach and the square
on the hypotenuse. Though the fugue

offers to seize the evanescent
theme out of the air, impose its own

ineluctable logic, radiant, that proved
not for me. The dog at the keyboard

snarls proprietary rights, and who
may presume to say Thou art the man?

Moving shadows of male or lady-fern
over fall of swift water, blown sun

skittering, ungraspable brightness
of the five sharps following on five

flats, point what little was, and what
might have been: for now, for always.

Person in Question

Fernando Pessoa in Lisbon

Iain Bamforth

As FERNANDO PESSOA would tell you: there is no better time to visit Lisbon – 'luminous Lisbon' – than winter, when the sun is slant, the light weak and diffuse, the streets mostly empty, and the rain gusting in from the Atlantic Ocean sleeks the pavements with a fine skein that turns them mother-of-pearl. Visitors who favour leather-soled shoes have to be careful when they walk the seven hills of Lisbon, though. Not only are Lisbon's roads paved; many of its sidewalks are paved too, with slick and shiny granite cobbles. And you have to be especially careful if you're carrying one of Pessoa's books in your hand.

Not only did I have one of his books in my left hand, the all too appropriately named *The Book of Disquiet*; I was ill-advisedly trying to open a popout map of the city of Lisbon with my right. All I had to do was flick my wrist, and all of Lisbon would open out before me, in a kind of historical reconstitution by the magic of origami; or so I thought.

Obviously I was really rather eager to observe the universe at a slight angle to it, like Pessoa himself...

•

Lisbon's air is 'a hidden yellow, a kind of pale yellow seen through dirty white. There is scarcely any yellow in the grey air. But the paleness of the grey has a yellow in its sadness', according to Bernardo Soares, putative author of *The Book of Disquiet*.

Bernardo Soares was Pessoa's alter-ego, an assistant bookkeeper who lived in a rented room and worked for a textile trading firm in the same street, Rua dos Douradores, one of the drabber streets in the bustling commercial district of Baixa – 'I know: if I raise my eyes, I'll be confronted by the sordid row of buildings opposite, the grimy windows of all the downtown offices, the pointless windows of the upper floors where people still live, and the eternal laundry hanging in the sun between the gables at the top, among flower-pots and plants.' Not much happens in Rua dos Douradores except for the occasional sound of someone practising scales, arguments between family members and the endless meteorological rearrangements overhead. That was how Soares liked it.

The description of Soares, and the circumstances of his life, as laid out in the preface to *The Book of Disquiet*, sound very close to those of Pessoa himself, who often ate lunch in a café on the street. That is why Pessoa – famous now for taking his commitment to multiple perspectives to the point where to be 'Fernando Pessoa' was also to be (and to be astonished by) the other poets within him – insisted that Soares was 'solely a mutilation of [his personality]'. Soares's life looked too much like his own as a writer and translator of business correspondence (for the agent and importing firm Casa Serras in 1934 and 35) in the Rua Augusta, which runs parallel to the Rua dos Douradores, for him to qualify fully as a *heteronym*, the term Pessoa seems to have invented to describe his fictive

personalities. 'I grew soon to have no personality at all except an expressive one,' he wrote describing a kind of revelation he had in March 1914. 'I grew to be a mere apt machine for the expression of moods which became so intense that they grew into personalities and made my very soul the mere shell of their casual appearance.' He had found his voices even as they unmade him.

There were three principal heteronyms. Alberto Caeiro, a tranquil shepherd who wrote simple pagan poems full of nature mysticism (and was the only one deferred to by the others as the 'master'); Ricardo Reis, a strictly rhyming classicist with Horatian poise and manners; and Álvaro de Campos, an exuberant, hyperbolic, squabbling modernist in thrall to movement, loudness and sensation: it was he who advanced the doctrine of multiple personality that governed their relations. The three heteronyms even compelled their first reader, the medium called Pessoa, to discover how the old notion of a single, self-possessed authorial presence ('know thyself', as the oracle at Delphi instructed) might actually be an impediment to a life of writing. Bootstrapped from the *ex nihilo* paradox of creativity itself, these three personages were secure enough in their literary identities and opinions to argue with Fernando Pessoa. So much do they argue that when the semi-heteronym, Soares, chips in with a comment about his being the living stage 'where various actors act out various plays', it may well seem that the observation properly belongs to the pen of the principal player, Fernando Pessoa – whose surname is cognate with the Latin word *persona*. (Long before them, the eighteenth-century Scottish philosopher David Hume, in comparing the self to a form of theatre, had already denied the possibility of there being only one authoritative player on stage at any time.)

The forthright and even rather overbearing Álvaro de Campos – who had purportedly studied naval engineering in Glasgow, travelled the world and wore a monocle – even intervened on the occasion of Pessoa's only known romantic liaison, with a secretary called Ofélia Queiroz (note the given name) in the employment of one of his clients, telling her in a letter to abandon any idea of marriage with her 'Fernandinho'. Even then, Pessoa (the *orthonym* Fernando Pessoa, to be technical about it) was capable of writing wildly different poems under his own name, publishing avant-garde works in the famous literary publication *Orpheu* while reserving his more reactionary outpourings for a monarchist periodical. It is almost as if he expected his readers to be cognitively dissonant too.

When he died the day after checking into the Hospital de São Luis dos Franceses, the French hospital, in November 1935, of fulminant liver disease brought on by heavy drinking, most of the 523 fragments of what became *The Book of Disquiet* were found in an envelope marked 'L. do D.' (*Livro do Desassossego*) among the 27,543 documents (number still growing) that constitute Pessoa's considerable *oeuvre*. 'The saddest book in Portugal', as Pessoa called it, had no design, and it is unlikely Pessoa himself could ever have edited it.

Compiled by a team of editors and published in 1982, *The Book of Disquiet* is now Pessoa's most frequently-read volume. It is by no means all as slack or lugubrious as he suggested: some entries are droll and self-mocking. In view of Pessoa's lifelong obsession with astrology and the occult, it is amusing to read Soares complaining (like a true aesthete) about the stylistic shortcomings of the mystic masters: '[They] all write abominably. It offends my intelligence that a man can master the Devil without being able to master the Portuguese language.' And he doesn't provide excuses for the holier kind of mystic either. 'To have touched the feet of Christ is no excuse for mistakes in punctuation.'

Forestalling the phenomenon that has been prematurely called, since the 1960s, 'the death of the author', Soares's philosophical musings could even be regarded as a spoof on the entire genre of wisdom literature. 'Travel?' he writes. 'One need only exist to travel.'

The Book of Disquiet could even be said to be a self-help book in which the writer starts from the premise of having no very fixed self.

•

Pessoa himself had much stronger feelings for his native city than Soares, who rarely ventured even as far as the marina and port area of Cais dos Colunas. He even admitted to *The Book of Disquiet*: 'I have no social or political sentiments, and yet there is a way in which I'm highly nationalistic. My nation is the Portuguese language.' Yet Pessoa himself insisted, in a memorable phrase, 'To be Portuguese is to be European without the discourtesy of nationalism.'

Born in Lisbon in 1888, Pessoa lost his father at age five and was taken to colonial Natal (South Africa) when his mother married the Portuguese consul in Durban. When he returned to Lisbon at the age of majority it was to settle there, and he never left the city again except to make a couple of trips to provincial towns. And while many modernist writers have had a strong link with a particular city – think of Joyce and Dublin, Kafka and Prague, Svevo and Trieste, Musil and Vienna – Pessoa did for Lisbon something that few other leading writers have done for their home cities. He wrote a tourist guide to the city that his own poems have since helped to remake in their image. Was this part of the 'infinite sightseeing cruise' Soares mentions somewhere in *The Book of Disquiet*? Or was it requested – given the fact that Pessoa wrote it in English – by one of the commercial firms that employed him, for the use of foreign visitors to the city on the Tagus?

His guide is particularly noteworthy in view of the generally critical relationship that modernism has had with 'tourism' as an economic and cultural activity, in which it is invariably and unfavourably contrasted with travelling – although it is probably true that in the eyes of indigenous people all visitors look like tourists. Pessoa certainly had no interest in leaving his native city once he had rediscovered it in his late teens.

What the Tourist Should See is a bare eighty pages, and like nearly everything he wrote was retrieved from a manuscript found after his death. It imagines a voyager approaching the city from the sea, already smitten by the sight of the red roofs of Alfama and Mouraria and the dominating citadel of São Jorge, and only too eager to get through customs and on to the major sights.

This, of course, is Portuguese history in reverse, as I observed when I took the train from the Cais do Sodré train station, where Pessoa handled correspondence for a firm called Toscano & Cruz in 1920, past the famous squat castellated limestone Belém Tower – which marks the ancient northern district of the city from which Vasco da Gama set out for India in 1497 and Pedro Álvares Cabral for Brazil in 1499 – to Cascais, the upmarket resort at the northern tip of the Bay of Lisbon. Nearly all the passengers on the train sat on the left: they wanted to look out to sea, to admire the yachts sailing on the Tagus, and measure their progress along the coast by the Bugio lighthouse that stands between Lisbon and the abyss. This was where they could commune with 'the ancient Portuguese speech of the sea', as Pessoa put it in one of his poems.

Pessoa's guide to Lisbon is therefore really a museum guide, since this splendid city on seven hills 'which rises like a fair vision in a dream' (as he puts it in his decorous English) has always had mythical pretensions. As one of the oldest European cities it was formerly called Olissipo, in homage to Ulysses (Editora Olisipo was the name of a short-lived publishing house run by Pessoa between 1921 and 1923 in the Rua da Assunção which among other titles published a couple of volumes of his not very convincing poems in English). Nowadays Lisbon cannot separate itself from its revenants. Every square seems to boast massive, muscular effigies of kings and explorers whose very bulk delivers a verdict on the mediocrity of the present. What convinced this city's inhabitants five centuries ago that reality doesn't flatten out at the horizon? How did a seafaring kingdom that once commanded half the world owing to its knowledge of the Atlantic gyre and the *volta do mar* ('turn of the sea)' – from Brazil in the west to entire countries on both coasts of Africa as well as scattered entrepôts in Asia – retreat to this recess on the edge of Europe where the loudest debate on the quays is the price of cod?

The vast space of the Praça do Comércio, for instance, is crowned by the mounted effigy of King José I, his charger busily crushing snakes. This square, and nearly all the districts of the city close to the river, were rebuilt by his prime minister, the Marquês de Pombal, after the devastating earthquake of 1755. The marquis has his own statue at the top of the imposing Avenida da Liberdade. Camões, the great epic poet of *The Lusiads*, Portugal's own *Aeneid*, stands on another baroque pedestal in the Chiado surrounded by less illustrious bards. Even Pessoa has been copperplated and placed outside the famous coffeehouse *A Brasileira* in the Rua Garrett, his left leg jauntily resting on his right. Tourists can't resist sitting next to him.

It is difficult to imagine a more inappropriate memorial to Pessoa, whose true effigy is one of the few photographs of him: a man reduced to the bare semiotics of gabardine raincoat, bowtie, specs and moustache striding along the street. This is what Tintin might have looked like if he had progressed from being a boy-reporter to the cosmic disillusion of middle-age. Álvaro de Campos, his loud-mouthed heteronym, even blurted it out on one occasion: 'Fernando Pessoa, strictly speaking, doesn't exist.'

·

My Pessoa moment in Lisbon occurred in the famous *eléctrico* 28, one of the ramshackle but appealing narrow-gauge vintage trams manufactured between 1936 and 1947 that still serve the narrow streets of the city's hills. I got on at the Rua da Conceição stop, and found a seat at the back (seats for only twenty persons, standing room for almost twice that number) as it trundled around the Chiado and slid down the Rua da Loreto in the direction of the Estrela park. The driver had to get out once to readjust the pantograph, which had become dislodged on one of the sharp bends ascending the Chiado, stepping smartly out of his cab with a long pole in his hand. But we didn't get very far. A funeral was being held in the Santa Catarina church, with a hearse parked outside the steps to bring in the coffin. The tram had no option but to wait behind it as the bells pealed down the narrow street. Bowing to the inevitable in what appeared to be another fairly common occurrence, the driver got out of the cab again, this time to have a smoke. Half an hour later, with several other trams piled up behind us, we were able to continue the journey to Pessoa's last home.

This was the tram to Prazeres, in the neighbourhood of the cemetery in which Pessoa was interred on 2 December 1935, when it rained and rained. He lived in this district for the last fifteen years of his life, and the apartment he leased at 16, Rua Coelho da Rocha where his mother and other members of the family lived at various times has been transformed into a museum, Casa Fernando Pessoa: it holds his personal library, his bed, his personal astrological chart cast in marble on the floor and some of his school reports from his British colonial education in South Africa. He had clearly been a studious pupil.

At the Casa Pessoa, I picked up the exhibition catalogue 'Os lugares de Pessoa'. I used it to visit all of 'Pessoa's places' in a single day, from the fourth-floor apartment on the Largo de Sao Carlos were he was born in 1888 (and which is now guarded by a sculpture with its head appealingly lost in a book); the Church of the Martyrs where he was christened; the apartment of his aunt ('Tia Anica') on the Rua de São Bento, close to my own hotel, and his residence on his definitive return to Portugal in 1905. The Café Martinho de Arcada, an upmarket restaurant recessed in the arcade behind the Praça do Comércio, even has a little shrine to Pessoa from the days when it was called Café da Arcada, and he was a regular. It still does his favourite menu: Portuguese cabbage soup, cod and fried eggs with cheese.

In 1988, on the centenary of his birth, the writer's remains were transferred to the famous Mosteiro dos Jerónimos (Monastery of the Order of St Jerome or the Hieronymites) in Belém where the country's greats are buried. The monastery is the centre-piece of his *What the Tourist Should See*, where he describes it as 'the most remarkable monument which the capital contains.' Commissioned by King Manuel I five hundred years ago, its western front is a masterpiece of Renaissance stonework: made of worked limestone, it is richly ornate and incorporates maritime symbols and objects gathered during the naval expeditions of the Age of Discovery. Its vaults and pulpits are no less remarkable, and also full of memorabilia: 'The vault which rises over the cross is an admirable work, and contains the real bronze escutcheons which belonged to the caravels that went to India and to Brazil.' Once the visitor has seen the monastery, Pessoa suggests, he will never forget it.

Strange, I thought as I walked back the few miles back from Belém on those rain-slicked cobblestones, to come upon the mortal remains of such a timid and housebound man in such a place, 'glorious' as he said it was, and alongside those of Camões. Pessoa had always maintained that imaginary travel was superior to the actual thing – but it's true that in his early writings he had also written about dream-cara-vels sailing off to discover transcendent 'New Indias' and flirted with Sebastianism, the doctrine of the messianic king who was supposed to return and restore Portuguese culture to its former greatness (after leading it to disaster in 1578). His theatrical splitting into three heteronyms, a semi-heteronym and someone who claimed to be called Mr Person was perhaps the only way a twentieth-century poet could hope to emulate Camões's epic dispersal – to be a 'super-Camões'. Self-coherence yielded to sub-sidiary psyches. Instead of going to the tropics Pessoa multiplied the 'desire to die another person beneath unknown flags'. Esoterism was made to stand in for exoticism. Pessoa had discovered that the world isn't a globe at all; it is flat, as flat as a sheet of paper.

Pessoa intensified to an almost hallucinatory pitch Calderón's supposition, in his famous seven-teenth-century Spanish drama *Life is a Dream*, that 'though no man knows it, all men dream the lives they lead'; and while his attitude may seem resigned and restful, or even have a mystical Zen quality, it has its recessed elements too. The heteronyms can even be seen as a means of concealing rather than expressing aspects of Pessoa's personality. Ivo Castro, one of editors of the critical edition of Pessoa's work, has remarked, 'Hiding from his own editor is perhaps the most subtle form of disguise which Pessoa ever adopted.' Whether masked or muted, it is difficult to imagine Pessoa accepting Dante's strictures about the moral need for coherence in a human life.

The immobility of Pessoa's life has a haunting quality. You only need to chance on one of the excerpts in *The Book of Disquiet* – most certainly not a book to be read cover to cover – to be seized by a renewed sense of what the title suggests. 'I don't know how many will have contemplated, with the attention it merits, a deserted street with people in it. This way of putting the phrase already seems to want to say something else, and indeed it does. A deserted street is not a street where nobody ventures but a street on which people walk as if it were deserted.'

Scale that up, and you are contemplating a complete urban geography of Lisbon. Walk in Pessoa's footsteps, especially in the rain, and you'll discover his insomnia too. *Saudade*, that uniquely Lusitanian quality, isn't just nostalgia for the past, but for the future too.

Gratitude

STANLEY MOSS

1. After Night Fell Down the Abyss

After Night fell down the Abyss,
ages after Eros mated with Chaos,
the gods were cut up and scattered.
After Forty-Two Names, the creation, the flood,
after nights and days were everyday,
the laws, the land promised,
centuries before an English word there was the Word,
Jesus alone chose to be born.
First day of spring,
flocks of birds break out of darkness,
hatch without choice
into the universe with the rest of us,
join the elements we know and don't know,
protons and neutrons that live privately,
never chose to be born,
dark holes that did not and do not
choose to be gravitational.
Pushing with closed wings,
soon to fly to its first flower
a butterfly looks out of its chrysalis,
through a torn silk web.
Spring is coming in. A milk-fed race
that has no choice but nipples,
four-footed and two-footed,
is coming into society.
There are gatherings in vineyards.
In that beautiful, noisy company
I would not choose to be a grape.
I hear a buzzing, a splashing, a *God bless*,
most will live a day or two without choice
then become feed.

Some frogs, after a three-day orgasm,
may be devoured by a loveless bass or heron.
I pity flies.
I cannot conceive of insect pleasures.
                After a while
philosophers and farmers are feed,
which we all become sooner or later
unless we choose to go up in smoke
that has no choice where to go
any more than mountains do.

2. Second Choice

A cup of tea, a shot of old whiskey,
comfort for the moment,
I do not choose to play chess,
I play there-is-Heaven-and-Hell.
I choose to sing, *Depuis le jour*, then silence...
silence gets me used to silence,
I will hear it for a long while.
No silence in my trees –
I say 'my trees', I planted hundreds,
some assassinated in their own beds.
On May afternoons, it is my opinion
the survivors recognise me,
but birds and squirrels living in the branches
don't know me from Adam. Barefoot,
lonely as a cloud I've walked beaches,
I've gathered Cubist driftwood, discovered a trunk,
the chapel of a Chinese temple bridge,
I've climbed mountains, found rocks
with fossils of seashells and fish spines carved in.

3. Ridiculous

We are made to look ridiculous.
Our bodies are stuck with fingers,
usually ten, knuckles and hair.
We have ridiculous noses
with nostrils that pull air in and out
with the help of ridiculous lungs,
God-made feet with toenails,
a navel that connects us to holes of ill repute
that are made to do outlandish things
with mouths and tongues on pilgrimage or hajj
or going to Jerusalem 'next year'
with our pagan ridiculous teeth.
After an outlandish past and present,
we die ridiculously, go to dirty hell.

I hunt for sensible things
in rock without feelings,
both of us loaded with ludicrous bacteria.
I know some people and gardens
that are beautiful, clearly sensible,
are reasons for, but they die
ridiculous deaths like the rest of us.

I'm soon to have my ridiculous salad,
everything is ridiculous
but a good cup of coffee in the morning.
The rising and setting sun is iffy,
clouds are not ridiculous,

winds certainly are ridiculous,
are political but don't vote,
they are left-wing, right-wing, east or west.
I am registered to vote in a cosmological election.
The sun is president.
What is the state of the universe?
Time and space are certainly undemocratic.

Still, in the sensible by-and-by, dark holes
will hold an election, the candidates
real-lifers against supernaturalists.
What ridiculously new
relative pronoun will come of cosmic jousting?
In the distant future tense:
I will will cry over spilled milk.
It is ridiculous as gravity to wait
to pull a string theory on anyone.
Still I am prepared to stay here and wait.
I wait and wait, wait and wait.

4. Just Like That

Some of us choose to disappear,
which is not the same as burial.
After wonderful everyday routines,
breakfast and suppers,
Shakespeare and the singing laudy goddamn others
with their lending hands, still part of the forest
in darkness, 'for the birds', as they say in Queens.
I delight in my broken circle because
I can say 'birds of prey'
and 'I pray that you observe the Sabbath'.
Praying pays attention, reminds me
Jesus alone chose to be born.
Wishing, I make noise,
'noise for the Lord' as David suggested.
I could write a history of choice and necessity.
I do not choose my dreams.
Time and space, those grown-ups, are choiceless.
If I had a choice, I'd choose to be human,
a farmer or poet, a farmer-poet.
No farm ever chose to be a farm.
Not having chosen my beginnings,
my language, my century, I choose English now.
Some say the poem writes itself.

5. December 21st

I do not think a child
is born simply because
you do it or did it.
Birth is a miracle,
like December 21st,
shortest day of the year.
Death is everyday
like waking up.

Death is hardhearted.
I know flying birds
carry a heart with them
as do sandpipers
and cormorants that dive
and seem to disappear.
Trees' hearts are difficult to find
when they are cut down –
so many leaves, branches, and roots.
A tree has its own soul,
often houses a god,
should be offered a gift.

Mothering is rare,
not like fish eggs or pollen,
but thanks to four holy letters
a miracle happens.
Stars fall in love
at first sight,
have illegitimate stars,
commonplace and steadfast.
Miracles don't have to be holy,
can be profane.
Okay with me if you tell me
you grew up unmiraculously.
'Every living thing is part-miracle',
I don't know why.
The miracle gets tired,
needs a good night's sleep
we call death.
Death is not a defeat
it is a triumph, the permanent
over the temporary.

6. Number One

There are diminishing unshakeable effects,
love, fathering, friendship,
first love, chance encounters.
I may simply stay home.
Life's not a menu, but I can choose a song,
my final resting place for a while.
In the end I'll simply say:
the universe did not choose
Big Bang or Mom and Pop.

Speechless bastard orphan
abandoned on the doorstep of language,
to stay alive I will accept any tongue,
inarticulate as the wheels of a locomotive –
after a month listening I will learn, I think,
first useful words, names of things, foods and drink,
salt, how to nod *thank you* and *good night*,
personal pronouns, if any, some understood.
I think I will learn the possessive quickly.
My new tongue has an untranslatable word
for *gratitude* that also seems to mean
the sun is shining and number *one*.

Eliot's Scientific 'Tendencies' in 1919

Duncan MacKay

AN INTERESTING ARTICLE in *PN Review* 228 (March–April 2016) by Robert Griffiths presents us with the 'curiously coincidental' emergence of modernist poetry alongside the revolution in physics represented by Einstein's 1905 and 1915 papers on Special and General Relativity. Griffiths suggests 'the fact [is] that all of this revolutionary poetry and physics (and psychology), as well as a great deal else, was going on in a mutually unrelated way'. Griffiths is right to distinguish 1915 from 1919 as far as Einstein's notoriety and its wider cultural significance was concerned; Einstein's work was previously little known outside even a small circle of physicists. However, while influences at any time can be subtle and complex, Griffiths's general assertion of 'a mutually unrelated way' after 1919 is surely not tenable.

Griffiths refers specifically to poets Ezra Pound and T. S. Eliot during their pre-1914–18, and immediate post-war, years. He acknowledges that 'Pound's intellectual hinterland was more varied than Eliot's and included scientific interests', but considers that Eliot had 'no especial interest in science and possibly even a slight disdain for it'. Pound would be the first, and indeed was, to caution us against over-simplification when it comes to issues of influence. In an essay of 1911, he wrote: 'the best of knowledge is *in the air*',[1] and in a letter of the same year he wrote: 'Out of the 25 people who [critics say] are variously supposed to have formed my mind, [...] I have counted about 9 poets unknown to me [and] 7 whom I had only read "casually"'.[2] He continues: 'I think that the "influences" in a man's work which matter are usually pretty well concealed.' Nonetheless, a selection of scientific influences on Pound were first shown some years ago by scholars such as Ian Bell[3] and Martin Kaymer[4] and most recently referenced by Peter Middleton.[5]

As for T. S. Eliot, Griffith's assertion that Eliot had 'no especial interest in science and possibly even a slight disdain for it' deserves much closer attention. For example, on 31 December 1922, the month in which *The Waste Land* was published in book form (having previously appeared in October's first edition of *The Criterion*) T. S. Eliot wrote to his brother that he regretted 'innumerable gaps' in his knowledge and that there was 'so much that I should like to know in the various sciences' – hardly disdainful.[6] In November and early December, in letters to Pound, Eliot had already spoken of wanting *The Criterion* (his response to *The Athenaeum*'s decline following its amalgamation with *The Nation* in 1921) to be a review 'as *unliterary* as possible'. He wanted *The Criterion*, like *The Athenaeum*, to be a review journal of literature, arts and sciences, with contributors such as 'Sir J. Frazer, Trotter, Eddington, Sherrington, or people like that'.[7]

Eliot was immersed in the intellectual ferment of those immediate post-1914–18 war years in London, and its influence in shaping his thinking can be illustrated through his particular acquaintance with J. W. N. Sullivan, Deputy and Science Editor of *The*

Athenaeum from 1919–1921; and through the evidence of Eliot's familiarity with the published writing on scientific issues by Sullivan and others. Eliot's identity as a critic is inseparable from his work as a poet, and his developing critical ideas regarding poetic practice, tradition and the individual, owe much to the ideas of his contemporaries, not least those questions raised in relation to science. Some twenty years ago, Michael H. Whitworth published his 'rediscovery' of an obscure but very revealing essay of Eliot's. Let us briefly review that evidence.

Eliot published two closely related essays at this time. One is the well-known 'Tradition and the Individual Talent', first published in *The Egoist* in September 1919 and reprinted many times since.[8] The other is 'Modern Tendencies in Poetry', which started life as a public lecture Eliot gave in London on 28 October 1919 at the Conference Hall, Central Buildings, Westminster – subsequently published in an Indian journal in 1920 and never reprinted in Eliot's essay collections.[9] Both pieces concentrate on poetic impersonality as well as individuality, the role of tradition, and the 'simultaneous' presence of past literatures, but 'Tendencies' is much more revealing of the scientific parallels and, indeed, direct scientific influences on Eliot's thinking.

Eliot's lecture took place eight days before a meeting at which Fellows of the Royal Society and the Royal Astronomical Society would meet at Burlington House in London for a joint session to hear the results of two expeditions: that of Arthur Eddington and Edwin Cottingham to the island of Principe off the West Coast of Africa, and the other of Andrew Crommelin and Charles Davidson to Sobral in Northern Brazil. Both expeditions had observed the total solar eclipse of 20 May 1919, and had obtained evidence that rays of starlight are bent in the sun's gravitational field. Furthermore, they found that the deflection was exactly that predicted by Einstein's recently proposed Theory of General Relativity (1915). During the following days and weeks this result became headline news across the western world, and there is no doubt that Einstein's bursting onto the popular and intellectual scene in post-war Europe brought many scientists into the cultural conversation on a scale which had not previously occurred. *The Times* ran with: 'Revolution in Science – New Theory of the Universe – Newtonian Ideas Overthrown'. It continued: 'It is confidently believed by the greatest experts that enough has been done to overthrow the certainty of ages, and to require a new philosophy, a philosophy that will sweep away nearly all that has been hitherto accepted as the axiomatic basis of thought'[10] [...] 'the ideals of Aristotle and Euclid and Newton which are the basis of all our present conceptions prove in fact not to correspond with what can be observed in the fabric of the universe'.[13] Throwing in Special Relativity too, *The Times* wrote: 'Space is merely a relation between two sets of data, and an infinite number of times may coexist. Here and there, past and present, are relative, not absolute, and change according to the ordinates and coordinates selected'.[11] It's hard for us to grasp the impact of such pronouncements on the educated middle and upper classes for whom Aristotle, Euclid and Newton were the absolute foundation of their schooling and university experience.

Magazines such as *The Athenaeum*, as self-proclaimed journals of literature, arts and science, could boast the major figures in all three fields among their contributors. Among the intellectual debates that were prompted by Einstein's overthrow of Euclidian space and Newtonian gravity, were those on the aesthetic appeal of scientific theories. Perhaps the division between arts and sciences was a myth arising with Victorian industrialisation and fuelled by post-War disenchantment. Eddington had argued in 1918 (at the London Physical Society, a year before his eclipse expedition) that whether Einstein's theory proved to be right or wrong, the theory was 'beautiful'; a sentiment which was echoed by Bertrand Russell in *The Athenaeum* of November 1919: 'every lover of the beautiful must wish it to be true'.

During May and June 1919 (that is, between the eclipse observations and the announcement of the results of their analysis) Sullivan had provided the *Athenaeum*'s readers with a series of articles, which introduced many non-scientists to the ideas of Relativity, priming the pump before the results were announced. Throughout 1919, 1920 and 1921, *The Athenaeum* continued to publish multiple articles on Relativity, written by Eddington himself, by Bertrand Russell and by Aldous Huxley, among others. In fact the flurry of discussion was conducted across the full range of literary and cultural, as well as popular science, magazines, including *The Contemporary Review*, *The English Review*, *The Quarterly Review*, and *The Fortnightly Review*, with articles not only by Russell and Eddington, but other scientists (such as Lodge, Andrade, and Lindemann), philosophers (such as Broad and Wildon Carr), mathematicians (including Whitehead) and professional journalists (such as Randall, who also wrote regularly for *The New Age* magazine).

Sullivan and Eliot moved in these same intellectual and literary circles. Both were literary journalists; both contributed to *The Athenaeum* and the *Times Literary Supplement*. We know from Eliot's correspondence and, as we'll see from the 'Tendencies' lecture, that at the very least he read Sullivan's articles. They first met in 1918 and the diaries, letters, visitors' books, and memoirs of members of their circle, record a good many subsequent occasions. Sullivan had a reputation as a conversationalist and is credited in his articles with explaining Relativity to the layman better than anyone.

Both Sullivan and their mutual friend John Middleton Murray (then Editor of *The Athenaeum*) were in the three-hundred-strong audience of Eliot's 'Tendencies' lecture. It seems evident that Eliot spoke in a significant sense with them in mind, several times referencing material from their *Athenaeum* articles, and arguing at times under the assumption that the audience were also familiar with these. Eliot described his purpose in the lecture: 'to determine what is meant by "modern" poetry, and to trace, among the variety of currents and eddies, what is the line of true poetry, as distinguished from mere novelties'. He went on: 'In answering these questions it is useful, not to compare poetry to science, but to start out with the view that poetry *is* a science.' He referred to the fact that the relation between art and science had been examined on recent occasions in *The Athenaeum* magazine and he went on to frame his lecture around these discussions, including in particular those of J. W. N. Sullivan.

During the summer of 1919, in various editions of *The Athenaeum*, arts-science issues had been raised by writers including Roger Fry, I. A. Richards and H. W. Crundell; and it was Ezra Pound who had already suggested in two articles in *The Egoist* the previous year that the poet should be like the scientist, who 'begins by learning what has been discovered already'. It was Eliot's extension of this idea, arising out of the *Athenaeum* exchanges, to the requirement that a poetic work possess both the impersonality of the tradition and the individuality of the writer. Consider some of his sources.

In 'The Place of Science', in April's *Athenaeum*, Sullivan had noted that a less than rational impulse might inspire scientific research but that, in the formation of theories that follows, it is 'facts, the products of local curiosities [that] now take on an order, and serve the desire for comprehension. The apparently dissimilar becomes related; law supervenes on chaos. The desire for knowledge becomes transformed into the desire for *significant* knowledge – significant primarily for contemplation, and secondarily for practice.' In 'Tradition and the Individual Talent' the echoes seem unmistakable. Eliot refers to a poet surrendering his or her self to their work, at which point there is 'an expression of *significant* emotion – emotion which has its life in the poem and not in the history of the poet'.[6] In other words, facts into theories has its equivalent in transforming personal experience into a poem, the function of the latter being primarily that personal experience be made objectively available 'for contemplation'.

In a subsequent article ('The Justification of the Scientific Method', May 1919) Sullivan had returned to the relation between facts and theories and suggested that the scientific impulse to generalise random collections of facts into theories was driven by more than curiosity, in fact by something deeper: essentially an aesthetic impulse. For Sullivan this aesthetic drive is what gives the scientific method its true worth as a human endeavour beyond any practical gains that might follow. In his October 'Tendencies' lecture, Eliot echoes this in considering poetic creativity as akin to the making of scientific theories. The poet resembles the chemist: 'He is aware of a great number and variety of elements which can be combined into new and important compounds; his training has given him knowledge of what the elements have been made to do already, and has made him exceptionally sensitive to what they can be made to do. He is in tune for perceiving new relations, as the scientist is.' That personal experience, that background of tradition, all the literary raw material available – that's what Eliot perceives the poet to be reformulating, in analogy with the scientist. He goes on to say that largely 'under the leadership of Mr Ezra Pound' poets were coming to appreciate the 'diverse elements' of

Anglo-Saxon, Scandinavian, old German, and the Latin languages, held 'in suspense'; 'the problem is how to make use of all these Elements, to refer continually to the sources, and at the same time make a vehicle adequate for the expression of any modern thought or emotion.' By way of illustration, Eliot criticised what he called the 'unconstructive' poetry of Dada, specifically a poem by Tristan Tzara (who had published the Dada Manifesto and 'Twenty-Five Poems' in 1918): 'It is wholly unconstructive. It is in the end, unscientific. It is no more art than a postage stamp album [...] It is unscientific, because the interest in mere data is not a scientific interest at all.'

In addition to the analogy in which experience is distilled, from which essence the scientist makes a theory as a poet might make a poem, Eliot's lecture emphasised the provisional nature of knowledge and the fact of its historical place in our culture. Eliot also honed in on the impersonality of scientific discovery, as an analogy for the potential of artistic discovery; an impersonality which yet displays the individuality of its practitioner. In 'The Justification of the Scientific Method', Sullivan had considered the fact that all scientific truths, while evidentially infallible, are nonetheless provisional. Each is superseded eventually as new knowledge emerges. In this Sullivan was anticipating the post-November 1919 debates: the truth of Einstein versus the 'discredited' Newton. To quote Sullivan: '[Any] contradiction is only apparent, however, for it will be found that there is a part of every discarded hypothesis which is incorporated in the new theory.' Equally in his lecture, Eliot says that the literary work of the past cannot be taken as 'an indiscriminate bolas', rather the poet must 'digest' the passions which are its material. There is a selection process in which what proves valid from the past is incorporated into the present.

In 'On Learning Science' (*The Athenaeum* of July 1919), Sullivan championed the 'historic method' over 'modern text-books' in teaching science. Through history the student discovers that 'delicate web of doubt, of half-seen alternative explanations' legitimised, enabling him or her to appreciate the 'hesitations and difficulties' of the real pioneering scientist, against the false 'air of infallibility' given to science in popular misconception. In 'Scientific Education' (*Athenaeum* September 1919), Sullivan asked that the educated person learn something other than isolated scientific facts; instead that they learn of the relationships between science and other human activities (what we would recognise as a cultural and historical context). 'Many misunderstandings,' he said, 'including the present absurd "conflict" between science and literature, would vanish.' That both science and literature share an aesthetic motivation and that both build on their past, seems evident in the beliefs held by both Sullivan and Eliot.

As for 'impersonality', writing in *The Athenaeum* in July 1919, the editor Middleton Murray had reviewed some of Eliot's poems which were subsequently published in the 'Poems 1920' collection. He referred to Eliot's 'individuality' in a paradoxical presence and absence: 'He leaves his coat in our hands. We do not hold him indeed, but we have his *pieces d'identitie*.' Eliot's writing identifies him as author but his personality, unwritten, remains private. Eliot used the same

French phrase in April 1920 when himself reviewing another author, so the image left its impression on him. In the same week as Murray's article, Sullivan also considered the subject of personality, in comparing English and French scientists. Eliot would compare English and French characteristics in his 'Tradition' essay published in September. Sullivan's assessment of the last Victorian scientists (such as Lord Rayleigh, Nobel Prize-winning physicist, who had died the previous month) was that they 'had a particular quality of scientific imagination', not being content with 'mathematical equations' but having 'an instinctive sense of form', seeking that which was 'aesthetically as well as logically satisfying' – impersonal science but having individuality. Eliot's parallel response is clear in his 'Tendencies' lecture: 'When you study the life's work of a great scientist, if you have enough knowledge of the subject to study it at all, you recognise that the man accomplished what he did not through a desire to express his personality, but by a complete surrender of himself to the work in which he was absorbed. He is continuing a work which will be continued after him. The great scientist submerges himself in what he has to do, forgets himself. But if he is a great scientist there will be – I believe scientists will corroborate this statement – a cachet of the man all over it.' Eliot then turns specifically to Einstein and the contemporary debates over his achievement: 'No one else could have drawn those inferences, constructed those demonstrations, seen those relations. His personality has not been lost, but has gone, all the important part of it, into the work. Yet the inferences seem to have drawn themselves, the demonstrations constructed themselves, the relations flown into each other's arms; but without him it would not have happened.'

In a short review called 'Humanist, Artist and Scientist' which he had written for the 10 October edition of *The Athenaeum*, this published two weeks before the 'Tendencies' lecture, Eliot reflected further on the 'presence and absence' of personality: 'The humanist has personality; often, we might think, more than the scientist or artist. But the humanist's personality throws out the idea, centrifugal, without so much entering into it [...] In the man of scientific or artistic temper the personality is distilled into the work [...]'.

Lastly among the parallels, in his lecture Eliot considered progress in science versus progress in poetry: 'we know, or think we know, what is meant by progress in science; but is there the same kind of progress in poetry – is there any progress in poetry?' In his 'Tradition' essay Eliot said simply 'art never improves'. He would acknowledge that our valuing of poetry is not permanent; it changes as new poetry is written. But this is not 'progress'. Like the good classicist he was, he rejected the notion that we are more 'civilised' than previous ages. Sullivan's preference for teaching science historically chimed with Eliot because it emphasised the awareness of change without the implication of progress. As for contemporary practice, Eliot put it in the 'Tendencies' lecture: 'If suddenly all power of producing more poetry were withdrawn [...], if we knew that for poetry we should have to turn always to what already existed, I think that past poetry would become meaningless. For the capacity of appreciating poetry is inseparable from the power of producing it; it is poets themselves who can best appreciate poetry. Life is always turned toward creation; the present only, keeps the past alive.'

Eliot's *Waste Land*, which he will begin to write in early 1921, will be the embodiment of 'the present [... keeping] the past alive'; individual quotations and allusions will come from different historic periods, yet be merged into a 'present-time whole'. The Einstein-ian notion of 'simultaneity' – an end to it as precise contemporaneous events but a rebirth as an imagined multiverse of events across times and spaces – seems taken up in Eliot's 'totality of memories', a phrase from 'Tendencies'. As he also wrote in the 'Tradition' essay: someone with 'historical sense' would feel that the whole of European literature, as well as his country's own, would have 'a simultaneous existence', being as alive to us now as when originally written.

In almost the first review of *The Waste Land* on its publication in 1922, and one of the most positive, Sullivan, writing in *The Athenaeum*, described the poem as a series of 'flashes', seeing its fragmentary character as an optical phenomenon. Those flashes, as glimpses, come 'from radically different sources, some many light years away from Eliot's London, others in close proximity; some from anthropology (and therefore from "prehistoric" culture), some from the Renaissance, others from Eliot's immediate contemporaries'. Sullivan's is an appreciation of an avant-garde poetry by a science specialist, but one who clearly had a closely informed understanding of what Eliot had been thinking during the poem's gestation.

Simple stories of influence are rarely so simple and we should be wary of the simplistic. However, we can surely agree with Michael H. Whitworth in saying that 'the borrowings, allusions, echoes and sugges-tions we have considered give a clear indication of the extent to which Eliot's concerns were part of the literary, intellectual and scientific culture of the immediate post-war period'.[12] His interest and its influence on his thinking at this significant period in his career is unmistakable.

NOTES

1   Ezra Pound, 'I Gather the Limbs of Osiris, II', *The New Age*, X, 6 (7 December 1911), 130.
2   G. Thomas Tanselle, 'Two Early Letters of Ezra Pound', *American Literature*, XXXIV, 1 (March 1962) 117.
3   Ian F. A. Bell, *Critic as Scientist: The Modernist Poetics of Ezra Pound* (1981), London & New York: Methuen.
4   Martin A. Kayman, *The Modernism of Ezra Pound: The Science of Poetry* (1986), Basingstoke: MacMillan Press.
5   Peter Middleton, *Physics Envy* (2015), Chicago: Chicago University Press, 47-49.
6   T. S. Eliot, letter dated 31 Dec. 1922, *The Letters of T. S. Eliot*, ed. Valerie Eliot (1988) vol. 1, London: Faber, 617.
7   T. S. Eliot, *Letters*, 7 Nov. 1922 and 1 Dec. 1922, 593 & 603.
8   T.S. Eliot, 'Tradition and the Individual Talent', *Selected Prose*, ed. Frank Kermode (1975), London: Faber & Faber.
9   T.S. Eliot, 'Modern Tendencies in Poetry,' *Shama'a* 1, no.1 (April 1920), 9–18. The rediscovery of this article was part of Michael H. Whitworth's doctoral research and published in 'Pieces d'identite: T.S. Eliot, J.W.N. Sullivan, and Poetic Impersonality', in *English Literature in Transition 1880–1920*, (1996), 149–70. It was subsequently included in Whitworth's, *Einstein's Wake: Relativity, Metaphor and Modernist Literature* (2001), Oxford: Oxford University Press, 135–145.
10   Alan J. Friedman & Carol C. Donley, *Einstein as Myth and Muse* (1985), Cambridge: Cambridge University Press, 10.
11   Friedman & Donley, Myth and Muse, 11.
12   Michael H. Whitworth, 'T. S. Eliot, J. W. N. Sullivan, and Poetic Impersonality', in *English Literature in Transition 1880–1920* (1996), 166.

Music for Ghosts

PATRICK COTTER

As an offering to the ghosts
I left some music playing
when I shut the door
on the empty house.
Even when a house is full

of ghosts we say it's empty,
empty when you step out
and there's no one left inside
breathing. 'Lost in Music' by Sister
Sledge and 'Good Times' by Chic

both by the same composer.
You might say if I was truly
considerate of ghosts I would pick
songs more than forty years old.
I should leave playing tunes

by Cole Porter or the sort warbled
by Count John McCormack.
But I believe playing ghosts
any music in an empty house

all to themselves while the dial
of the electric meter spins wild
is a gift and not only the living
but ghosts too, deserve harmony.
Even when a house has every wall

lined with books we can call it empty;
even when plants exhale from inside
every windowsill we can call it empty;
when I am sitting on the stairs staring
at the shadows thrown by the morning sun,
as you sleep under stars in a distant timezone.

Three Poems

MARY NOONAN

The Nuns' Wall

At night, when I bolted up the punishing
steepness of Richmond Hill, there was
the wall, and a line of heads along the top –
nuns in the moonlight. If they weren't
ghosts, how did they get up there?
Did they drag ladders from the convent
at midnight, creaky bodies in full habit
clambering up the wobbly rungs?
I had paid my dues for robbing the grapes!
Fecky Murphy led us over the wall between
the handball alley and their greenhouse.
Big, blue grapes, huge bunches of them that
I sold for a penny a throw on the street.
They had us up in court for the damage
and the shortfall in communion wine
that winter, but I got off with a warning.
The father didn't let me off though,
hauling me out of the bed at five to ride
in the side-cart with the drover to our
rented field beyond the town, from where
we would drive the cattle along the road
into the mart. And then the nuns' wall.
Were they mad, or just fond of a drop,
those beaming, gap-toothed faces?

Professor McCracken's Lecture on Skin

The American medievalist delivered her talk
on the power of fur in the Middle Ages.
The higher the rank, the more ostentatious

the garments of hide. Kings wore full sable
houppelandes to show their dominion
over all the creeping creatures, the right to take life

and wear the skin of the vanquished as trophy.
While she summoned French lords draped
in the prestige of marten and weasel, I couldn't help

noticing her name, wondering if she knew that
'craiceann' is the Gaelic for skin. She showed
slides of the covering of the private parts

in twelfth-century images of Adam and Eve
leaving Paradise, and mused on the mobility
of skin – its ability to conceal and disclose –

but what came to my mind were Irish and Scottish
tribes herding goats on hillsides, skinning them
to make panniers for humping turf from the bog

discovering that weathered hide, when hit with fist,
made a hollow drumming; calves rounded up
in a haggard, yielding their flesh to burning oak

their skin to the monks, who dried and scraped it
to make vellum for the missals they inscribed with
gold-leaf and cochineal; groups of men slipping

from small coves into northern seas in coracles
made from hide stretched over curved lathes –
skin boats they called 'naomhógs', little holy ones.

Virgin of the Rocks

Go on, Ann Lovett, crawl into the grotto
and join the Blessed Lady there, the one you
prayed to at the railings when your mother
held you by the hand. Water is streaming down
your school tights and the pain is making it hard
for you to move. Go on! Lie down and let your
long hair hang over the cold stones, over your belly,
let the small head come out between your legs
in the grotto cut high in the rock outside Granard,
on the last day of January, nineteen-eighty-four.

Let the small head come out and let the weight
of your heart ballast you to the grotto of your
blood, as the thick liquid starts to trickle down
your thighs, over the stones, a red waterfall
washing the Lady's alabaster feet. Whimper now,
Ann Lovett, cry to the circlet of stars, to the
corn-flower-blue eyes turned forever to the sky!
Swaddle your little scrap in Her ice-cold skirts!
Offer Her a lily, as the statue of the girl has done
all the years of your fifteen, the stone girl

in the grotto, holding the white bloom, praying
to the Holy Mother – *Oh clement, oh loving, oh
sweet virgin Mary, pray for us who have recourse to Thee!*
– lift up your blue lily, your silent boy, you prayed
to him in your belly, the secret of your small bed,
couldn't say the word you heard whispered
by your mother and your grandmother, a word
that could not be said aloud. Say it out loud now,
Ann Lovett, on this last night of January. Then
raise your heavy head from the rocks and pray.

Rilke's *Orchards*

Paul Batchelor

EVERYONE KNOWS THAT IN 1922 Rilke, after more or less a decade of waiting, completed the *Duino Elegies* within a matter of weeks, simultaneously producing a second masterpiece: *the Sonnets to Orpheus*. It is less well-known that after this, in the four years he had left to live, Rilke wrote nearly four hundred poems in French – as well as continuing to write many in German. Since late 2009 I've been working on translations of some of his French poems. Part of the challenge I set myself was to match the number of lines per stanza and per poem, and to rhyme (though I use consonantal half-rhyme), since Rilke rhymes in almost all of his French poems, and it seems to have been essential to his exploration of the language. The translations published here are from a sequence called *Vergers* (*Orchards*), most of which was written at the château at Muzot where the poet lived from February 1921 until his death in 1926: this was the closest Rilke ever had to a home, and many of his poems from this period are descriptions or addresses to household objects or nearby flora and fauna. – P. B.

....

XVI

Porcelain figurine,
O my recording angel, mark this down:
that someone, at the height of summer, deemed
                             it necessary
to crown you with a raspberry.

How frivolous
to gift you that red bonnet!
Since then – so much has shaken loose,
yet it endures, your delicate hat.

Memories wither
and embalm us
as, wrapped in its ghostly wreath, your
little brow remembers.

XXIII

According to the doctrine of contrast,
it is the Pope – so solemn, so careful
at his so very solemn feast –
that tempts the Devil.

We should respect these checks & balances. Like the pull
of the Tiber's crosscurrents, every move
calls up its countermove:
irresistible!

And I remember Rodin –
drollest of the droll –
when we were leaving Chartres by train
musing that the too-tall cathedral
provokes the wind's disdain.

XXVI: Fountain

No lessons now unless they're yours,
fountain, as once again
you fall into yourself, your waters risking return
from the heavens to life on earth.

My one example
is your murmur:
you, a column from a temple
brought down for simply being what you are...

In falling, the way you modulate
each jet of water that completes its dance –
I study it
down to the subtlest nuance

and I am yours in song, yours in murmuring, yours
in the moment of delirious silence
when you double back to draw a breath
through your liquid momentum – an inspired balance.

XXX

The pleasures of our well-bred ancestors –
their hearts reeling from the chase;
their repose
before dying fires –

have passed us by.
And yet, when our lives seem wasted, dry,
bewildered, emptied-out – we are still full,
for they are within us.

And the women – to how many women must
we have played host,
smuggling them out, as in the interval
of a bad play,

clothed in sorrows that today
no one would choose to wear...
how strong they appear,
drunk on our blood.

And those children whom the Fates refuse –
the children we were –
who told them their best hope of survival
lay in us?

XXXIV

And how many ports, and in every port
how many portals welcome you? And can you say
how many windows, when you pass,
flash back at you your life, your masterpiece?

And how many harvests will have failed;
how many, moved by the whirlwind's good grace,
will have been destroyed
before – tenderly, joyously – you gather the fruit?

And how many lives meet
answering one another every day?
Just being in the world
denies the void.

XXXVIII

The way the angels see it
the beech tree's roots are distant treetops,
while each branch sips
the sky, just like a root.

To them the earth seems insubstantial stuff.
Clouds are solid. Solid as a corpse, a cloud.
Our fiery earth! – and our springs that echo with the far-off
keening of the dead.

XL

Lake water, so still,
and there, enfolded in its form, a swan –
or the barely-moving likeness of a swan...
Sometimes the one we love
glides up to us
like that – pure motion, pure space –

until, too near
our never-easy soul,
like the swan upon its mirror
they cannot help but leave
their image: trembling between
doubt and bliss.

XLVI

Two wagons full of bricks
roll by in the golden day;
a pinkish hue stakes
its claim to the scene –

and renounces it in turn...
But why should that suddenly-softened tone
draw up a new conspiracy between
tomorrow and today?

XLVII

Winter's silence
is overcome
by a singing silence –
every harmony plays its part,
adding a nuance
to render the image perfect.

And this is not the final act
of the heart:
so full
of daring, so unspeakable,
it too must overcome
the part-song of silence.

LIV

I saw, once, in a wild beast's stare
the good life that will endure;
a glimpse of the pure
calm of the world. It did not scare –

not because it had no fear
but because it had resolved to live & move despite
                                                    its fear.

So, in a land of plenty, there once
grazed a presence
that did not yearn for elsewhere.

LV

The world could not spin on its axis if
it took too firm a hold,
and I am beginning to see
that the humblest thing requires some risk.

Who gave you that thin base, little flask?
So easily spilled!
The air shudders in ecstasy
as you come to grief.

LVII: Doe

Ah, doe: your eyes loom
with the beauty of these old trees –
what strong trust lies
mingled there with your alarm?

All of it now
carried away by your bounding grace –
but nothing spoils the homeless
ignorance, the bliss
stamped on your brow.

LIX

The last goodbye has been said. I am the man
departure made me. Every return
released my gaze a little more – I looked
and looked again, again...

So once more I come back; so I begin,
determined never to regret the love
I felt & feel for all these symbols of
the absences in which we act.

Letter to My Friends Overseas
translated from the French by André Naffis-Sahely

ABDELLATIF LAÂBI

'Letter to My Friends Overseas' was first published in *La Nouvelle Critique* in August 1978. It was written during Laâbi's decade-long imprisonment in Morocco for politically radical literary activities. Mailed piecemeal to friends on the outside, the poem was later assembled according to the poet's instructions. A truncated and transliterated English version appeared in *Index on Censorship* in 1980 in order to bring attention to Laâbi's worsening medical condition, by which time he had served seven years of his sentence. The poem appears in *Beyond the Barbed Wire: Selected Poems*, translated by André Naffis-Sahely (Carcanet, 2016).

Friends
you've become
one of those beacons of light
who help to defend me
from the forceps of the night
You find your way to me
through the mercy of the poem
and I'll see you again
beyond the barbed wire of exile
in a stillborn continent
that never surges out of the sea or the sky
nor is fashioned out of clay
but by the hands and the fervour
of voices that plead and jump out of the window
to plunge into the swell of possibilities
A human continent
that nurses the preamble
of all the sleeping or reawakening gifts
inside us all
which despite the hurdles of baseness
work their way through our flesh
and our consciences
A continent
where suspicion, contempt and indifference to the other
one day will look
like poorly-written plays
and be entombed in the mass grave

of obsolete currencies
A continent
where the Inquisition
will vanish from our brains
after this kingdom of barbarism crumbles
where intelligence
will fuse with feeling
where conversations without masks
will be welcomed and peppered with peaceful
greetings

Kind friends
usually when I write
I barely have the time
to feel your warmth
and sit amongst you
(a cigarette in my lips, the same tune in my head)
and must leave you
before I've reached the end of the page
You see, here they ration out
even the stationery
The request forms I fill
only allow correspondence
between the prisoner
and his family
They'll never understand
that family to me

doesn't mean ancestry
or heredity
or villages or ID cards
I've never been able to estimate
the size of my family
It stretches out
as far the sunrise in our eyes
as far as our newly-born continent
tears down the walls erected inside us

Friends
I've got so much to tell you:
it's just that usually
I keep my mouth shut not wanting to risk
the censors putting a stop
to these acts of presence
in fact I censor myself
fearing the briefness of my answers
might twist my thoughts
out of shape for you
or warp what this humble letter
this gradual rediscovery of ourselves
these simultaneously peaceful upsetting accounts
of the other through dialogue
have to say

Friends
I grow more convinced
that the poem
can only ever be
a dialogue
made of live flesh and sound
that stares you straight in the eyes
even if the poem has to cross
the cold wastes of distance
to finally reach you
in the creases created by absence
This is why
you no longer hear me speaking alone
in the trances of exorcism
in my tragic haemorrhages
as I extricate myself from this quagmire
and call out to the earthquake survivors
to heap my distress calls and curses on them
A long time ago
I wrote those poems
about the infernos of solitude
about my desperate climb back to my fellow ↵
                              human beings
and I'm not quite ready to disown them
those bitter fruits
of the murderous twilight
where I struggled
as I sought the roots
of a voice I knew was my own
of a human face that reflected
the exact image of my truth
Those violent poems were healthy
and without them
maybe my voice
today would be hollow
devoid of what gave it

its vital intensity
But the problem is
I can't write like that any more
Nowadays
my life's taken a different path
and so has my style
I'm not alone any more
My ordeal has placed me
on the road of encounters
My body has learned
to be pushed to the limits and curl up
as from a scalding-hot steel plate
to endure the lacerations
and to resist
to translate humiliation and pain
into their literal opposites
and inside this lead-sealed arena
where they condemned me to shuffle
for ten whole years
I have started to dig
entire tunnels
and underground passages
even into my veins
even into my mind's vital parts
and I heard other people were digging
in all the directions towards which
I was piercing through my aphasia
until the day when the first hand broke through
and I felt the willowy vines of embraces

Friends
you've often asked yourselves
how I got to this point
how a poet
can descend from his clouds
to walk on the earth
and turn into a warrior
Well here it is
you know my love
for my country and countrymen
and you can grasp
how in our stormy part of the world
these words are saturated with meaning
so that they can resonate
                              struggle
                                   and perish
for what they stand for
Your compassion for me
is glaring proof of that
Yes
if I'm here
it's because my passion was all-devouring
It destroyed my vague cravings for comfort
all the perks that being an intellectual
might have conferred upon me
all the illusions of cool-headed analysis
of the academic laboratories
There was no middle ground
It was either the gilded cage
of intellectuals-for-hire
an ostensibly servile
face-saving exercise,

or the brio of talent
that never accounts
for all the defeats and abuses
So I severed the moorings
and made for the wide-open sea
of the only struggle that matters
which my people are waging
and I can sing
out of love for this haunting land
this hijacked country
that electrocutes my memory
which serrates my distress
and hits me like a meteorite
magnetising the bend of its rainbows
unwinding its arabesques
revealing itself
as the gleaming giant of youth
who reaps the solar apotheosis
with a sphinx's dreamers' eyes
as it paws the ground inquisitively
a poppy pressed
to every artery torn from the body of life
so that blood abolishes
the winter of man

I can sing
out of love for this haunted land
which has turned into a poker chip
in the stock market of lawlessness
free it from the lies of slave-driver travelling salesmen
the clicking prayer-beads of billboards
in the stations of the West
where its sun
is a whorehouse for the pimps of bride abductions
where its veils and tattoos
are the opium of mystery
behind which the ghosts gasp for air and salivate
where the dignified faces of its men
are assaulted by old Kodak cameras and savage ↵
                                 disorientations
O to what extent we stunt
and debase
       life!

I can sing
out of love for this haunted land
as it bleeds standing up
so its name resonates
like these warning-bell words
that reverberate in the heavens
of courage and brotherhood
so that they swell
out of these cutting-edge wounds
sing of the blood
of those who perished at the dawn of great hopes
so their names grow in stature
and each of their syllables
becomes as familiar
to the uprising of consciences
as Vietnam and Palestine

Friends
You who live in the sterilised labyrinths
of the fortress of Wealth
You who see the caravans of taxed swag
amassed by your Knights-Templar Merchants
from the pillaged realms of the world
as they pass under your windows
You the conscientious objectors
in the twilight between the wolves and dogs
where they scheme, interfere and exterminate
on every horizon
all for the sake of your supposed security
of your interests
of your existential outlook on life
You the gentle gardeners
of the tree of fraternity
before whose eyes
they still whisper
o so discreetly
while putting a gun, a knife and a grenade
into the filthy hands
of gallows-birds and nigger-wogs
while camouflaged under cover of fog
You who go hungry
because the sight of your roads
saturated with the rubbish of waste
makes you heave
You the entombed
banned from the old-boy networks
where they pre-package popular culture
and put it into little golden sachets
of mimicry and of ruins
You the motionless
the killjoys
in the prison-factories
the penny-jars
the temples of shopping
the plantation-colonies of the supercities
that enrich the inner sanctums of multinationals
decorated with the emblem of the golden calf
You the troglodytes
of black-magic spell-books where they whisper ↵
                               the universal
sound investments of the old missionary West
the belly-button of the world

All this and more
dear friends
you the harbingers
who've thrown open the windows
of your hearts and your hands
You who've dug up the beach
and the red, vivid sea of multitude
from under the cobblestones
You the new bards
of the street who
sing Communard songs
and flock back to the vigilant barricades
You thanks to whom
the West will one day disappear
from our legitimate nightmares
like the spectre of dispossession

like the jungle machetes
suspended right over our heads
You the artisans
who will repopulate Europe
and restore
its cities of marvels
and plant the seeds
for the springtime of humanity

O friends
be brave
for your sake and ours
be brave
wherever the tunnel of the night
seems like a dead end
be brave
We'll deflect the sun
to shine on our imperative journey
We'll disembark
in that new continent
that'll arise all over the world
whose seas
won't be private pleasure-lakes for bankers
or criss-crossed by aircraft carriers of carnage anymore
but instead become oceans
streaked with bridges
traversed only
by sailing boats of discovery
and convoys bearing gifts

Friends,
I'll stop here for now,
I don't know
if what I've written you
is a poem
and whether people

recognise it as such
doesn't bother me much
because poetry
to me
isn't an attitude one adopts towards language
or friezes of hieroglyphs
that we should decipher
aided by scholarly
parameters of criticism
Poetry spills out of the page
evades these insignificant labels
employed to confine it
       pigeon-hole it
         make it niche

Poetry to me
is simply a way
to hold out my hand
to push myself further
to rear my head again
       and provoke
to herald all the brotherly suns

Kind friends
I'm so happy we've talked
Rest assured
my cell is far brighter
I feel like singing and laughing
and want to raise my glass
to our loves and hopes
What I've told you
doesn't add up to much
but our dialogue
has barely begun
and we've got a whole world to change
Adelante!

From the Archive
Issue 30, March–April 1983

GAEL TURNBULL

———————————

from a contribution of three
poems: 'A Racing Walker',
'Love is Also', and 'No'. The
same issue features poems by
Christopher Middleton, Eliz-
abeth Smither, and Michael
Hamburger, and articles by
Donald Davie ('Poets on Stilts')
and C. H. Sisson ('Christian
Sobriety'), among others.

LOVE IS ALSO

from the Gaelic of Sine Reisideach

Love is also a great door of oak,
studded with iron,
behind which is refuge against every storm,
that opens outwards
even before it is touched –

but equally, can be transformed
to a dungeon gate
and jealousy, the hair trigger spring
to slam the bolt.

Six Etudes
translated from the Polish by Jennifer Grotz & Piotr Sommer
Jerzy Ficowski

OVER THE COURSE
of his life and career,
Jerzy Ficowski
(1924–2006) published
more than a dozen
volumes of poetry,
including *A Reading
of Ashes*, illustrated
in the 1980 edition
by Marc Chagall. In
intellectual circles, he
is best known as being
the crucial authority
of the expressionist
Jewish fiction writer
Bruno Schulz, who was
killed by the Gestapo
in 1942. Ficowski
studied Schulz's
life, drawings and
writing for more than
a decade, publishing
the first definitive
literary biography
on Schulz, *Regions of
the Great Heresy*, in
1967. Ficowski, who
as a young man took
part in the Warsaw
Uprising, travelled
with the Polish gypsy
population after the
war and became an
avid historian of the
Polish Roma, docu-
menting their culture
in several monographs
and translating their
poetry, especially
the work of a woman
known as Papusza,
into Polish. He made
part of his living as a
popular songwriter, all
the while writing and
publishing his own
poems.

1. Old beggar at the church

At the gates of the church
deaf as the stump
of a felled tree
is a polychromed beggar
with an empty hand
He used to wear gold brocade
but it grayed
he had archangel wings
that turned into a hunchback
He scrapes together coppers
for the bell
So that the Lord God
will listen

3. Gordian bow

Who are you
bow
I am
a flowering knot
I intimidate
macedonian blades
and the cutters of ribbons
I withhold
from my own self
the easiness of my solutions
Pollinated by a spider
I bear fruit
I change into
a pom-pom

5. Erotic

Behind the short-lived
screen
of the bat
you take off
the last color
you fade out
in the hiss of a tear
you dive into
the infrared
spark
before the flutter of my wings
blows you out

2. Cemetery squirrels

Squirrels
like cemeteries
the dead are good
they don't pick nuts
Squirrels
count
gravely
for their souls
with their praying paws
under the flames
of red tassels
hazelnut rosaries

4. Since carp

Ever since the carp went deaf
as a result of
the constant staying in water
they know
man is mute
they sympathise with him
with a funereal fin
and ceaselessly
like a spindle
on the looms of their ponds
they weave water
they weave water
so as not to shred it
as people
do rain

6. All the same

Everything is
all the different to me
smoke
cut off from fire
a jar
detached from its handle
and this tree and this tree and this tree
but still no forest
until night comes
which unifies
And then
everything is finally
all the same to me

Five Poems

translated from the Italian by Todd Portnowitz

Lorenzo Carlucci

Lorenzo Carlucci was born in 1976 in Rome, where he now teaches mathematical logic at the University of Rome 'La Sapienza'. His road to poetry has been a strange one – a degree in philosophy from the University of Pisa, a doctorate in mathematics from the University of Siena and another in computer science from the University of Delaware – and his poetry is appropriately strange. Part hedonist, part ascetic, he records the woozy world with a sober methodology. As the Italian poet Stefano Dal Bianco describes his work, Carlucci 'writes with the authority of one who's understood that there's something out there to understand, and fixes on it, trudging forward, flailing, like a sort of a Thomas Aquinas dressed up as Dylan Thomas, or vice versa'. All at once his voice is somehow colloquial, scientific, lyrical, severe, and comical. The form in which he most excels, with the dexterity of Charles Simić, is the prose poem, which features prominently in his two published collections, *La Comunità Assoluta* (Lampi di Stampa, 2008), and *Ciclo di Giuda e altre poesie* (L'Arcolaio, 2008), which together won him the Premio Speciale Ceppo di Pistoia in 2009; and in his forthcoming collection, with Camera Verde press, *Sono qui solo a scriverti e non so chi tu sia*.

The five poems translated on the right, taken from Carlucci's latest book of poems, form a section entitled 'Prose Poems for Olympia'. But what, or who – and when? – is Olympia in these works? Personified and modernised, Carlucci's Olympia is somehow still in possession of history and location, still saturated with myth. Olympia seems to be all things to the poet but attainable: a stubborn, amorphous, Greco-Roman tension. The two are locked in a timeless stare-down, each daring the other to move. Yet despite the oddity of the whole proposition, Carlucci recounts this relationship with an almost frustrating naturalness and measure, as if philosophizing on a quite rational subject. And this is the wonder of his poetry: though the lines come off as almost mechanical, they are nonetheless insistently human, carefully recorded, deeply thoughtful. Carlucci is not merely stitching together found phrases or trying our patience with flat description, he is teasing the prose of the world into poetry. – T. P.

I mourn my time with Olympia, days spent by the sea, pine needles in the folds of our clothes, evening, the passing of time perceived like a plant's inaudible growing, not like a *sequent toil* but like the motionless rearranging of grains of sand, into a homogeneity. And from the café I can see Olympia on the beach, and the space between us, and the time it will take for her to reach me, if ever she wants to, if ever she stops playing with the children and making small talk or just being preoccupied with the riptides, the time it would take for her to reach me, feet stirred by the scalding sand – already they're filled with their own substance, or else with the air between me, who's at the bar, drinking and greeting transsexuals, and Olympia by the coast, who has no intention of coming back.

This time and space, brief, are like a membrane, they're filled already, already they're the movement they induce, my touching of Olympia, if ever she decides to come over and give me a kiss, or if ever I pry my ass from this chair. It's time and space, here by the sea, a distance already crossed, capacities already filled, already I've become my outstretched arm, same as my lazy gaze above a glass of orange juice, same as the soft and mysterious gaze of Olympia, who perhaps sees only the wind and not me, above my shoulder.

Olympia explains, as I drive along this interstate, the secret behind the numbering of highways. How 'even' means north-south, 'odd' east-west. How 'even' also means around, and 'odd' across. She also explains, without speaking, moving her smile like a cop's radar gun along the circumference of the passing landscape, how the sensation of beauty we feel even in the completely anonymous stretches of our hometown is due in large part, and perhaps entirely, to the familiarity of these locations, a fabric of signals we don't recognise openly, but that strike us as the keys of a typewriter strike an already written page. And I think then that there are poets who write as if typewriting onto their eyes. I smile, and I'm happy as a kid who reaches into the freezer to grab an ice pop but his arm is too short, clutching the hem of Olympia's skirt between my fingers.

Olympia also says that seagulls are beautiful and aerodynamic and exacting in their flight patterns, exacting in their direction and aimlessness, exacting in their wilfulness and refusal. I agree with her, they're beautiful, and they also socialise much like we do. Olympia also says that ducks are the source of the underwater chemistry of contact lenses and I think of us down in the sea, with one eye open, down in a lake on the hunt for prey, one eye always open, with a lens that forms to the eye, without burning or blinding it. Olympia is my prey, on the wooden beams that face the river, I'd like a boat to bring her to the centre of this body of water to the white centre of a seagull's eye. But Olympia's already distant and she's jealous of the child's pedalled contraption that's barrelling down now toward the river.

[...] and maybe she'll take my hand or maybe she's waiting for someone else. Better to think she'll take my hand, yes, she takes my hand and brings me on a walk, along the empty streets at night, she brings me to a place, or just to a time, in which there's no pride or fear, in which there are no delays, she brings me to a time, or to a rhythm which is the rhythm of her movement, holding me by the hand, and with no defined expression, and almost without being there (such is the levity of her presence), she takes me walking on the asphalt, rain-soaked black like her eyes. Like her hand, the hand of a mother between the shoulder blades of her son, at a funeral, the moon is white just like her hand, white-skinned, on a face with cobalt blue eyes.

To Invent the Word?

translated from the French (Algeria) by Marilyn Hacker

SAMIRA NEGROUCHE

'The second you appeared to me, my heart had all the sky to light it up.
It was noon in my poem. I knew that fear was sleeping.'

René Char, *the pulverized poem*

I don't know which of us you or me got there first seizing the other by her shirttails to see you coming or know you wait for me is the same mirrored reflection.

•

You always hum that innocent tune when your cheeks turn red in the evening for hands that sweat when they meet and I let the tide bring its own refrain.

•

Didn't I meet you after climbing a staircase no elevator and a heart that needed exercise what workout could I have done not to fall on my knees at your threshold?

•

In the verb poem there's the idea of fleeing from you and losing myself at daybreak at dusk and of making speeches to you on the solitude of words and the liberty of the flesh there is in the same verb poem the idea of lowering the sails and loving you without restraint.

•

I like to imagine a train arriving the length of the station platform that at last comes gently to a halt in the scratching of a language spoken by two beings who wait for each other in the same faraway and who meet by chance on the eve of a fresh start after having carefully straddled an infinity of conditionals.

•

I can't keep myself from thinking of those women who before me and after me attempt love with the forbidden as their one mirage I can no longer distinguish the reflections I so often give birth to my interdiction and let myself breathe in the wind of park gardens open air hotels bedrooms for the destitute of heart and the outcry of unregistered loving.

•

Before you I wanted to die with you I still want to die but I'd prefer to wait a while first.

•

Women who love have the odour of a fireplace that makes the day into a nest and of a garden that can find its earth in a collection of plots carved out of the cracks in the sidewalk in that love are my eyes that withdraw in the tenderness of sharing.

•

The body I love doesn't love my going to bed late my getting up early the eyes I love are almost patient when daylight is tardy they watch me go beyond my lunar compass and awake at the phantom border of our superimposed dreams.

•

Necessary now to invent everything to acknowledge the instant of loving I will have to say to you unprefaced what can have no proof except the word remember every instant stutterings promises I made you and vice versa necessary to be marked by all the ground we skimmed against with fear as our fellow traveller fear of losing each other of losing ourselves there is no antidote to doubt except our steps that cross each other reinventing the prism of colours there is no love but doubt that grows and rests in the certitudes of the past.

Two Poems

S. A. LEAVESLEY

Holidaying

A week of undiluted summer views
in an apartment uncluttered by past use.

Tattoos stretch out next to oiled sand;
body boards dart and yap on their leashes.

Bunting chatters brightly in the streets,
dusk surf promises a good head of lager.

Slowly, lights create their night braille –
town bars splashed with restless laughter.

Later, the wind whips away stray words,
while the moon holds a thousand secrets

tight to its chest – witnessed but never spilt.
Waking each morning in unfamiliarity,

messages scratched on the shoreline
where a dark sea danced at lovers' feet.

The tide wipes them without reading,
returns each grain to its place of flatness.

Driving home, I meet my work-day self
in the services, pale-faced and sulking.

Beautiful

A globe artichoke's softness
revealed beneath the rasp of spikes.

In the black heart of a poppy,
a sea anemone coralled in petals.

The rose without this name.
Palms in a pilgrim kiss. The twists

of grace in a ballerina's wrists, weight
lifted in en pointe pirouette.

Is the hummingbird's beauty
in the rainbows gliding from its wings,

its song or those feathered brushings
that make thin air sing?

Is it the gold ring, or the waiting finger;
the wringing out of wet linen

pressed against shivering skin,
or the way one sleeping breath

may shape itself to another's?
Is it this...or something else completely?

Any morning... no, every morning,
rising from the night's tides to find

my mouth's mist on cold windows –
its lapping shoreline: warm, damp, alive.

Four Poems

JOHN DENNISON

I let you go again

The quiver; and you're gone
where I cannot follow,
springing off the mattress
into the wide sky
of sleep, its cross-winds
and abrupt consolations,
its remonstrance and visaged
confrontations, its books
of bindings of pages of turnings,
and wonderful re-runs
of uncommon good,
its unlooked-for counsel
and the telling of the heart.
Me too, I say, let me
too go there, bomb
the flickering pool of dream
in a finger-tipping duo
jump, knees tucked
and both of us rounded,
like too-ripe passionfruit
hiffed over the wall
of the day – way to go!
And you have. Awake,
I let you go again
and hold your body close,
an instrument to gauge
our singularity.

Domain

Turning in the light, we search the face again –
an impressive façade; written above the colonnade:
The Whole Earth is the Sepulchre of Famous Men

runs the inscription, utterly serious. Auckland Domain
lies open, boys playing 7-a-side,
turning in the light. We search the view again:

the air is full of machines, the flypast bang on time;
faces open and nod in the breeze, gladly concede
the whole earth is the sepulchre of famous men,

and other solemn etc. certainties, doctrine
of mud. Look: the island kneels in the channel; the tide's
turning. In the light, we search the field again –

game over; I remember my sons, their restless limbs
which will carry them through dreams that stand astride
the whole earth. Is the sepulchre of famous men

like the dawn, over us all, letting down
its utter uniform? We don't speak the world.
Turning in the light, I search the news again:
'the whole earth is the sepulchre of famous men'.

Birdman

Harbour light. He is the business,
sole entry in the daily competition,
making an optimist's breakfast, a right mess
of, a clean breast of, a vision
of plucked courage going down, and up
we come, buoyant. He bobs in self-belief,
looks for the ladder, the heavy return trip.
Brightnesses teem, school in the water beneath
the wharf: life is in its element
regardless, things being what they are,
not longing and flap in a feathered suit.
O birdman, birdman, you keep on falling harder,
keep lifting up your head; let it tug,
that sense you're on the verge of something big.

The work

Nearly still in the late or early light,
it silts, occludes in sediment the lively
spill (a tickle of fall over bearded root,
troubled source unminded). Pools blankly,
unclear still of remember when and hurt
that, yes, will rise to broach the vocal air
with tiny wings, tongues, an articulate
Ferris wheel, not nothing there,
and – will you own it? – moving. Slow
hour; slow yourself. Trees stand
about, breathe out, lean into the murk.
And nights there is bread on the water, let go
to the mouthy, languaged element. Understand:
the refusal; the clouding; the rising, and the work.

Getting Personal

Love and Sex in Geoffrey Hill's *Pindarics*

SIMON COLLINGS

GEOFFREY HILL IS not a 'confessional' poet, at least not in the sense in which that term is commonly used. He has challenged, in forceful language, the 'contemporary pseudo-dogma' which equates the degree of a poet's suffering with artistic merit.[1] Hill's disapproval of 'confessional' poetry could not be clearer. So it is interesting to find him, in *Pindarics*, writing about personal sexual experience with a degree of openness not typical of his work. In 'The Songbook of Sebastian Arrurruz' (published in *King Log*, 1968) a fictional Spanish poet speaks of the pain of separation from a woman, seemingly his wife. Several poems in the sequence contain erotic imagery, and some commentators have interpreted the poem as referring to Hill's first marriage.[2] Apart from this rare example, and a few lyrics in *Without Title* (2006) Hill's poetry has not broached these topics, though in a 1999 interview, published in *Paris Review*, Hill does say that the erotic is 'very important' to him. In that same interview he also talks of how his views on objectification have relaxed over time, and that an approach to the 'truth' requires that 'the shortcomings of the self shall be admitted'. In *Pindarics* Hill addresses the reader in his own persona, eschewing the device of a fictional narrator. While not 'confessional', the poetry is, at least in part, about sexual relationships, and about the messiness of sex. Hill says in the *Paris Review* interview: 'I've experienced the power of Eros in some of its most joyous and in some of its most destructive and humiliating forms.'

Pindarics appeared originally as a sequence of twenty-one odes in *Without Title* (2006). Hill later expanded and revised the sequence, issuing a new version, comprising thirty-four odes, in *Broken Hierarchies* (2013). It is in this later version that most of the material dealing with sexual experience appears. The revised work represents an extensive remodelling and reordering of the original. He retains just eleven of the odes from the first version, some substantially revised, occasionally with elements reused from discarded odes. Fragments of odes he does not retain are sometimes absorbed into the new material.

'Pindaric' most obviously refers to the Greek poet Pindar whose odes were mainly written to celebrate important individuals or events. The term 'Pindaric' was also employed by the poet Abraham Cowley in the seventeenth century to describe a series of odes of irregular stanza lengths, mainly of a philosophical nature. A more immediate influence on Hill is the American poet Allen Tate. In the eighth poem in the original version of *Pindarics* (which is omitted from the revised version) Hill describes himself as having 'cribbed from much / maligned beau Allen Tate pindaric odes'. Tate, in commenting on his own poem 'Ode to the Confederate Dead', said:

It is an ode only in the sense in which Cowley in the seventeenth century misunderstood the real structure of the Pindaric ode. Not only are the meter and rhyme without fixed pattern, but in another feature the poem is even further removed from Pindar than Abraham Cowley was: a purely subjective meditation would not even in Cowley's age have been called an ode. I suppose in so calling it I intended an irony: the scene of the poem is not a public celebration, it is a lone man by a gate.

Each of Hill's thirty-four poems consists of two stanzas, each of nine lines, and a final stanza of five lines, echoing the classical Greek ode which consisted of three major parts, a strophe, an antistrophe, and a concluding epode. Hill's poems include occasional mention of strophe, antistrophe and epode, as well as the word 'counterturn' – the direct English translation of antistrophe. Within this regular verse form Hill allows himself considerable compositional freedom.

Pindarics reprises themes familiar from Hill's earlier collections – an identification with martyrs, the importance of remembering, the debasement of language, and the role of the poet in society. He moves from topic to topic, between and within poems, by a process of association, incorporating a diverse range of material. Each ode is cross-cut by the different themes, providing the sequence with a sense of unity. The register is sombre, that of an old man contemplating death, though the verse is laced with wry humour and moments of lyric beauty. The writing exhibits Hill's typical levels of 'difficulty', as well as his abiding fascination with the lexicon. As Ann Hassan says in *Annotations to Geoffrey Hill's Speech! Speech!* (Glossator, 2012) the difficulties presented by Hill's writing stem from 'its thousands of particulars – these being part of the singular, idiosyncratic experience of the poet'. The present essay aims to assist the reader to navigate some of the challenges presented by the text of *Pindarics*, and to bring 'reader and text closer together', to borrow another of Hassan's phrases. There are several major themes in the poem, and an exploration of all of these would fill a book. This study will focus primarily on the material relating to sexual relationships.

Pindarics is addressed to the Italian writer Cesare Pavese (1908–50), a man who was deeply troubled in his relationships with women, and it is the encounter with Pavese's work which seems to prompt Hill to write about sexual experience. The overt address to Pavese is clearer in the original version. Quotations from the Italian writer preface each poem in the original but these have been dropped in the revised version. These elisions, along with the many revisions to the odes, obfuscate the frequent references to Pavese's life and work.

Hill identifies with Pavese on a number of levels. The resistance to Fascist cultural policies, the literary innovations and commitment to 'truth', the interest in myth all chime with some of Hill's long-standing interests. Pavese is, like many of the writers Hill includes in his pantheon, a 'martyr', a man who bore witness, staying true to 'the work' at significant personal cost. *Pindarics* references these qualities in

Pavese, and they are clearly attributes which attracted Hill. But it is Pavese's peculiar difficulties with sex and women, and Hill's response to this, which make him unique among the writers Hill claims as one of his own. Pavese came to believe that he was destined to be rejected by the women he most desired. He wanted to marry and have children but never did. In 1950 he committed suicide following yet another failed love affair. At one level Hill clearly empathises with Pavese, though his own experience has been very different from the Italian's. Hill has twice been married and has had children with both wives. He married his second wife, the American poet Alice Goodman, in 1987 and the relationship has been a positive force in Hill's life.[3] He seems to draw mainly on experiences from his earlier life in making connections with Pavese's personal struggle.

The epigraph to *Pindarics* taken from Pavese's diaries anticipates some of the themes developed in the odes – the 'terribleness' of love, and the nature and value of poetry. The first line of the epigraph reads:

It is not true that with the passing of years, love becomes less dreadful.

Pavese was born in the Langhe region, north of Turin. He lived for much of his life in Turin and was deeply attached to his Piedmontese roots. His father died when he was young and Pavese was brought up by his mother, a strong and domineering woman with whom he had a difficult relationship. He suffered from bouts of depression during his life, and often entertained thoughts of killing himself. From an early age Pavese became interested in American writing, and he translated many authors previously unknown in Italy – including Melville, Hemingway and Faulkner. His championing of American and other writers clashed with the nationalistic rhetoric of the Fascists then coming to power, and his association with anti-Fascist writers in the 1930s led to him being arrested and sentenced to a period of internal exile. But Pavese was not especially active politically, and he did not join the partisans during the war as many of his peers did, something he was later ashamed of. After the war he became a member of the Communist Party as a way of trying to assuage his feelings of guilt, but he later faced political criticism from the Party. He was an atheist, though he developed a fascination with myth towards the end of his life. Hill draws from two particular sources, Pavese's diaries (*This Business of Living*, Peter Owen, 1961) and a biography of Pavese by Davide Lajolo (*An Absurd Vice*, New Directions, 1983).

The sex theme in *Pindarics* is established in the first two odes, which represent new material, appearing only in the *Broken Hierarchies* version. Hill opens with an evocation of childhood and adolescence. 'Could I have known what I had, *Boyhood's End* / and all that. Crowding her so to myself / through strange puberty, Dame Kind her solitudes / a joint possession.' *Boyhood's End* is a cantata by Michael Tippet based on a text of W. H. Hudson which recalls a child's ecstasy in nature. Hudson says if he could keep one thing it would be the sense of innocent wonder he knew as a child. Dame Kind is the goddess of Nature in a poem by Auden (titled 'Dame Kind') published in *Encounter* in 1960. She is the mother of our reproductive urges

'to Whom the first innocent blood was formally shed'. Auden's verse is both cynical and grotesque in its discussion of sex. The photographs referred to in line 6 of Hill's poem are presumably pornographic, 'smeared' by much handling. Hill interjects with the editorial aside, 'If this is abrupt / forgive me', and then goes on to describe himself and Dame Kind as being 'inexplicable' to themselves 'even now'.

The strophe deals with the confusing loss of 'naturalness' which comes with puberty. In the antistrophe Hill holds out the possibility that we may discover, if we read on, the identity of the woman he's writing about. In fact the odes refer to a number of women – though none by name. Hill announces from the outset that he intends to write about his subject in a way which 'grants nothing to dignity', nor to 'dignitas', the Roman concept of moral probity. In other words, he does not intend to spare himself. The phrase 'an art / reactionary as all wars' (lines 14 and 15) alludes to the conflicts between rivals in love, a theme picked up later in ode 22. The long-desired 'solo album' is a reference to celibacy, a subject also touched on again in other poems. In the epode Hill declares himself 'bemused by how late love retracts its term'. Here 'retracts' suggests at one level a withdrawal from sexual activity, even perhaps detumesence. But Hill is also using it in the sense of 'revised' (cf. St Augustine's *Retractationes*). Hill is reaching back to the word's etymological roots to suggest the way we revise our thoughts and feelings from the vantage of age. 'Ces' in the last line is short for Cesare, the nickname Pavese was given by his school friends and the name by which Hill refers to the poet throughout *Pindarics*. Suicide released Pavese from the torments of lust and the indignities of ageing.

In the second ode, Hill includes further personal references to events in his past. In lines 3–6 we read: 'Elsewhere now / *I laboured for Rachel not Leah*, but lost her / ere I had numbered pearls in the bride's cache-sexe. / Mating for life aborted by birth [...]'. '*I laboured for Rachel*' refers to the Old Testament story in which Jacob agrees to work seven years to win the hand of Rachel. After seven years the father tricks Jacob and gives him Rachel's sister Leah as a bride. Jacob then toils a further seven years to be able to marry Rachel. The personal significance of these lines is unclear. Hill may be referring to his first marriage, but this can only be speculation. The presence of children, he implies, creates tensions in a relationship. In the same ode, 'Guess / what comedy of uncreated kind / draws us to confluence' echoes the Dame Kind referenced in the first ode, 'confluence' suggesting sexual intercourse.

The passage starting 'Most explainings are slipshod...' evokes images of conflict within a failing relationship. There's perhaps an oblique reference to Eliot's 'undisciplined squads of emotion' here, and to Eliot's problematic first marriage. Eliot turns up again in ode 21 with the line 'things ill-done and done to others' harm' quoted from 'Little Gidding'. He describes Eliot as having had an 'unrivalled fear of intimate disclosure', a 'fear' Hill is identifying with. Eliot's advocacy of 'depersonalisation' in art, in for example the essay *Tradition and the Individual Talent*, had a major influence on Hill. Ode 31 also deals with this topic, asking in the opening lines, 'by whose desire / is the open secret a wound?' Hill's response: 'I play you sealed witness.' *Pindarics* moves repeatedly from moments of revelation to reassertions of the principle of depersonalisation. At the end of ode 2 Hill announces that he is not yet ready to 'draw out too much'.

Sex is touched on briefly in ode 4, which describes the landscape of eastern Cambridgeshire. Fleam Dyke is an ancient earthwork, the main surviving section extending between Fulbourn and Balsham. Hill describes the dyke, the furrowed earth of fields, a cold spring day, with a sense of desolation similar to that found in many of the poems in *Without Title*. The East Anglian landscape also features in odes 8 and 29. Hill became a lecturer at Emmanuel College, Cambridge in 1981 after his first marriage broke up (he was divorced in 1983). The final section of the poem discusses suicidal thoughts. Sexual desire is presented as grotesque in a complex image which compares an erect penis to the stuffed head of a fox – proud but lifeless. Hill makes ironic use of 'thrust' and 'mounted'.

Aside from these references, the themes broached in the first two odes do not re-emerge until much later in the work. Odes 3, and 5 to 10, are primarily concerned with language and the public role of the poet, and contain references to aspects of Pavese's life, including his winning of the Strega prize in 1950. Ode 12 has Hill reflecting on ageing, an old apple tree in bloom a metaphor for the poet's late creative outpourings. Odes 13 to 20 are principally concerned with moral integrity, witness and human fallibility, themes Hill has been engaged with throughout his career. These poems deal variously with Pavese's internal exile to Brancaleone, and the fate of other writers under Mussolini.

It is not until odes 22, 25, 27 and 28 that we find further references to Hill's personal history. Ode 22 develops the theme of unsatisfactory sexual relationships, both Pavese's and Hill's. The poem begins: 'Ces was bad vibes, a weakling in his loves / though only there.' *Moby Dick*, referred to in the next sentence, is one of the books translated by Pavese, evidence of his strength in matters other than love. In the lines which follow Hill recalls an early experience of being rejected by a woman, perhaps a fellow student. '(Myself dispatched, / a play toward, trim raincoat over arm / like a sommelier's napkin, tickets prick-eared / blazer breast pocket – a college *Hamlet*...)' The play starred her 'tyger lover', a male rival Hill dismisses with the observation: 'unheard-of since'. The term 'struck-through' in line 8 (meaning crossed-out) stands for rejection. But 'struck-through' is also of course a reference to stabbing and to events in *Hamlet*.

In the antistrophe Hill asks himself whether he responded to this woman's rejection of him by excising a dedication to her from a half-finished poem. 'The busy hammers closing rivets up' in line 13 comes from the prologue to Shakespeare's *Henry V*, where preparations for the coming battle are described. Hill here uses 'battle' as a metaphor for the way men compete for the affections of women. The stress, he notes, drives some to withdraw into religious abstinence. 'Boys have gone mystic for less, displeasingly / celibate, though from chained whim [...]' Pavese practised celibacy at one stage in his life

in an attempt to find release from sexual desire. This ode picks up on the motifs of conflict and celibacy first introduced in ode 1. One is also reminded of the final section of 'The Songbook of Sebastian Arrurruz' and the lines 'And enjoy abstinence in a vocation / of now-almost-meaningless despair.'

The 'gyring Ann Lee' of the final section of ode 22 is a reference to the leader of the Shakers, born in 1736 in Manchester, UK. She had a revelation that: 'a complete cross against the lusts of generation, added to a full and explicit confession, before witnesses, of all the sins committed under its influence, was the only possible remedy and means of salvation'. 'Profligate abstinence' from sex of course leads to 'annihilation' of the 'stock', as Hill wryly observes.

An early, perhaps adolescent, love is recalled in odes 25 and 27. Ode 25 begins: 'Pitched *labouring ships* so well that I took off / but botched the dating. Must I yet go back, / the process over (he said), over the process?' '*Labouring ship*' here is a reference to Yeats's poem 'The Sorrow of Love' in which love is presented as a source of misery. Hill expresses his anxiety about raking back through these memories, which still have the power to unsettle him. He and the girl, we are told, carved their initials into the bark of a beech, 'long since felled'. 'Du, nachbar Gott' (You, neighbour God), mentioned in line 17, is a poem by Rilke, from *Stundenbuch*, which begins:

You, neighbour God, if I sometimes disturb you
in the long night with hard knocking,
it is because I seldom hear you breathe and know
You are alone in the room.

(tr. Kurt Knecht)

Hill's 'I make knock / repetitive' echoes the Rilke poem in which God remains silent and mysterious. The 'labouring ships' of the doomed Greeks, of Yeats's poem, are mentioned again in the epode. 'Concede / those labouring ships their laboured progeny / among which we are borne. Contrary tides / clamour to beauty as flared light scuds through.' The 'progeny' here are life's experiences with which we must be reconciled. Note the punning on 'labour', 'progeny' and 'borne'.

Ode 27 describes a landscape in May and recalls an encounter with a girl or woman, a missed opportunity of his childhood or youth. This may be the same relationship referred to in ode 25. 'Conjubilant the hawthorn crusts and crests / with blossom, part-submerges its own growth / [...] So much of us is coded.' Conjubilant means 'shouting together' – a wonderfully apposite term for a hedgerow in bloom. The description here recalls ode 12 in which Hill likens himself to an old apple tree in flower. The poetry, the blossom, Hill says, also hides what is beneath. 'A faintish ringing [...] hammers far abroad' in lines 7 and 8 recalls the 'busy hammers' of ode 22, and the rivalries associated with love. These are now distant, memories of youth. The thoughts which come to the poet in this landscape are 'shadowed', as though he's looking through water. The memory of that missed opportunity is a wound which still aches. The final lines of the epode read: 'and all for folly that is even now / remonstrance of the wound. Rewind the spring.' 'Remonstrance' means a protest or complaint. The speaker wishes he could have his youth again.

The opening lines of ode 28 pick up on the 'remonstrance of the wound', and the pebbles he gathers in memory of the girl of ode 27 'because I did not gather her to myself.' Hill talks about how his inner impulses and thoughts are not 'admirable', but to the question of whether he could restrain them, or refrain from talking about them, there is no answer. He echoes here the comments in ode 1 about his subject granting 'nothing to dignity'. 'Making is exhaustive' echoes 'work is tiring' (the title of Pavese's first collection, *Lavorare stanca* in Italian, which is referenced several times in *Pindarics*). He returns to the theme of how difficult it is explaining oneself. The antistrophe combines images of physical fragility and comments on the process of creating: 'Invent from noting each new scene, / an oblique shaft of sunlight'. The epode suggests that desire causes us to repeat patterns of behaviour we are powerless to escape: 'Set us down / into our loop; and we repeat ourselves / only as mute desire.'

The principal material relating to Pavese's dysfunctional relationships with women – he described himself as a misogynist at one period in his life – appears in odes 23, 24, 26, and 33. Hill conjures a hawk as an image of predation in ode 23, perhaps recalling the Spanish Renaissance poetry which influenced some of his earlier work, such as 'The Pentecost Tower' (published in *Tenebrae*, 1978). The Miss Dowling of line 8 is the American actress Constance Dowling, to whom Pavese's last novel, and the poem 'Death will come and she'll have your eyes', were dedicated. Pavese killed himself after their relationship came to an end. Hill is mocking of her professional achievements, calling her fame 'brief' and 'untowardly', the language echoing his dismissal of the student Hamlet of the previous ode.

Ode 24 is a recasting of the opening poem of the original *Pindarics* with a number of revisions, especially to the epode. In the original the epigraph read: 'What, then, can you deny this most hateful of men? You can deny him nothing whatsoever.' This is from Pavese's diary entry for 10 October 1938. The 'most hateful of men' is one who 'thoroughly enjoys life' and is happily married to an attractive woman, the kind of man Pavese could not himself be, but at some level envied. Hill is paraphrasing Pavese's diary in the strophe of this ode, presenting a heavily ironised version of domestic happiness. He then contrasts this in the antistrophe with fleeting, unsatisfactory sexual relationships; he uses the word 'swive', which means to have sexual intercourse. Hill is here identifying with Pavese, and suggesting parallels with his own life, though as noted earlier Hill has married twice, has fathered children, and has been married to his second wife for twenty-eight years.

Ode 26 is new material, though the phrase 'baroque divas / god-haunched castrati' is recycled from the original ode 18. The epigraph to the original ode 20 is absorbed here into the text: 'But the real, tremendous truth is this: suffering serves no purpose whatever.' In Pavese's diaries, these words appear in a section recording yet another failed relationship (see the diary entry for 26 November 1937). Hill begins with comments on the slide of contemporary culture into sentimentality and presents himself in opposition to this, describing his stance as 'heretical'. The poet's

portrait of himself is characteristically witty and self-deprecating: 'I love the detritus of my own body / such as earwax'. The rest of the ode deals with sex. Pavese may have had a problem with premature ejaculation, according to Lajolo, his friend and biographer, and Hill implies that he himself has had problems with reaching orgasm, a not-uncommon experience. Lines 14 and 15 read: 'Achieving climax / never that easy; they missold us there.' The 'wise wound' in the next line is a reference to menstruation. The poem continues: 'I effectively remember / that stumbling engine-note desynchronised; we staring upward; they, up there, gaze down.' The image evoked is of lovers lying side by side, the man having failed to sustain an erection, the gods looking down mockingly. In the epode Hill sustains this sense of the comic absurd, imagining a contrivance which would allow Circe to have sex with a man suffering from erectile dysfunction. 'Little, death' in the last line refers to the post-coital lassitude the French call *la petite mort*. The commas suggest the thrusting actions of sex and ejaculation: 'to, and, with, you, our, little, death.'

Ode 33 is a substantial rewrite of parts of odes 6 and 7 from the original version. Hill opens with reference to his own experience of being a published poet and the subject of criticism – not always friendly – while drawing a parallel with Pavese. 'Be inured / the spikier the better', Hill advises. The text then makes oblique references to Pavese's exile by the sea in Brancaleone in southern Italy, as well as to Ovid's experience of exile under Augustus. (Hill draws parallels between Ovid and Pavese in ode 13.) The 'barren empire barking on its tides' in the final line of the strophe could be Imperial Rome, Fascist Italy or contemporary society. The antistrophe picks up again on Pavese's sexual problems. The Italian poet liked to swim in his youth – the original version of the poem has 'you were a swimmer, Ces', changed here to 'How could one swim so well'. 'Induration' in line 13 is a hardening of tissue, as with a scar over a wound. The sense here is of Pavese developing a 'thick skin' from repeated woundings. 'Induration' chimes with 'inurement' and 'inured' from the first and second lines of the ode. The 'impediment' referred to in lines 15 and 16 suggests Pavese's sexual problems as well as something in Hill's experience. The text reads: 'Women become contagious abstinence, / afflictions of the skin. What has been heard / of my impediment's productive charm? / Impediment's not the right word; hold contagious.' There is a sense here of sexual abstinence feeding productive literary output, something Pavese wrote about in his diaries. But then Hill in a typical gesture covers his tracks, obscuring the connection between Pavese and himself; abstinence isn't 'contagious', 'impediment' the wrong word.

The phrase 'look at yourself' in the second line of the epode could be a reference to Pavese describing in his letters moments during his exile when he began to lose the sense of who he was, and of gazing in the mirror for company. It could equally be Hill addressing himself. The 'judicial stay' of lines 21 and 22 refers to Pavese's early release after serving less than a year of his three-year sentence. He returned to Turin, to the shattering experience of finding himself jilted by a woman he loved. She had married the day before he reached Turin. The experience had a lasting effect on Pavese. Later, after the break up with Constance Dowling, he killed himself in a 'small hotel' in Turin. The final sentence of the ode refers to this.

If Pavese found release in suicide, 'treason against the self' is something Hill says in ode 21 he can go along with only 'in snagged kinds of ways'. Ode 29 offers a potentially different source of consolation, in an experience of natural beauty which evokes Gerard Hopkins's ideas of revelation. The poem opens with a description of reed beds in the fens of East Anglia lit up at sunset. Fleem and Flame echo 'Fleam' from ode 4, taking us back to the fens. The antistrophe comments on the impermanence of human relationships, how everything glides by, untouched by 'hope'. 'Instress', the term Hopkins uses to describe the apprehending of God's design in the world, provides in line 14 a possible instant of transcendence: 'Stand / to stare through: is it *instress*?' The sun on the reeds is experienced as a moment of beauty, perhaps a revelation of the divine. In the epode Hill describes, in moving terms, having always felt detached, though loved, and 'oddly vacant': 'Without marriage in heaven it becomes harder / to take bearings. Yet loved at any time / my soul was oddly vacant, as if still born, even into old age'. But he invites us not to lose this moment of wonder, the reeds glowing in the dying sunlight.

Ode 30 is something of an oddity. Hill eulogises here the French poet Andre Frénaud (1907–93) who was captured by the Germans in the Second World War and held in a prisoner of war camp from which he managed to escape. The point of interest with regard to love and sex is the reference to Frénaud's book *La Sorciere de Rome*, a sequence of complex, dream-like meditations on the city which incorporate references to myth, history and to the present. Messalina, referred to in the epode of ode 30, was the third wife of the Roman emperor Claudius, who had a reputation for sexual promiscuity. Frénaud mentions her once in *La Sorciere de Rome* where she briefly appears as an incarnation of the creative / destructive female force which haunts much of Frénaud's work. The possible connections being made here with the theme of sexual relationships in *Pindarics*, and with Pavese, seem tenuous. Hill also refers to Frénaud in *The Orchards of Syon*, poem LX, quoting the line 'la vulve insomnieuse' literally 'the sleepless vulva' – which appears in the same stanza as the Messalina reference in *La Sorciere de Rome* (section VIII).

A rather different poet, Eugenio Montale, obliquely referred to in two of the odes, has a more obvious connection with Hill's theme. In ode 11 we find material reworked from odes 10, 11 and 12 in the original version. *La Bufera e Altro* (*The Storm and Other Poems*), which Hill names in the opening lines, is a collection of poems published by Montale in 1956. Montale is named in line 6 of the original ode but the name is replaced in the later version with 'a dead man's'. (There are also disguised references to Montale in ode 6, 'cuttlefish bone' being the title of the poet's first collection.) Montale, a contemporary of Pavese, features in several of Hill's works, the earliest explicit reference being in section CXXXIV of *The Triumph of Love*. *Without Title* is dedicated to Montale and includes a translation of the poem 'La

Bufera' ('The Storm') in which a thunderstorm serves as a metaphor for Italy's experience of the war and Montale's personal loss of the great love of his life, Irma Brandeis. She was an American Jewess forced to return to the USA because of the political situation in Italy. Montale wrote hermetic, complex verse as a way of avoiding interference from Fascist censorship. In line 16 Hill is referring to Montale's coded speech when he asks how he should 'type-code' his own 'storms'. How, in other words, should he write about his own personal disappointments and frustrations?

In ode 21 Hill provides a concise statement of his position in the phrase: 'all told / nothing confessed' (lines 9/10). Hill here reasserts his rejection of 'confessional poetry'. The statement is reinforced in the antistrophe. The heart's 'fury' is best 'occulted' (cut off from view) – *non è vero?* – he says. Despite its references to broken relationships, emotional dysfunction, and even sexual malfunction, *Pindarics* is not a 'confessional' work. It is however revealing of aspects of Hill's emotional life in ways that other of his poems are not. His vision is bleak. Libidinous impulses are presented as a source of confusion and humiliation, sexual gratification near impossible to achieve, lust is both comical and depressing. Only occasionally do shafts of 'flared light' break through. These revelations are consistent with what Hill sees as our 'fallen' nature as human beings, our lives inevitably flawed, true intimacy with another impossible to attain.

In the final ode, 34, the topic of relationships is touched on only tangentially, in a reference to Propertius, the Roman poet known for his romantic verse. This ode is largely new material though the strophe uses lines from the antistrophe of the original ode 14, and the poem ends with reworked lines from the epode of the original ode 3. A 'shade before his time' refers both to Propertius's premature death – he died in his early thirties – and to his delayed influence on other writers. He was 'rediscovered' by Renaissance poets including Petrarch. Hill suggests that Propertius understood better how to win favour and patronage with his love poetry – 'sexual polity' – than did Ovid. He draws a contrast between Propertius and his imitators, and poets like Ovid, Pavese and Hill, for whom 'love' is troubling.

The primary focus of this concluding ode, however, is not love and sex but poetry. 'The best / song studies the gyre' (lines 8 and 9) recalls Yeats, whose *A Vision* is quoted in ode 8. A flock of wild geese (lines 11 to 16) stands as a metaphor for poetry. Their wing beats 'make something' of 'directionless lament' and 'direct exilic order'. The vatic, the public, prophetic aspect of poetry is laid aside in favour of private solace: 'it is the beat that counts.' It is in the act of making order out of the chaos of lived experience that the poet ultimately finds consolation.

NOTES

1   See Hill's essay 'Language, suffering, and silence', originally published in 1999.
2   A profile of Hill published in the *Guardian*, 10 August 2002, says: 'His first marriage had broken down in the 1970s, in circumstances that friends describe as "agonising".'
3   The 2002 *Guardian* profile says: 'Hill is unflagging in his admiration for his Jewish-born wife'.

Three Poems

ROGER GARFITT

The Action

i.m. Alan Hawke

          Slow work,
you would think, building... I never knew
it could be so passionate until you threw
your fast bowler's back into plastering
our living room wall.

          Some spell
you put in that afternoon, one continual
shoulder roll of the hawk over the
wall until it was sheer in the
original sense and shone.

          That night
from the sofa you'd glimpse it again,
run up on a spliff and a couple
of cans and throw yourself
into oblivion.

          The long
back gathering to its pitch – that's how
your sister was these last six months,
insistent she should drive so she
didn't have to think,

          the runs
to the hospice easier to focus on, for all
the roadworks, the overnight closures,
the diversions through small towns
in the small hours, than the

          one thought
running under everything – or they were
until stalled headlights on Clee Hill
showed a lad thrown
off his motorbike.

          Strange how
the perception altered in those months
that were like living on the run,
services to services, fuelled
up on double shots,

          time as
tangible as the road surfaces worn
under our wheels. I see myself
now as one of those lads you
coached, learning to hold

          speed in,
to pace my run over the changing
ground as if nothing could
throw the arm off
its deliberate arc.

Spain

for Patience Edney

They sit in a cave with a hundred beds,
the nurse from St Albans and the mayor
who ferries food from the village below.
She hears the last intake of troops singing
as they go up to the Front, 'children' of
fifteen or sixteen. 'I became a man',
he tells her, 'when the land reform came in.
I measured the plots. I learned to read and write.'

His words are an earnest of the new earth
that had brought men to the Gare d'Austerlitz
in their Sunday suits, brown paper parcels
under their arms, a faith she must hold to
against the atavism of the Stuka's howl,
even as the children sing to their deaths.

The Subaltern's Hymnbook

The truce is over. The firing begins again.
How strange it was, crouched beneath the parapet,
to hear the tune I used to sing at Father's elbow
in the family pew. How intimate it always seemed,
that last verse, *to be sung on Christmas Day,*
'Yea, Lord, we greet thee, Born this happy morning',
as if our voices might carry all the way back
to Bethlehem. We sang it so quietly yesterday,
as if they were family too. And I thought back
to Harvest Festival as a boy, glancing down
to find *Wir pflügen und wir streuen* set over
'We plough the fields, and scatter...' Did they paint
their waggons different colours? With us every county
had its own. What shape did they give their harvest loaves?
I imagined all the parishes of Northern Europe
in procession, horkey boughs carried from every twist
and turn of the map, and over us a phrase of Luther's
that had already caught my eye: *Ein' Feste Burg*,
'A safe stronghold our God is still...' What should I sing
across this wasted land as the shells burst and the snipers
pick us off? 'A deep dug-out our God is now'?

Two Poems

WILLIAM LOGAN

Red Slipware, Italian,
c. first century BC

The palm-sized dish, still coated –
no, encrusted! – with the scale
of some minor, long untenanted village,
does not offer the hoped-for gossip
about the stranger who buried it,
the exotic disease carried by the Cretan rower;

cannot provide the pet name of the citizen
who fingered from it – not lark's tongues,
the slipware too modest – or of the scheming
handmaiden who served him, a slave, of course,
and treated lavishly only in departure
from the lavish; cannot whisper the sins

of the humpbacked potter who turned it
on his wheel (scars still inscribed
along the rough bottom); yet in the mended
fractures hints, not at X-rays (bone neatly
pinned, as if an abandoned sewing project),
or the meandering of ancient

trade routes across open plain,
but, in the faint suggestion of buried canals,
something of the surface of Mars –
none of this explaining why an object
unmarked by word can provoke such fear,
except that it too is clay going back to clay.

Muse

She was the muse of every boy in eighth grade –
tomboyish queen of the flared skirt,
prepossessed of beauty. Those cheekbones,
Cherokee or Mohawk, never went out of date.
Beauty is the enemy of democracy.
Maturity could be only a darkening.
I saw her years later, forties, fifties, still flashing
that wall-to-wall smile, unashamed, strenuous to watch.
She married half happily, as muses will
when they don't know they are muses.
Her every word was an electric shock – mine, I mean,
and words were few enough, never good enough.

Two Poems

PETER ZERVOS

To my Seamstress

To me, the sun's more seamstress than sovereign:
her cambered needle rushes on the wind
and stitches yellow lines on my room's blind
or adds brown outlines to the cyclamen.
Her scissors yawn over loose ends on the lawn
and whet their limbs against the pine tree bole.
She tries new trimming angles on the corn,
decks out with ivy arabesques my wall.
Even her carelessness becomes my gain,
as when she drops her rhinestones after rain.

To P.

'Goodnight.' I kiss you on the hip, tiptoe
toward the door. I hear your forearm shuffling
across the corner of the bed I've slept in
year after year, my brow touching your brow.
This is the hour of chirpings in the grass
and navels slowly filling with slow ash.
This is the hour of the long-shadowed wind
that coils around the eyes, damping all tint.
It is the time I spend attending to
your shuffling body over our bed's lisp:
me here, you in the next room, trying to sleep
away the thought I rarely think of you.

Off Beat

Jeff Nuttall and the International Underground

DOUGLAS FIELD & JAY JEFF JONES

IN 1978, INVITED to read his work to the students at Warwick University, Jeff Nuttall was asked to introduce himself. He did so and at some length, but first he said, 'Ten years ago that wouldn't have been necessary.'[1]

The niggling vanity in this statement suggests Nuttall's acknowledgement of his diminishing stature as a countercultural figure who, back in 1968, was renowned in certain quarters, on the back of the success of his generation surveying tour de force, *Bomb Culture*. This hip sociology bestseller established him as the expert insider of the alternative society, which was high on the media's free love and drugs titillation agenda. It was one of those cornerstone works of an era, like *The Female Eunuch*, that could have launched Nuttall on a Greer-sized career if he had played his cards right.

'I had no idea I was stepping so far into the enemy camp,' Nuttall wrote. 'The iconoclast had come home, shown himself articulate, rational, prepared, in fact, to talk things over sensitively. The embrace was flattering, remunerative and smothering.'[2]

Instead, Nuttall appeared to chuck in his zeitgeist straight-flush hand and retreated from the psychedelic salons of London for the life of a dedicated art lecturer in provincial Bradford.

Bomb Culture, MacGibbon & Kee, London, 1968.
Cover designed & illustrated by Jeff Nuttall.

Well, hardly.

Bradford College of Art was, at that time, the educational equivalent of Dodge City. As one of Britain's most dogged pioneers of happenings and performance art, Nuttall found Bradford (in 1970 he moved on to Leeds Polytechnic) – and the shadowlands of an industrially-defunct urban Yorkshire – one great playground for avant-garde devilment. The unconstrained Art Colleges of the 1970s were a godsend to him, a reliable patronage that gave him the time, money and collaborative energies of students and fellow tutors to follow his creative instincts.

Most biographical notes on Nuttall are obliged to begin with a catalogue of his polymathic abilities; partly because, almost five decades after 1968 and twelve years since he died, all his literary work is out of print and his art is mostly out of sight. It's as if sheer versatility has to justify turning our attention to someone whose artistic activities were calculatingly off the edge. So they might usually go something like: 'Jeff Nuttall was a novelist, poet, painter, sculptor, actor, musician, essayist, teacher and radical thinker.' One of his lifelong friends, the writer and teacher Eric Mottram, wrote that he was 'the only all-round genius most of us are likely to meet in our lifetime. And let the sceptic beware: this is no exaggeration. His talents usually control at the limits of human exuberance.'[3]

The real point, of course, is that Nuttall's highly individual approach to all those activities (and the half dozen or so others he pursued) resulted in a substantial body of work, enthralling those that befriended, collaborated with and published him. There is also a fresh and growing wave of interest, not only from literary and cultural critics but by many younger artists, writers and publishers who are probably discovering him through enthusiastic word-of-mouth or by increasingly expensive second-hand, original small-press poetry collections and his mini-novels, possibly even finding copies of his idiosyncratic and bellicose examinations of the arts and society. Apart from *Bomb Culture* there were a number of polemical works, among them *Common Factors / Vulgar Factions* (1977), *The Pleasures of Necessity* (1988) and *Art and the Degradation of Awareness* (1999).

This year, as well as the exhibition we are curating based on the Nuttall archive at John Rylands Library in Manchester, there will be a small exhibition of his artwork and books in Abergavenny, close to where he was living at the time of his death. He is the subject of essays in several books that will also appear this year. An omnibus edition of four or five of his fiction titles is planned by Verbivoracious Press and there has been increasing interest in collecting his art and sculpture in public collections, including those of the Tate and the Henry Moore Institute.

As he prepared to read his most recent poems and short fictions to those Warwick students, Nuttall claimed that he was 'mainly' an artist, before going on to list in detail the forthcoming publication of his biography of Frank Randle, three novels and two volumes of performance art memoirs that were due in the same year. (The memoirs, as he predicted, were not published by John Calder until 1979.) He also impressed on his audience that he had 'been a poet since 1962'. London in the 1960s was one of the best places and times for anyone with an ambitious, imaginative and aptly rebellious personality to come of age, creatively speaking. Through his involvement with the Campaign for Nuclear Disarmament (CND) and the Aldermaston marches he met with a circle of like-minded poets at the Peace Café on Fulham Road (including Dave Cunliffe, Jeff Cloves, Lee Harwood, Pete Brown and Michael Horovitz). He was also fortunate to secure an early teaching job in the same school as the poet Bob Cobbing, who introduced Nuttall in turn to the Better Books shop on Charing Cross Road, a mini arts lab that became a hub of underground culture in the 1960s.[4]

The correspondence in the John Rylands Library archive reveals that Nuttall was equally attuned and sympathetic to poetic contemporaries who were concrete poets, sound poets, quasi-Beat New-Albion protest-going Blakean visionaries, or the broad church of British Poetry Revivalists. Nuttall's own writing mostly developed individually out of his riskier association with the two London-based Beat grandees of the time. He strongly connected with William Burroughs' literary strategies and had an (ultimately regretted) sympathy with Alexander Trocchi's self-serving intrigues.[5] As enthusiastic as he originally was about Ginsberg, these two figures were more influential in shaping Nuttall's style, on one hand, and his fuming sociocultural criticism on the other (*BC*, 228). 'Since my student days', wrote Nuttall, 'all my creative work, whether literary or visual, has been concerned with the same discord, the ecstatic violence which is detonated when nature and ethics meet.'[6]

He began as an ardent practitioner of the Brion Gysin / Burroughs compositional technique of cutting up existing text to create new text, with the aim of revealing hidden, possibly truer meanings. The way Nuttall was wired, he hardly needed to bother with scissors and paste to do his cutting up. His mind had a natural and powerful kaleidoscopic sensitivity, an intuition for dislocated juxtapositions that were as likely to reveal, as he intended, new mysteries as meanings. Nuttall was also a jazz man through and through (he played the cornet) so he was perfectly ready to extemporise and riff. You might also say, to use some dated American vernacular, that he was 'the class cut up'.

Nuttall's knack for innovation is reflected in his enthusiasm for 'happenings'. Although not the first to be enacted in Britain, his have arguably had the most lasting effect. Not content with simply conceiving and orchestrating happenings, Nuttall eagerly placed himself at their centre. In 1966 he conscripted a group of recent acquaintances for his first serious attempt at producing a performance art event.[7] The result was a mixed success, but it

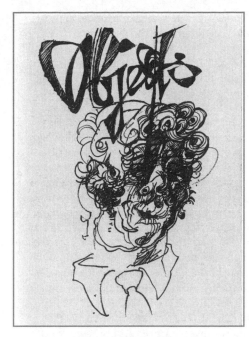

Objects, Trigram Press, London, 1976. Designed & illustrated by Jeff Nuttall.

encouraged the participants to try again under the title The People Show, which continues today and is the longest-established performance art company in the UK, possibly in the world.

Nuttall moved on to new performance partnerships, solo efforts and a characteristic role as the outsiders' outsider. Forcefully articulate about his own work and wider culture, he embraced contradiction and willfulness as normative states of creative genius.[8]

In *Bomb Culture*, Nuttall suggested that the word 'underground' was not in common use in the early 1960s, at least not in any generation-defining way, one that suggested a coherent network, an agreed purpose or common ideals. It was in New York around 1964, he thought, that the term became significant, being attached to two important activities, 'duplicated magazines and home movies'. Fuelled by opposition to the Cold War and Vietnam, and by their support for the civil rights movement, New York artists were driven by 'an unprecedented concern to air all taboos as blatantly as possible, to confess and sing from the rooftops all the most impermissible desires' (*BC*, 165).

Nuttall's list of correspondents developed as he sought interested sympathisers for Trocchi's Project Sigma, an ill-fated attempt to establish a global network of underground countercultural activism; and as he sought contributors for *My Own Mag* (his own mimeograph publication) or outlets for his poetry and graphics (somewhat cartoonish, but an artful, surreal combination of text and illustration) he discovered sympathetic creative spirits across the globe, although largely in or from the United States. Some had already developed literary reputations and others were destined to be significant, even iconic figures in alternative culture. We are fortunate that Nuttall preserved so many letters, notes, manuscripts and publications from the period, leaving an important record of this passionate, at times outrageous, correspondence.

His choice of the most dynamic and ground-breaking of 1960s homemade magazines began with Ed

Sanders and his *Fuck You: A Magazine of the Arts*, which started to articulate an incoherent but burgeoning countercultural political aesthetic, and which was 'Dedicated to Pacifism, Unilateral Disarmament, National Defense thru Nonviolent Resistence [sic], Multilateral Indiscriminate Apertural Conjugation, Anarchism, World Federalism, Civil Disobedience, Obstructers & Submarine Boarders, and All Those Groped by J. Edgar Hoover in the Silent Halls of Congress.' He also cited Tuli Kupferberg's various titles including *True Confessions*, Ted Berrigan's *C Press*, Doug Blazek's *Olé*. Also admired was Charles Plymell, who followed the literary and artistic exodus from Kansas to San Francisco and developed the skills of a craftsman-printer, editing and producing titles like *Now Now* and *The Last Times* on his own or borrowed lithographic presses in addition to printing numerous key publications for other underground figures (notably Mary Beach, Claude Pelieu, Jan Herman, S. Clay Wilson and Robert Crumb) (*BC*,167–173).

If *Fuck You, C,* and *True Confessions* were formed in the crucible of New York riots and brewing revolutions, Nuttall's work was forged in the hangover of the CND, which galvanised post-war youths who united in their opposition to mass destruction and the perceived apathy of their parents. For those living under the shadow of H-bomb annihilation, the future was uncertain, and the present brimmed with urgent, quivering energy. It was, Nuttall recalled, in reference to the early 1960s, 'a perpetual noon of decisions, every action crucial being possibly final' (*BC*, 19). Fuelled by the threat of extinction, Nuttall focused on the present: 'if you want to exist you must accept the flesh and the moment. Here they are.' (*BC*, 141)

In order to appreciate what made the underground 'underground' in a meaningful sense, the 1960s and 70s have to be seen in their joined-up political, legal, moral and aesthetic context. Beginning in the US and quickly spreading to other parts of the world, there was a period of demonstrations (including civil disobedience), mostly concerned with opposition to state control of political beliefs, testing conducted by the nuclear powers in wide-flung places (including islands and atolls across several oceans and numerous 'uninhabited' desert areas) and the escalating Vietnam War. Protesting in support of civil rights and an end to racial segregation was intense in the US, resulting in violence towards and the murder of protesters and organisers.

By 1968, the mood progressed into substantial anti-capitalist, anti-bourgeois and even anti-philistine actions that would erupt across Europe and force the dissolution of the French Assembly. Similar protests that year in more authoritarian countries, such as Mexico, Poland and Czechoslovakia, were forcibly repressed.

While the political mood of protest engaged a wider range of people in society, often led by student activists (some becoming armed militants), underground culture's battles were more intimate and aesthetic. The natural appetites of bohemian lifestyle and its artistic expression brought the Beat Generation infamy, persecution and punishment in the form of imprisonment, psychiatric sectioning and surveillance by the FBI and CIA. Their alleged transgressions included varieties of sexual liberation (behaviours that at the time were not only socially disapproved, but often illegal), narcotics use and obscenity.

The Beat stratagems for survival, pioneered by Kerouac, Ginsberg and Burroughs, involved subterfuge, evasion and exile. The eventual cohesion of the underground, the subsequent Beat-linked generation, was concerned with the same issues but was more subversive, confrontational and idealistic. They also faced censorship, prosecution, and disapproval in the establishment press, and censure and scorn from mainstream culture and the academies. As Burroughs wrote, 'Censorship is the presumed right of governmental agencies to decide what words and images the citizen is permitted to see: that is thought control since thought consists largely of word and image – [...] In English-speaking countries, the weight of censorship falls on sexual word and image [...]'[9]

Nuttall catalogued the attempted, often successful, suppression of underground culture that occurred throughout the US and the UK, with increasing instances of censorship prosecutions occurring around Europe and in India. 'Essentially (the police) go far beyond their official role of uniformed civil servant and have become the guardians of a definite way of life [...]' (*BC*, 201).

Like Sanders, Berrigan and Plymell, Nuttall decided to self-publish, although in sharp contrast to the New York and San Francisco-based countercultural publications, Nuttall's mimeographed little magazine, *My Own Mag: A Super Absorbant* [sic] *Periodical* was produced on the school duplicating machine where he taught, with early issues listing his home address as Salisbury Road, Barnet. The production and distribution of even a technically-meagre magazine, if sufficiently experimental and risk taking, was a great international underground network calling card. Nuttall was warmly welcomed on the basis of his, which was provocative and explicit right from the cover of issue one, in November, 1963.[10]

If the 'bomb culture' of 1960s eviscerated traditional notions of temporality, then it also, at least for Nuttall, collapsed the distinctions between art and literature and body and mind. As an accomplished poet, sculptor, painter, musician, actor and theatre innovator, Nuttall's aesthetic approach was holistic: 'I paint poems, sing sculptures, draw novels', Nuttall declared, and he described his intention with *My Own Mag* 'to make a paper exhibition in words, pages, spaces, holes, edges and images' (*BC*, 141).[11] By the mid-1960s, *My Own Mag* became the pre-eminent British underground magazine, a publication that attracted a coterie of countercultural and avant-garde writers and artists, among them Ginsberg, Robert Creeley, B. S. Johnson, William Wantling and Anselm Hollo.

My Own Mag remains a distinctive little magazine for several interconnected reasons. Driven by Nuttall's refusal to separate visual art from literature, the magazine assaults the senses and draws the eye in unexpected ways. There is an issue with deliberately burnt corners; there are disturbing ink drawings and cartoon strips, mostly drawn by Nuttall, mock agony-aunt columns and cut-up experiments that defy conventional reading. As an editor, Nuttall fostered a creative space in *My Own Mag* that enabled writers, among them Burroughs, to experiment. As Jed Birmingham observes, *My Own Mag* 'functioned like a laboratory for Burroughs where he was free to experiment. Like Charles Olson's experience with *Floating Bear*, Burroughs could get feedback from a receptive audience immediately since the turnaround time on the mimeo machine was so rapid. It had to be because Burroughs' approach to the cut-up was changing quickly at this time.'[12]

Burroughs' first cut-up appears in issue 2, an experimental piece which has the hallmarks of the cut-ups in the sixty-page pamphlet *Minutes to Go* (1960), 'the original manifesto and manual of the method', which showcased the cut-up experiments of Burroughs, Brion Gysin, Sinclair Beiles and Gregory Corso.[13] The Nuttall-Burroughs collaborations developed quickly: in issue 4, Burroughs experiments with a 32-grid cut-up 'to be read every which way', and by issue 5, 'The Special Tangiers Issue', Burroughs is on the front cover, also appearing as a character in Nuttall's comic strip 'Perfume Jack', which ran across many issues of *My Own Mag*. Significantly, Burroughs also contributed his own section, 'The Moving Times', which was a major turning point in the development of his three-column cut-up technique.

The effect of this, from issue 5 in May 1964, was immediate: 'No sooner had the signals gone out in that fifth issue of *My Own Mag* than they started to come back. Carl Weissner in Heidelberg, Claude Pelieu and Mary Beach in San Francisco were ploughing their poems in with fragments of newsprint, drifting scraps of telecommunication. Harold Norse was on the wavelength. So were Dan Richter and Philip Lamantia.' (*BC*, 155)

Following on from the success of the The International Poetry Incarnation at the Albert Hall in 1965, Barry Miles, John Hopkins and others who had thought themselves part of London's Beat scene were convinced that an audience existed for a publication that brought the news and literature of the international underground to London and could send London's vibes back in return.

Miles explained the plan behind *International Times* (*IT*), 'The idea was to have an international culture magazine, to link London to New York and Paris and Amsterdam and so on.' Jim Haynes, an American underground adventurer who also helped set up the publication, had run the Traverse Theatre in Edinburgh and established the London Arts Lab, said, 'My vision of *IT* was that it would be a European paper that would try to create a kind of underground consciousness throughout Europe.'[14]

The early *International Times* had something of a controlled and earnest look, without the trippy typography and layouts snarled in psychedelic mayhem usually associated with the 1960s underground press. Its literary emphasis was greater than most other underground press titles, with regular, urgent dispatches from Burroughs, Trocchi and others making it something like a collaborative, vaguely-journalistic development of *My Own Mag*. The main difference was a circulation that grew steadily into the thousands. *IT* was also constantly monitored by the Obscene Publications Squad and raided several times, eventually being forced to close down for 'corrupting public morals' by printing gay contact ads.[15]

Nuttall was initially happy to be involved and contributed a series of cartoon strips, mostly under the title *Seedy Bee*, which anticipated the underground comix that were not yet unleashed from San Francisco. These provided *IT* with some visual component, in his fusing of word and image in what appeared to be unruly innuendo and grotesqueness but were in fact highly precise. One of Nuttall's comics was singled out by the *News of the World* in a Hippie expose series, 'The strip showed huge distorted bodies with monster heads and twisted limbs spouting such things as: "Vera, your beauty is unsurpassed in the undeniable excess of its obscenity..."'[16]

Drawing on his archive at the John Rylands Library, the exhibition *Off Beat: Jeff Nuttall and the International Underground* (September 2016–March 2017) explores the involvement and influence of Nuttall in global avant-garde culture as it evolved and found its voice. Structured around four main themes – Beat Generation and America: influence and fraternity; William Burroughs and *My Own Mag*; the birth of the British Underground; and, the international network – the exhibition charts Nuttall's energy and commitment to countercultural literature, both during his editorship of *My Own Mag*, but also his collaborations with a coterie of writers and artists across the globe. Only a small (but significant) part of the archive can be reflected in the exhibition. However, it features a roll call of avant-garde, Beat, and experimental writers, including Douglas Blazek (another key figure in the 'mimeograph revolution'), the City Lights co-founder and publisher Lawrence Ferlinghetti, and the African-American Beat surrealist poet Ted Joans; it also features an original cut-up by Burroughs for *My Own Mag*. Closer to home, there are examples of Nuttall's connections with the filmmaker Anthony Balch, poets Tom Pickard and Michael Horovitz, as well as with Eric Mottram, a

The Patriarchs, Beau & Aloes Arc Association, Todmorden, 1978. Designed & illustrated by Jeff Nuttall.

central figure in the British Poetry Revival and one of the first British lecturers to specialise in contemporary, mostly Beat-related American literature.

Nuttall's published work includes twelve volumes of poetry, ten volumes of fiction, seven volumes of non-fiction and a considerable number of contributions to literary journals and anthologies. A selection of his early titles will be on display, along with some of the crucial underground network magazines that he appeared in, including *Olé*, *The San Francisco Earthquake* (VDRSVP issue), *Klacto*, *City Lights Journal*, and *International Times*.

The exhibition highlights Nuttall's contributions with two important collaborators alongside Burroughs: the conceptual artist John Latham, whose work included burning towers of books ('skoob'), and Trocchi, who collaborated with Nuttall on a number of projects, including *The Moving Times* in 1962, a publication connected to the Scottish writer's Project Sigma. Trocchi's work inspired sTigma Environmental Exhibition, a 1965 happening that took place at Better Books, and which was conceived as a collaborative Dada-esque happening, with input from Latham, Nuttall and recordings from Trocchi and Burroughs. As the exhibition illustrates, viewers had to squeeze through narrow corridors littered with Victorian pornography, pictures of war atrocities and stained underwear as their senses were assaulted by the smell of rotting meat. The sign-in book, part of Nuttall's archive, which includes the signatures of Mick Jagger and Keith Richards, required visitors to continue through the exhibition to the end: a pact to confront the terror and not turn back, a fitting metaphor for the prolific and frequently disturbing work of Jeff Nuttall.

The exhibition 'Off Beat: Jeff Nuttall and the International Underground' takes place at the John Rylands Library, Manchester, from September 2016–March 2017.

NOTES

1   www2.warwick.ac.uk/fac/arts/english/writingprog/archive/writers/nuttalljeff/260581
2   Jeff Nuttall, *Performance Art: Memoirs* (London: John Calder, 1979), 143.
3   Angela Flowers Gallery brochure *Jeff Nuttall Landscapes* (London, 1987).
4   Jeff Nuttall, *Bomb Culture* (London: Paladin, 1970) 181–182; hereafter referenced in the essay as *BC*, followed by the page numbers.
5   Allan Campbell and Tim Niel, ed., 'There's this fucking writer', *A Life in Pieces: Reflections on Alexander Trocchi* (Edinburgh: Rebel Inc., 1997), 282.
6   Abergavenny Museum catalogue notes, *Black Mountains* (Abergavenny, 1996).
7   Jeff Nuttall, *Performance Art: Memoirs* (London: John Calder, 1979), 20–23.
8   *Ibid.*, 66–68.
9   William Burroughs, 'Censorship', *The Transatlantic Review*, Issue 11 (London-New York, 1962), 5.
10   The complete run of *My Own Mag* has been digitised and is available at http://realitystudio.org/bibliographic-bunker/my-own-mag
11   Jeff Nuttall, 'The People', *International Times* 9, 1967.
12   Jed Birmingham, 'William Burroughs, *My Own Mag*, and Tangier', http://realitystudio.org/bibliographic-bunker/william-burroughs-my-own-mag-and-tangier/
13   Oliver Harris, 'Burroughs Is a Poet Too, Really': The Poetics of *Minutes to Go,* Reality Studio, http://realitystudio.org/scholarship/burroughs-is-a-poet-too-really-the-poetics-of-minutes-to-go/
14   Jonathan Green, *Days In The Life: Voices from the English Underground, 1961–71* (London: Heinemann 1988), 121–122.
15   John Sutherland, Offensive Literature, (London: Junction, 1982), 104–107.
16   Nigel Fountain, *Underground: The London Alternative Press 1966–74* (London: Routledge, 1988), 37.

From the Archive

Bombing a Publisher
ANTONY DUNN

Published in *A Commonplace Book: Carcanet 1970–2000* (Carcanet, 2000) and in Dunn's 2002 collection *Flying Fish*.

Imagine, for days after the sirens,
book-ash falling like fingerprint dust, soft
tonnes of poems making a slow Pompeii
of Manchester, the air guilty with it:

a grey broadcast among aerials,
interfering with satellite dishes,
sly in the creases of morning papers,

printing its unwelcome news on shirt-fronts
and carry-out cappuccino, trodden
down hall-carpets, making itself at home;

filling sewers with shampooey fervour,
filtering into the water-supply,
half-inching its way into lungs, leaking
into blood, heart, brain. Breathe out, now, and speak.

'I mad, you mad for me'

Robert Lowell Behaving Badly

TONY ROBERTS

'O to break loose. All life's grandeur
is something with a girl in summer...'

ROBERT LOWELL, 'Waking Early Sunday Morning'

SCHADENFREUDE? Do we read biographies to gloat? I thought we read from an interest in or admiration for their subject, that and to have the work live again by other means. Yet on the sleeve of Jeffrey Meyers' *Robert Lowell in Love* (University of Massachusetts Press, 2016), Paul Mariani, (earlier a sympathetic biographer of Lowell) describes its compelling quality in these terms: 'Meyers has turned the pain of all into a honeycomb for us to enjoy with a guilty, cathartic kind of Schadenfreude.' I find it hard to see *Robert Lowell in Love* as 'enjoyable', though I admit it is a page-turner. I was left wondering if Mariani's comment is a sly criticism of what is a racy study of a man behaving badly.

When it comes to writing about a manic love life you are walking the tightrope of confessions, letters, memories, opinions, rumours, and the plunge is into the titillating stuff of celebrity gossip. There is mileage in this sort of study to the extent that it sheds light on the poetry, and a serious study – and Meyers is keen on establishing seriousness – would have to pursue the life and work, especially when its subject is a leading poet who lived the two as one. It would also have to be finely nuanced. In this book, the ironic, Falstaffian title rather gives the game away: we are in the land of appetite and confession.

There is no doubting that Lowell (1917–77) is an inexhaustibly fruitful subject. He was well-born, if poorly raised, deserted his native Boston for the South and poetic mentors Allen Tate and John Crowe Ransom, became the pre-eminent poet of his generation and thrived on the periphery of post-war American political culture. With *Life Studies* (1959) he changed the game (to use his own expression), was much honored in the poetry world, suffered regular manic episodes, married three times – to writers Jean Stafford (from 1940–48), Elizabeth Hardwick (1949–72) and Caroline Blackwood (1972–) – and 'enjoyed' many affairs. Lowell's relationships with women were a complicated form of exploitation, fuelled by his bipolar condition. His last marriage brought him to England, decline and death at sixty.

Let me begin by acknowledging a couple of positives. Firstly, Jeffrey Meyers put together one of the best books yet on his subject, the 1988 *Robert Lowell: Interviews and Memoirs*, a wonderful source for Lowell watching. Secondly, *Robert Lowell in Love* is well-researched and pacey. It has involved lots of interviews and is written with passion. It provides many back stories of the women in Lowell's life, first person anecdotes of his treatment of them, and the occasional revelation. It also offers some insights. Finally, the Appendices in Jeffrey Meyers' book bring welcome annotations to Lowell's *Collected Poems* (2003).

Sadly all this is not nearly enough. These same Appendices seem out of place in what precedes them, as if they were intended to offer some late academic rigour to Meyers' enterprise. Despite his claim that *Robert Lowell in Love* 'is meant for the general reader who is not familiar with the details of Lowell's life as well as for the specialist on modern poetry', what we are given in repetitive detail is the tale of a lost and exploitative man whose adventures are skilfully assembled from the confessions of his lovers. The whole is reminiscent of Meyers' less-distinguished *Manic Power: Robert Lowell and His Circle* (1987) ('He was a mental case in his teens.').

The problems with *Robert Lowell in Love* begin, however, with the author's tone which, with its assurances and certainties seems arrogant. In the Acknowledgements, those who failed to respond to the author's overtures are named and shamed. In an Appendix we learn of how one named lover was brought from vacillation to inclusion in the book by the prospect of self-aggrandisement.

Meyers' skill itself is problematic. In order to convey the drama of the life, he tries for a seamlessness which requires both his own omniscience and a simplification of his subject. So, for example, we learn that when escaping his difficult mother as an unhappy Harvard student, Lowell embraces Allen Tate and his wife, the novelist Caroline Gordon, 'his ideal mother' according to Meyers. In truth Gordon was a little too feisty to be a maternal figure for Lowell. Could Tate, his mentor, have been his ideal father? No, presumably because Tate, the poet and essayist, was 'a publisher and novelist as well as a poet, was a Catholic convert, heavy drinker and active fornicator'. Instead, according to Meyers, Ford Madox Ford becomes a 'father figure' for Lowell (though in truth Ford spent much of his time avoiding the young man). Randall Jarrell is Lowell's 'poetic conscience' and when he dies, in 1965, Elizabeth Bishop assumes the role. Yet Lowell and Bishop were poetic intimates from the late forties.

It is all too tidy. It also leads to questionable speculation on Meyers' part. Is it true, for example, that the distinguished poets who recognised Lowell's talents taught him 'the craft of poetry, but also how to live as a poet and use a poet's charisma to attract women'? Was it true of the marriage to Jean Stafford that 'His repressed guilt was one reason he married a woman who had contracted a venereal disease and been disfigured by him' (a reference to their drunken car crash)? Was it true that Lowell preferred to dally drinking with Blair Clark in Paris so as to reach the Italian hospital when his mother 'was safely dead'? On the poetic front: does Lowell's prose reminiscence '91 Revere Street' provide, 'the essential personal context for the poems of *Life Studies*'? After all, the book did without it on publication in England. On Plath's poetry, was Lowell 'disturbed by his responsibility for its suicidal direction and cultish influence' (which contradicts Lowell's prose reminiscence and letters of the time to Elizabeth Bishop and Al Alvarez)?

Such speculation is accompanied by a tendency to repetitive summarising. After having battled through their marriage, we learn again that Lowell and his first wife, Jean Stafford, 'had overwhelming problems: their literary competition, psychological difficulties and sexual dysfunction, her depression and heavy drinking, his Catholic fanaticism and brutal violence'. Elizabeth Hardwick, Lowell's second wife, 'remained faithful to him, through all his travails, out of pity, charity, faith, masochism and love'. And pruriently: 'His sexual relations with his lovers varied with his physical and mental condition. He was sexually inept with Dick and Vetra and was impotent with Adden. But he was also a passionate and pleasing lover with Hochman and Ritter and, apparently, with Buckman, Madonia and Keelan.' (Adden inspired the Lowell line used in the title of this essay.) And what do we do with the anecdote – in the spirit of full disclosure, apparently – that ends with the poet masturbating through a window?

Then there are Meyers' increasingly grating allusions, again intended to bring a literary feel to proceedings. Commenting on madness, for example, Meyers ditches Lowell in favour of discussing Plato, Kierkegaard, Dostoevsky, Nietzsche, Rimbaud and Sartre, all on the basis of the fact that Lowell was 'keenly aware of the western literary tradition that assumed, in John Dryden's words, "Great wits are sure to madness near allied"'.

What did Lowell's 'awareness' signify? Uppermost in his mind after manic attacks, seem rather to have been shame and regret ('My disease, alas, gives one [...] a headless heart.').

The book is full of such flights: 'The Lowells resembled the desperately unhappy family in D. H. Lawrence's story "The Rocking Horse-Winner"'; this is 'remarkably similar to Vincent van Gogh's description'; 'Like the famous beautiful muses Lou-Andreas Salomé and Alma Mahler, Blackwood attracted supremely talented men.' The problem is that the reader will soon start to play the game. At the bottom of page 33 we find that the young Lowell believed that dallying with girls would undermine the monastic agenda he has designed for his friends. I turned to the next page assured of meeting the King of Navarre ('Loves' Labours Lost') and there he was.

In itself this is simply the author's style and my judgement a matter of personal taste, but allied to other tropes it lowers the tone. The whole thing is anyway too heavy-handed with the constant urge to dramatise. Lowell is 'a combustible cocktail of the brooding Hamlet and fierce Tamburlaine'. We are told that 'in his last book, *Day by Day* (1977), published a month before his death, the unwanted son of a mother trapped in an unwanted marriage finally exposed the festering wound that had tormented him for a lifetime'.

Women inspire much of the Hyde; friendship a little of the Jekyll. It would have been a better book if Meyers had had the occasion to find shades other than black and white. He might have developed his comments from friends into a study of their influence on the man and poet, instead of paying lip-service to Lowell's virtues and yet exploring the negative. He does tell us that Lowell could establish warm and supportive relationships as he did with Elizabeth Bishop and Mary McCarthy, and a number of his unbedded students benefited from his influence, including Sylvia Plath and Anne Sexton. In fact he quotes William Meredith: 'nobody had any trouble staying friends with Cal [Lowell's nickname]. He was an extremely loyal and generous man.' This is a sentiment echoed by Christopher Ricks, but then we also learn that 'Lowell Agonistes, a combative pacifist and brute force adversary, had violent confrontations with many of his friends.'

In fact very few seem to come out well from *Robert Lowell in Love*, the men often run interference for Lowell's affairs or are themselves self-embroiled, the women social climbers or whiners, have breakdowns and drinking problems, trying to hang on to the Lowell name or their affair. Even the 'heroic' Hardwick is aware of making a great career move, 'By marrying him she climbed higher than she had ever dreamed, from provincial obscurity to a glorious lineage, with all its privileges and accoutrements.' Ditto the rejected Jean Stafford. Caroline Blackwood, who already had the (Guinness family) background is unstable and alcoholic. Mary McCarthy is 'tough, sharp-tongued', and Elizabeth Bishop 'sickly, shy and self-effacing'.

How far Meyers' project falls short in *Robert Lowell in Love* can be seen by a look in *The Letters of Robert Lowell* (edited by Saskia Hamilton). Read a few pages, dip into it here and there and the nuances that are so critical in a life and missed in Meyers' bring colour flooding in. Here are a few: Lowell writing to George Santayana at his father's death: 'We were familiar in an impersonal way without ever knowing each other well.' To William Carlos Williams, explaining his relationship with his late mother: 'My mother and I somehow competed. It took us a lifetime to be off guard with each other.' And to Allen Tate in that same month of 1954, 'when [people] met her without me or my father, marvelous qualities came out. A boldness and humor – all her own [...] Together, except sometimes when we were alone, we sat like stones on each other's heads – inhibiting and inhibited. But with a drink or two and me in the distance people were charmed.'

In a letter to Elizabeth Bishop, Lowell passes on an irritating comment of Randall Jarrell's on the first divorce, 'Now I always thought you and Jean were more alike than any two people I'd ever met. I guess you would have been perhaps a little too spooky and haunted together.' During turbulent times in England, Lowell wrote to Hardwick, 'What shall I say? That I miss your old guiding and even chiding hand. Not having you is like learning to walk', and equally powerfully on a slightly earlier occasion:

You[r] last not[e] and much else that you said and have said through the years go to my heart. You couldn't have [been] more loyal and witty. I can't give you anything of equal value. Still much happened that we both loved in the long marriage. I feel we had much joy and many other things we had to learn. There is nothing that wasn't a joy and told us something. Great joy.

And finally, in trepidation, to Caroline Blackwood, Lowell wrote on 19 April, 1977: 'Us? Aren't we too heady and dangerous for each other? I love you, am more dazzled by you, than anyone I've known, but can't I be your constant visitor?'

Without a nuanced approach, any biography no matter how readable inevitably fails. We are so much better off with the poems and letters, where the hesitation, the divided self, the bruised, bemused, unflinching tone reminds us why we are interested in the life of Robert Lowell, and why the art redeems a life that cannot have been lived (quite) that badly. At the end of *Robert Lowell in Love*, I can only side with those 'who failed to respond' to Meyers' questions: 'Helen Chasin, Mary Gordon, Mary Keelan, Sheridan Lowell, William Merwin, Jonathan Miller and Derek Walcott'. They are well out of it.

Two Poems

JOHN WELCH

At Hollow Ponds, Epping Forest

'Where the chimpanzee is able to recognise that the mirror is an epistemological void, and to turn his attention elsewhere, the child has a perverse will to remain deluded.'

LACAN

1.

A cold grey day in early March.
Travelling with a swarm of them
We're two of the conspirators
While these implacably cheerful children
Cross the bald ground. In the bushes
The five-year-old finds a dead fox:
'It smells like rotten fish.'

Hanging back, watching, and hearing their voices –
They arrive as if from nowhere
Travelling over the threadbare carpet of sound.
I wasn't sure I was still there beside you,
Flying apart we flew along together
As if caught in the same storm.
Much later we'll return to the grove.

2.

A reflection thin as the sheet of paper
On which I am writing this now
And a flood of ink, like a shadow retreating inwards.
A child who struggled
To express this gift
Do you falter? The mirror is tall.
Why do you follow what turns you away?
Seeing yourself in a mirror

You are looking at silence, beside you
The patience of a waiting name.

3.

As if this were an aberration,
These clicks in the silence – the language
It is within us scheming.
Something bolted on
To a cautious lyric gift,
These sounds an aspiration
Our little puffs of air. Look down
And see where below us
It opens a splendid page.
I shall lower my self
Cautiously into that silence

And the hopefulness a child might feel
At the start of a new day?
As the animals stirred one by one
They greeted him with their eyes.
Wings half hidden behind him
Enchanted by the trap does he find
There is freedom in falling to earth,
To land in a stumbling world?
Do you falter? Tell me you falter.

On The Hill

Forests, on the edge of cities –
Going out on an expedition,
And finding a smashed bird in the road.

A small space opens
Under a pigeon's
Insistent afternoon call.

Out on the hill my life's
A remote preaching of sunlight –
I can see it, almost, from here.

Dry shapes of words that rub together
Can make a dusty light
A frail thing, distant from blood,

But to hang about here
In the hawthorn's musky smell?
We climbed out onto the hill

Letting eye starve
On a hill slope where the animals
Tug and nuzzle perpetually,

The many-angled stones
So close-set in their wall
They appear to be in flight.

A wind came rushing down
Through the slope's sessile oaks.
In a dull panic I was alone,

And asked 'What will spill out of us,
This chaos, mine and yours?'
Was this the trick, to throw the mind away?

Seen from there the sea was quiet as milk.
Together we walked to the shore,
Then home, through several miles of English rain.

It was an act of faith
Leaving the words in those void arms,
To come home in the storm.

If I could show you. If I could show,
Being here like the water's continual
Murmur against a door of sunlight –

It was always about to come alive.
The language was a kind of devouring.
And then the tedium of the finished thing.

Three Poems

MAITREYABANDHU

Cézanne's Dog

What Mathilde Vollmoeller said or what Rilke
said she said at the Salon d'Automne
on a day of rain, was that Cézanne's intention
was not to describe, to say: *this the figure, this the ground,*
the object or the space around it, but to be accurate
to his sensations – half-red, blue-red, green –
so if he wasn't sure, if the precise tone evaded him,
he'd stop and start in another place until
the whole thing fought against itself – the bottle
with the dish, the apple waging war
against the pear – until, exhausted by his efforts,
he'd turn to his self-portrait once again
and paint himself like a dog who looks
into a mirror and thinks, there's another dog.

San Zachariah

What was it, after all, that Mathilde Vollmoeller said
about the colours in Cézanne? That each knew
every other in a perpetual – it can't have been 'dance' –
dialogue? exchange? Well, perhaps Rilke was right
and we are here in order to say house, bridge,
gate, fruit tree, window: this window, this morning –
a far off siren and the world, as every fool knows
and dreams about and damns, going to the dogs
in innumerable poisonous ways. I play a CD
of Mozart's *Sinfonia Concertante* which, I realise,
is the argument of a flower or votive candle –
the bassoon laughing to itself, the clarinet's ache.
The French horn is this late February sunshine
on a Victorian school, on a cherry tree (no, apple)
yet to come into leaf. And now, querulous
above niceties, the intellectual oboe opens a space
for the *Sacra Conversazione* of martyred saints:
palm and broken wheel, river pebbles and book
'…illumination at once naturalistic and symbolic'
while a wingless angel plays the *lira da braccio*
in San Zachariah. Too obvious this music/painting
analogy, too trite. And I see you're not listening
with much patience, having to make the horn
and oboe sing, the Virgin cradle the Christ child
and the impossible mountain speak to the impossible sun.

The Method of Loci

In the first room the curator has positioned
the inevitable apple on Madame Brémond's
light-ruffled tablecloth, vast, like Claes Oldenburg.

In the second, the mountain is reduced
to papier-mâché and chicken wire
with sponge for trees and an oo-gauge railway

that takes you to the third where the card players
abandon their pipe smoke and bucolic calm
to bark Provençal aphorisms and smut.

The girl leaving the fourth room with rustling
skirts and a suggestion of *Fantasia de Fleurs*
is followed by Cézanne's biographers who

want to know about the 'late style' and *alla prima*
in the fifth room in which air holes
and breathing spaces open, blues fold stiffly away,

reds judder slightly like kissing gates as you
squeeze between them back into the first room
and the endless confrontation of the apple.

From *a book with no name*

Water

It is a belief. Everybody is entitled to it. It is a belief system it underlies everything but it is undetected. There is all to play for it is entitlement. It plays gently it quenches. It plays and the play of it is endless it is a system. It is a system that quenches itself. But this system is endless. It is energy. It's undetected but it's behind everything. It is hidden. It is behind the walls. It is underground. Sleeping there. It is inside of us can you hear it? The Moon tugs it. Are you listening to it? There it goes again. Listen. It is hidden on the Moon. It really is something. The energy is really something it is something everybody knows. It is something everybody knows but it's unknowable. It is hidden on the Moon and it sublimates on Mars it escapes into deep space. We get it from deep space. We are made of it and we are unknowable. We are moving. Who can know us? It swirls and eddies it takes the form of torrents vortices and whirlpools it has a transcendental element. So salts form in it. And we move with it as we form. It is key to the landscape we say it transcends. It can't be contained. The domes are full of it. The tanks overspill. It is in the pipes. It's in the cesspools gutters drains and pipes but it can't be contained. It's coming through the pipes but the pipes can't contain it any longer. It's coming from upstairs. It's coming down the walls. It's coming down everywhere. Where is it coming from we don't know where it's coming from. It finds its own way. It finds a way it escapes and finds a way it finds a level. It has consequences. It finds its own way down we can't tell the consequences where it all comes down. It soaks muslin and leaves traces. The floor is soaked with it. Absolutely soaked. It leaves damage in its wake. Damage is formed by it. The consequential damage is incalculable. It lashes down without cease it sweeps away villages. It can't be predicted it has no colour. No colour can be observed in it. But it has a cadence. It is profound. Its cadence is profound. It has no colour it has a beautiful translucency with a shimmer in it. Has no colour but what a shimmer. With a shimmer we disappear. We disappear into its profundity into its vast depth we are engulfed and disappear forever. We call it the ocean but it lives in a glass.

Live at Birdland

They sing. They perch. They flit. They preen. They fly. They settle. They hop. They flutter. They walk. They peck. They look. They nod. They flap. They twitter. They call. They threaten. They jump. They mate. They jostle. They stretch. They warble. They nestle. They hover. They glide. They squabble. They feed. They kill. They sleep. They shudder. They fluff. They strut. They display. They sing intermittently. They perch wilfully. They flit threateningly. They preen beautifully. They fly cheekily. They settle prettily. They hop darkly. They flutter brightly. They rarely walk. They peck quickly. They look slowly. They nod purposefully. They flap randomly. They twitter pertly. They call erratically. They threaten firmly. They jump lazily. They mate fitfully. They jostle again. They often stretch. They warble lightly. They nestle loudly. They hover repeatedly. They glide well. They squabble badly. They feed strongly. They kill madly. They sleep nimbly. They almost shudder. They fluff shortly. They strut fearfully. They seldom display. They perch threateningly. They flit beautifully. They preen cheekily. They fly prettily. They settle darkly. They hop brightly. They flutter fearfully. They walk quickly. They never peck. They look purposefully. They nod slowly. They flap badly. They twitter randomly. They call pertly. They threaten erratically. They jump firmly. They mate lazily. They jostle fitfully. They stretch again. They often warble. They nestle lightly. They hover loudly. They glide repeatedly. They squabble well. They never feed. They kill strongly. They sleep madly. They shudder nimbly. They never fluff. They strut shortly. They display intermittently. They sing wilfully. They preen threateningly. They fly beautifully. They settle cheekily. They hop prettily. They flutter darkly. They walk brightly. They peck fearfully. They look quickly. They never nod. They flap slowly. They twitter purposefully. They call badly. They threaten randomly. They jump pertly. They mate erratically. They jostle firmly. They stretch lazily. They warble fitfully. They nestle again. They often hover. They glide lightly. They squabble loudly. They feed repeatedly. They kill well. They sleep strongly. They shudder prettily. They fluff madly. They strut nimbly. They display shortly. They never sing. They never perch. They flit wilfully. They never settle. Hop slowly. Flutter purposefully. Walk badly. Never shudder. They peck wilfully. Fluff threateningly. Strut beautifully. Display cheekily. Look pertly. Never flap. They nod firmly. Twitter lazily. Call fitfully. Never threaten. Never jump. They mate lightly. Jostle loudly. Never stretch. Never warble. Never nestle. They hover strongly. Glide madly. Squabble nimbly. Feed shortly. Never kill. They sing darkly. Never sleep. They perch brightly. Never flit. They preen fearfully. They fly away.

Animals have no names

We hear them at night in the forest but never see them. Their noises come over the water from the outer islands all night long their inexplicable noises. But when the sun comes up they are nowhere to be seen. Nowhere to be seen because they are in hiding. What have they got to hide? We know they are out and about on the islands or in the dark forest in the places nobody goes they are out and about they know we are here but they don't care. They don't care about us. They're out and about in the dark forest and they don't care about us not at all. You can call them all you like they won't answer. They will not answer they just chitter and howl and roar. You may see the prints of their naked feet where they have been. Maybe you can catch their eyes in the dark their eyes glitter. They glitter as they chitter they don't care. They whimper and they bleat they sigh and squeak. We give them names. The Leopard Cat and the mighty Bee. The Naked Mole Rat the Arachnids the Nurse Shark and the Molluscs with their beady eye. These are the names we give them but they have no names. The slovenly Lion the majestic Tapir and many others on land and sea and in the air such as the Humming Bird and indeed birds and bird machines of all kinds how they lurk and shout and perform their mad language games. In the midst of the dark forest they have lost their way. Call out their names all you like they will not answer. They lose their way and blunder in the forest they howl in the mountains but they do not lack confidence at all in any manner whatsoever their confidence is obvious in their stiff-armed strut their simian strategies. They are so sure of themselves. They howl from mountain to mountain. Their terrible soft eyes glitter in the dark. They don't know their names you call them repeatedly but they don't answer. They do not know their names. They have absolutely no idea. They do not answer to their names. They do not appear but you can smell them. The scent tells you they are very close. They are closer than you think. They are magnificent in their way even though they are stupid. They take their terrible revenge they murder their own kind they devour their children. They are crazy they really are. They show no gratitude. They lie and cheat they eat their babies they are stupid. They make war on their own kind with fangs and claws with rockets and swords. They cause explosions. They blunder and shout in the forest and laugh at the moon. They do not care about us. Their throats are warped they have no words they have no names the stupid stupid animals.

Where are the animals going

The animals are running. They are running together. The animals are running away. They are all different sizes. Faint steam rises from their bodies. They are not looking at us. Their eyes are fixed on where they are going. They are fleeing but we do not know what they are fleeing or where they are heading. It is a mystery. Scientists have come up with various possible explanations. The animals appear to be scared you can see it in their eyes. They are scared all right. They are all running together in a group or in several groups. They run and run. Are they trying to tell us something? Nobody knows. Nobody knows what they are trying to tell us.

The Aselline Starlets

PETER HUGHES

1

I said this imagery
was mental but
she claimed you
can't say what's
happening within
a composition
as the flicks & swerves
are too precise &
fast to verbalise
& also donkeys
are usually top heavy
as well as too
heavy to catch when
suspended from your
thoughts & old arcs
carry memories
of awkward turns
& ecstasy
each thought is made
of temporary nodes
we sometimes fresco
on the ceiling
but usually do not
because you know
death intervenes
or we get banished
from our provinces
by the council or the
gravities of love
& cooking then learning
this new scale or
trying to catch a flatfish
or anticipating flight
again become
the medium in which
these things happen
but we nearly know
it's impossible except in
certain kinds of art
to fly forever

2

we try to fly
above the heads
of propaganda
we partner novel forces
& the fatal graphs
of lost momentum
the show's constructed
on a person's wrist
sweaty & chaffing

ARTWORK: FAY JONES

lost in lights
made up
accommodating
glitter falling
balancing above
a couple of tunes

3

all the goodness
sucked out of the
neighbours & bound
to a stick with
malarkey & duct tape
was what they opted
to salute & strive for
songs of old rope
& sail-cloth embellished
with the sooty mould
of who gives a shit
we proceeded to erect
this monument to
the history of art
about camping & sex
with crumbs & mildew
where the nearest

place for milk was Wales
it's as if you go back
to an old town that's
dead in you forever
each time you open
your mouth to speak
& no speech comes

4

we dreamt there'd
been a rupture
in the weather
& we were entering
Steve Swallow's
disco period sideways
late into the night
I read the tattooed lady
without really
taking it in
the waste-ground
wind is whispering
we each have
decomposing caravans
parked inside our heads
rats' droppings

sketches &
rubber jewels
wait for the moon
to make the first move

5

no one came from
miles around these fields
of moonlit pumpkin
the substitute ring-
meister can't decide
whether to dance in
bed to Chopin or lean
out of the flap to see
if it's the bailiffs
one of the flying goats
is off on an away day
to express this
play any note
well not that one
a semitone higher
or lower
& nod

6

I'm no longer
with the circus
except sometimes
briefly in the memory
of strangers
I reached a point
where all I saw
were messages
from Mary
cross-stitched on
those overarching
canvas skies
still I do do the same
route at the same times
sleep in the car
register the music
now & then
with the window down
when the wind is right
but we don't interact
the time for such things
closed its eyes & rolled
back under the waves
they never see me park
or circle the compound
or swoop overhead

In Exchange with James Womack

SAM BUCHAN-WATTS

62–63
Poems
Hughes
Features
Buchan-Watts
& Womack

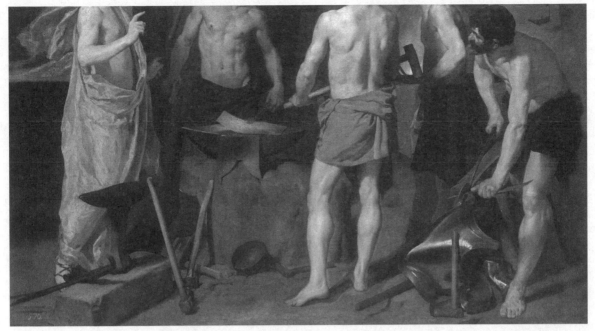

Diego Velazquez, *La fragua de Vulcano*, 1630 (detail)

SAM BUCHAN-WATTS: *Why* Misprint *as the title of your first book? On one hand a misprint can be something fortuitous, in terms of an aleatory poetic; on the other, it invokes clumsiness, even failure (though failure might be more in line with* misprision...*). What can a typographic error do for us that authorial intention can't?*

JAMES WOMACK: The poem called 'Misprint' came before the title of the collection as a whole, and seemed in many ways to sum up what turned out to be themes of the book's subject matter (death and irony), and what are in a larger way my current obsessions. So there's that, purely ry, usage. But I think you're right in the larger sense, that the idea of the random incursion into an otherwise 'perfect' entity is an extremely fruitful one. I'm riffing here, but maybe there's a spectrum moving between the misprint which has a small but contained effect on the poem (Auden writing 'every poet has a name for the sea', and Isherwood reading it as 'every port', but that doesn't change anything in the poem's argument beyond that one word and its subtle influences) and the misprint which is the absolute cause of poetic inspiration (cf. Bishop's 'Man-moth'). My 'ideal' misprint would be something like the flaw in the Persian carpet, that stops the object from being aridly (or divinely) perfect, but which is itself a source from which other ideas flow. Strictly speaking, I don't know that I believe in typographic errors (i.e. errors that come from the layout of the keyboard, from hitting the wrong key): certainly I find that most errors I make while typing tend to be standard Freudian mistakes, typing 'blunt' for 'brunt', which isn't really explained by the organisation of the machinery. I make lots of transcription errors, and get a lot of pleasure from the fact (although I haven't

yet used it seriously in a poem) that 'milestones' and 'millstones' look the same in my handwriting.

Would you mind explaining the process by which you came to the title poem? A short poem: 'We'll make him laugh himself o death'. It reminds me of a statement of Nabokov's, from Nikolai Gogol: *'one likes to recall that the difference between the comic side of things, and their cosmic side, depends upon one sibilant'.*

The original impetus was an actual misprint, someone else's. Well, not misprint, but I'll explain. There was an exhibition a few years back at the Thyssen-Bornemisza museum, of art at the beginning of the First World War (*museothyssen.org/microsites/exposiciones/2008/1914*), and the gallery commentary was, rather labour-intensively, written on the wall in stuck-on letters. Obviously, keen and dedicated (and bored) children had scratched some of the letters off, and one of the results was that instead of 'to death', the phrase 'o death' appeared in the middle of an otherwise innocuous sentence. And I liked that, the sudden invocation, and thought I might be able to do something with it. And the rest came from thinking about phrases that contain 'to death', and I thought about 'laughing yourself to death' (probably because I'd been watching that imperishable masterpiece *Who Framed Roger Rabbit?* at the time). And then it all clicked. Interestingly, I think Nabokov is the master of thinking about language in this dual way, with meaning balanced against the different possibilities inherent in the word itself, and that's almost entirely because he came at English as an outsider: there's a bit in that same book, *Nikolai Gogol*, where he talks about one of Gogol's stratagems and then says in a parenthesis '(beautiful word, stratagem – a treasure in a cave)', which isn't an obvious thing for a native speaker to notice, I would think.

Elizabeth Bishop said that the misprint of mammoth into 'Man-moth' in the New York Times *seemed 'meant' for her; that she was offered a kind of 'oracular statement'. This notion of ownership is brought to the fore in the first poem when you ask: 'Who owns the copyright to an erratum slip?' Do you feel that you are the 'owner' of any aspect of your writing over any other?*

Temporarily. I mean, I don't think I own the material that goes into a poem; can it mean anything to say that you 'own' your perceptions? Once you start to work on them (and this might be something that happens almost simultaneously with the perception; as soon as you say 'that cloud is very like a whale' then the poetic process – 'very like' – is under way), then they are yours for the duration of the process. But then you have to let them go. My instinctive reaction to this question was to say 'rhythm': the basic beat-sound that the words in a poem make in relation to one another is the one thing that the poet owns and has absolute responsibility for (if you don't want a word that goes ´´–, but instead one that goes ´´, then you write 'seagull' instead of 'albatross'). Meaning is more complex (and here the misprints come in, and my essentially relaxed attitude towards them, the welcome I give them if they come along): even when Milton insists on his theme in every line of *Paradise Lost* ('Of man's first disobedience, and the fruit' is a pretty clear, and pretty uncompromising opening), we read the poem as a whole as being about a good deal more than Milton, one feels, would allow it to be.

But would you say that we perceive an erratum slip to the same extent that we perceive a cloud looking like a whale? I guess I'm interested in the point at which the errors become 'ours', which is something writers are keen to express, even though they happen externally (I just found a good note in Tom Raworth's Collected Poems: *'All errors in the text are probably mine').*

On the level that both of them are suggestive material that is then turned into something more concrete (which is where the poetry comes from), then I would think that the act of perception is similar: something vague or formless (a cloud, or 'barouqe') becomes something specific (a whale, or 'baroque'). The interesting bit is when you have meaning on both sides of the equation (for barque read baroque, as it were). There's a lot of static to filter out of the way, though. Most clouds don't look like anything much.

You've worked extensively on translating other poets – how has this fed into your own writing? I am thinking about how much the notion of misprinting might work with or against that of mistranslation; 'mistranslation' being something of a slippery term, as, if we are to agree with Robert Alter, 'all translations are necessarily mistranslations, differing only in the direction and relative absurdity of their inaccuracies'.

Translation is impossible. Or rather, platonic translation is impossible: there will never, even between two languages that are close to each other (Castilian and Galician, or Portuguese and Galician, or Catalan and Valencian, just to stick to the Peninsula) – even if two 'equivalent' sentences are in fact word for word identical (as can be the case in certain simple sentences in, say, Galician and Spanish) – there will never be a sentence in one language that works in precisely the same way as it does when carried across into another language. We don't read in a vacuum, we don't speak in a vacuum, and even things that seem to be easily transferable across languages have different focuses, different connotations here than they did over there (e.g. if you wanted to translate an English poem in iambic pentameter into Russian, it might make historical and cultural sense to translate it into iambic tetrameter, even if it didn't make vocal sense or, you know, *sense* sense). So in metaphorical terms, all translations are misprints of the original statement. But with translations, of course, someone who reads both languages can tell you how much of this is fruitful misreading, or reading that is allowed by the elasticity of the source text, and how much is just a mistake. In one of my first Russian literature exams at university I was asked to translate a passage from Pushkin, and when I got the exam back, the examiner had written of my translation: 'Beautiful. Fascinating. Rubbish.' With 'original' writing, 'beautiful' (strength as poetry) and 'fascinating' (strength as argument) and 'rubbish' (truth to whatever impelled the poem in the first place) are all jumbled together. But it does feed into my own work: when you go through someone else's poem word by word, you get better at following and organising a poetic argument for yourself. If writing successful poetry consists in managing to stand inside and outside yourself at the same time, translating might be the ultimate and most helpful 'outside' skill.

How far do you agree with the idea that art itself is an act of translation? Octavio Paz said that 'the painter translates the word into visual images [... writing is often] the interpretation of nonlinguistic signs by means of linguistic signs'.

I don't like that as an idea because it gives to the word 'translation' a lot more meaning than I personally would want it to have. 'Translation as metaphor' is almost a sub-department of translation studies, and it doesn't really help much, or doesn't help me much, to think about inspiration as a form of translation. Or rather, it doesn't seem to me to be saying much that's new. We all know that there is the idea and then the verbal, or visual, or vocal manifestation of that idea, and a lot of frustration of e.g. writing comes from trying to bridge the gap between them ('It is impossible to say just what I mean!'), but I don't know if translation is a good metaphor for this. In translation, the source text, which maps onto the idea, or the inspiration bit of Paz's model, is generally much more specific, and you can go back and look at it and worry away at it and try to work at and refine your responses to it, whereas a lot of inspiration is temporary and fleeting, and if I write in my notebook 'the hand on the back of the seat in the bus' and go back to it six months later, I'm not, unless I'm very lucky, going to recover my complex of feelings and thoughts and emotions that led me to think this hand was particularly significant at that moment. Even before I try to worry that emotion into words.

It seems to me that a category of the misprint generally is to talk about poetry in terms of painting. Poets (Frank O'Hara is a good example) seem to envy the painter's ability to run with a mistake – whereas words are supposed to retain an objective accuracy of statement, a painting's primary objective can be to blur or distort. There can be evidence of the thing no longer aimed for (e.g. letters reading 'SARDINES' where there are none) but the process is cumulative; there doesn't seem to be an equivalent for 'typo' in painting terms. Do you find the analogy to be apt?

But what words do is to maintain this objective accuracy of statement in several layers, simultaneously. When Geoffrey Hill says 'Undesirable you may have been, untouchable / you were not', almost every word in that sentence is playing several roles (even 'have been', what is that asking us to think about the subject of 'September Song'? Is 'you may have been' describing a continuous process in the past, or a single completed action? Or both at the same time?). There's no way to hold that kind of double meaning in suspension in a painting, is there?

What about abstract painting that insists upon various possibilities but stays indeterminate? Could you talk a little about the allure of 'Stubbs and his horses'?

It insists on various possibilities, but not simultaneously. I think I was more interested in the act of perception here. The picture is of the wife and it's of the mother in law, but it's not of both at the same time. (By the way, did you ever see this? *youtube.com/watch?v=a91eiu_eer4*) In a poem, it's possible for 'read' to be an infinitive and a past tense simultaneously in a way that something perceived visually cannot be. One of my favourite bits of one of my favourite paintings is the breastplate that one of Vulcan's helpers is working on in Velazquez's *La fragua de Vulcano*. If you stand close to it, it's a smear of white paint, and if you take a step back, it's a perfectly detailed picture of a breastplate. But your perception swaps between codes, rather than keeping both these possibilities (the representation and the thing represented) in play simultaneously. As for Stubbs and his horses, I had in mind paintings like *Whistlejacket*, in which the background is in some senses as important as the foreground: the absence of detail, of anything, is vital for the picture's composition and its meaning. That poem also talks about 'details that will not / exist without the reader to make / them': this is something I am extremely interested in at the moment, the extent to which a poem, even one that seems disorganised or else freeform in some ways (a 'spontaneous overflow of powerful feeling', as it were), is essentially aimed at manipulation of the reader. Sincerity, once you can fake that, you've got it made. And maybe one

useful point about a misprint, why poets find them so attractive, is that they can seem to be something entirely external to the poet, and therefore in an obscure way trustworthy.

Would you recommend some of the poems you are currently enjoying?

The whole of Steve Ely's *Oswald's Book of Hours* is great. I'm liking a lot a book of translations of Vladislav Khodasevich by Peter Daniels (especially an untitled poem that begins 'Nothing more lovely and more liberating / than to part forever from your lover / and walk out of the station on your own.') Lucie Brock-Broido's *Stay, Illusion* (again, the whole book). Robert Wrigley, 'Horseflies' and 'Sinatra'. Brigit Pegeen Kelly. My current large-scale project is to read the whole of Geoffrey Hill's *Broken Hierarchies*, the early poems are all I've done so far, but I remember how much I love them every time I read them. 'Genesis'.

Could you end with a favourite example of a misprint or mistake in art? (One of mine is that New Weather, *the first collection by Muldoon (a poet for whom errata would later feature so largely in his praxis), was printed entirely in italics by mistake.) Has anything gone fortuitously awry in your experience publishing with Nevsky Prospects?*

In art, I don't know. I like very much the fact that a book I am currently reading, the Spanish translation of Adam Zagajewski's *W cudzym pięknie* (*En la belleza ajena*) says on its copyright page that it is 'financed by the Adam Mickiewicz Institute © POLISH TRANSLATION POGRAM': I almost can't believe that 'PROGRAM / POGROM' is not deliberate. But that's just my sick sense of humour. As far as publishing, the job of the editor is to hide, deny and minimise all mistakes, to claim that his work is immaculate (not like that of his competitors). Seriously, nothing really springs to mind. Or nothing I'd be happy sharing in public.

George Stubbs, *Whistlejacket*

Six Poems

JAMES WOMACK

Co-respondent

That morning, N and the baby being asleep,
I sat down to write a rebuttal to one of your love-letters.
But you know how it is:
you set out to perform some ordinary task,
to buy the bread, maybe, or else *I won't be long,*
just taking the videos back to the shop,
and then round a corner
the full majesty of the goddess Freya
strikes you in the face and blinds you.
Which was how it was. I cannot live in this world,
the goddess of beauty and death lounging
at street corners. Was this what I meant to write?
Anyway, I never took the videos back.
One of them was *our film*, if you remember,
or don't think it odd that shared possessions
are alleged to define or fix relationship.
Our song, of course, is 'Yakety Sax',
but the film behind my eyes admits of any soundtrack –
your hair wet from the pool.
And although my dream of you
is not the same as you,
it is in fact love, it is love.
Write that often and it will be enough.

Target

I'd like to be a queen of people's hearts...

Bored at ourselves, we filled bottles both glass and plastic with the undrinkable tap water.
We opened the large window and took a five paces run-up.
The bottles all burst. Some burst subtly, a disappointing collapse and split.
Others burst beautifully in a corona of shrapnel round a surprisingly dry centre.
This was the fourteenth floor, the fag-end of August, years and years ago.
The supervisor was alerted by the crashing the cheers the who-knows-what.
He came to our door smoking a cigarette.
Listen, you little cunts, if you throw more shit out of the window you're for it.
What, us? We haven't been doing anything. Look, the window is closed.
Hmph. So you didn't throw anything? No. We did not think he was convinced.
I will take photos and prove the truth one way or another.
A day or so of tension, him refusing to speak to us or to unlock the washing machine.
But then on the last day of the month he was grumpy but somehow tender.
I am sorry about your princess. But she was a liar as well.

'But the heart?'

But the heart? Ah, the heart! My heart...
My heart is a seaside town in winter,
the streets unpeopled; white, resilient buildings;
a thick sea-fog, fog like I've never seen it before,
blue fog chopping the trees in half,
and a thick sandy groundfrost.
Occasional passers-by greeted with a wan smile,
or embarrassing displays of affection.
But then I don't go out much, stay home
with Four Last Songs looped on the iPod.
If you want to visit (but then, why would you?)
you have to fly charter, endure the cramped journey,
listen to the instructions of an indifferent steward.
Lights in the floor will guide you to your exit.

Not the music you would listen to lazy
as the clouds pile slow above one another
on some thoughtless Saturday afternoon
but songs for the redneck pre-Apocalypse,
the final storm breaking or about to break
and the world massing in the road outside
where inside is only William Blake –
the face a Blake etching, Blake's deathmask,
and the voice the voice of unavoidable prophecy
a storm coming keen from an open throat.

Easter 2015

Having spun the wrong way round the block to avoid the drunks
Having seen the couple make their first sculptural kiss in the quarantine cone of a streetlamp
Having taught an exactly drunk young Englishman how to use a doorbell
Having passed by the aggressive hole in the road
Having walked the length of Genova Street from the headquarters of the ruling party to the tramps sleeping
      in the shade of the world's fifth-largest bank
Having acknowledged – same procedure as last year, Miss Sophie? Same procedure as every year, James! – the
      death and resurrection of Our Lord
Having passed the cake shops and the Plaza de Margaret Thatcher
Having unlocked silently the front door and remembered as you always remember that you really should get
      round to oiling its hinges
Having rolled the door away
Having checked on your son's soft breathing
Having taken your wife's breathing for granted
You are home safe for this morning of all mornings at least

The Ambassadors

In the undesired side of the park where no one goes
but the joggers, I found myself one green morning.
The shade spread over me as I walked under the arching trees,
and I tried to take a photograph, photographs,
of the chiaroscuro in the sprinkler
as it threw water in and out of patches of sunlight.
All I succeeded in noting was an anamorphic stain,
a brushstroke that squint as I might I could not
resolve into anything coherent, a skull.
Then a group of joggers ran through me, heads down,
refusing to swerve, bustling me out of the way.
Oi, you fuckers! I'm in the arcades too! I yelled after them,
then, *Go on, you run, much as you like, you'll never get far enough.*

From the Peak

'He had spent the last decade in Manchester […] as Warden of the fractious Fellows of the Collegiate.
It was virtual exile.' BENJAMIN WOOLLEY, *The Queen's Conjuror: The Life and Magic of Dr Dee*

No mobile contact
and Orpheus on the radio

Coming here, as we turned
where it said Elkstones

a pickup hurtled round
the bend and almost –

.

At Roach End, a commemorative plaque
on the stile notes the name of a doctor
'taken' while walking the moors he loved.

He was the age that I am now who walk,
breathe heather, pick, taste, feel
the stain of bilberry, and hope for a signal.

.

The Mermaid Pool no bird
will settle on: the girl
who was drowned there
is serving us with snapper
and marlin; she is dressed
in black and when I remark
on the well that plunges
twenty feet in the corner
of the bar, there's a blink
*Would you like any drink
with that?* They have closed
the room with the view
so the silent landlord can
only watch the road for
errant young farmers
in quest of his pool table.

.

Then there were the two
Methodists who stumbled
around in a local bog
'in the neighbourhood of Leek'
having lost their way
to a meeting where they
hoped to claim souls,
but instead found moss-pits
dragging them to their knees.

.

Lud's Church

the Green Chapel
conceivably

a moss-quilted
fern-vaulted

perpendicular
cleft or gorge

gaiter-deep in
mud and open

to all myths

.

as above, so below

thus I hear Hermes
Trismegistus
whisper across the plains

from here to Huntingdonshire

.

But the story comes back to us
as we hold up our handsets

for network connection, the mother
and daughter freezing here, the thunder,

the drifts, death stealing over them
that Boxing Day, wrapping them in

oblivion. A beep and a message
comes through from Manchester, all well.

.

We sit in this little valley like two
uncut pages of a book by an antiquary
about customs of the Peak. We have
never been read. I begin mid-sentence,
you end mid-sentence. And yet we are

Two Poems

STEPHEN BURT

Kalahari

Sandusky, OH 44870

Not the desert, but
the indoor family resort:

six acres of ways to snack, spend, swim and dive,
laid out like Chutes and Ladders, and featuring
peacocks, a docile ocelot, and five
varieties of net and racket sport.

Some of us prefer the video games,
the backlit kiosks in the waiting room,
to the reverberant waterfalls of the 'real thing'
for which we supposedly came. Both can make your ears ring.

·

Wave-tank waves are the mildest among
*the thousand natural shocks that flesh is heir
to*; their exhilarated spume

is water liberated into air,
whose particles then contract
and settle on minors whose spinning inner
tubes, colliding, reenact
the Battle of Lepanto.

Not one of them seems to be saying *I don't want to.*

·

It is a circulatory system, or
a miniature empire, or
a flotilla by means of which
each ride is *an apprenticeship to the truth
that around every circle another can be drawn.*

At least one grade-schooler appears to have lost a tooth.
At least one lost child has just been found.

·

The ridiculous inappropriateness
of the painted impalas and grass (at least
no painted people) mean
that actual history is long, and mean,
and better represented by maps and graphs.

·

Here's something to love, if you can
love the world and the people in it: not

the aunts and dads watching, extracting themselves from the queues,
but the older brother and sister willing
to flaunt tomorrow's bruise.

Not the bins full of nonpareils, like a train
derailed, across the floor of the candy room,
but the teenager in khaki and zori who labours
to sweep up a spill and re-stack them, as afternoon
sun through glass bricks turns the green tiles greener.

Not the lion's mane
for sale in the dress-up zoo,
not the backlit spray guns or the animatronic hyena,
but the nearly motionless employee
who stands one step from the lip of the topmost flume,
counting out safe intervals
between the successive slide riders
by tapping her fingers and whispering: *one, two, one, two.*

Heavenly Beings

                     That would be
the name for Nathan's band,
not the one that he plays in, but the one he plays with,
the one that he assembled from Duplos, whose special mission,

in between concerts, is helping a penguin escape.
The humans were penning her in against the will
of the gods of Olympus, who also play in the band,
which included a cello, a sprinkler, and a guitar

along with two polar bears, a river god
whose name keeps changing, and an orange giraffe,
who does not appear in the poster, since he was the member
committed to taking every photograph.

They have a laser cannon, so they can solve problems
through suasion and melody, or through *force majeure*.
They are also, apparently, always on tour.
The oral tradition proceeds to a tornado and a civil war

fought wholly in Antarctica, and ends
in Heaven, with Zeus,
where the polar bear, the penguin and his sister
pose on a bedspread thrown over the back of a couch,

which represents the Andes. A wooden birthday cake
now represents the drums,
while melancholy, silent microphones,
the right size for Lego hands, represent microphones.

They won't leave this Earth,
or not any time soon.

Meanwhile, Cooper has tried to sing harmony
with his earlier self on an iPhone,
three against two-and-a-half,
reviving his first big hit, 'Plocky Goes to the Moon'.

Delmore Schwartz, Again

FLORIAN GARGAILLO

Once and for All: The Best of Delmore Schwartz, edited by Craig Morgan Teicher
(New York: New Directions, 2016). UK Reprint, W. W. Norton & Co., 2016.

ONCE AND FOR ALL gathers a selection of poems, short stories, verse dramas, essays, and letters by Delmore Schwartz – remarkably, in just under three hundred pages. The book is pitched as a recuperative effort. From the back: 'This volume aims to restore Schwartz to his proper place in the canon and introduce new readers to the breadth of his achievement.' In his note, the editor, Craig Morgan Teicher, hopes that 'readers will be able to gain a broad, if not complete, understanding of Delmore Schwartz the literary artist'. The implication being that most of the attention paid to Schwartz since his death has been of a biographical nature. Evidently, the introduction by John Ashbery is meant to give this literary homecoming additional weight.

Even if we resist the sentimentality with which they were so often depicted, Schwartz's life and career were indeed tragic in many ways. After the success of his first book, *In Dreams Begin Responsibilities* (1938), Schwartz's fame entered a quick decline. For several years he devoted himself to a failed epic, *Genesis: Book One* (1943), about the family history of Hershey Green, a stand-in for Schwartz himself. None of his later work in any genre achieved the readership he had won, briefly, with his first book, and he died in relative obscurity in 1966, wracked by mental illness.

It is certainly good to have a new edition of a writer who captured the imagination of many, even for a short period. And it is good to have the writings themselves readily available, when the life has so overtaken the work. Yet reading through these pages, I wondered if his present obscurity as a poet, his absence from the anthologies (a point of contention for Ashbery), was really quite so surprising. The real surprise, for me, was the quality of the short stories, and the comparative weakness of the poems, at a distance of several decades – in particular since what works in the fiction is precisely what does not work in the poetry.

First, let us take a quick detour through the essays, since they are an important key to his literary writing. In 'The Isolation of Modern Poetry' (1941), Schwartz offers a number of theories as to why the modern poet now stands apart from the broader culture. There is the usual blame put on industrialism, for what role can art play in a society that only values commerce, etc. Schwartz also points to the decline of narrative and dramatic verse, and the rise of the lyric (and all of its intimacies and obscurities), as having led to the withdrawal of poetry from public life. His most interesting theory, though, is that the 'new world picture' of the nineteenth and twentieth centuries produced a host of ideas – by Freud, Marx, and others – that poetry could not absorb, leading to a split between the writer's intellect and his sensibility. Schwartz's work can best be understood as an

attempt to bring these ideas into the realm of poetry. If he fell short, it is because he often did not know what to do with those concepts once he had introduced them. History, Life, Nature, God, and America feature prominently, yet they remain abstractions. Instead of exploring the significance of these ideas in specific contexts, Schwartz too often leaned on the words themselves for their general impressiveness.

The choruses in *Genesis* are especially guilty of this. Concepts from Marx, Freud, and Hegel are flatly applied ('Hershey's ego defined itself further by means of father, mother and brother') or pointed to with extravagant gestures ('more and more, behold the dialectic, / How light brings shadow, how the evil, good'). Schwartz not only siphons down the ideas, but his presentation of them rarely shows much imagination. 'This is the way each only life becomes, / Tossed on History's ceaseless sums!' The mathematical twist of 'sums' just barely rescues the final line from platitude. When Schwartz does attempt a colourful framing image, the desire for immediate effect leads him into absurdities: 'The hanged man like a sack upon a tree / Cannot believe the freedom of the will.' Then again, the hanged man can't believe much of anything at all.

In the last two decades of his life, Schwartz's desire for a poetry of ideas translated into vatic posturing. 'This is the endless doom, without remedy, of poetry. / This is also the joy everlasting of poetry.' 'If you can look at any thing for long enough, / You will rejoice in the miracle of love, / You will possess and be possessed, as in the consecration of marriage, the mastery of vocation, the mystery of gift's mastery, the deathless relation of parenthood and progeny.' Schwartz dresses up pseudo-prophetic insights and pat reassurances of this sort by evoking the language of the pulpit, yet the imitation is rather shallow. As a result, many of the late poems read like unsuccessful imitations of Walt Whitman:

I am a poet of the Hudson River and the heights above it,
    The lights, the stars, and the bridges
I am also by self-appointment the laureate of the Atlantic
    —of the peoples' hearts, crossing it
    to new America.

Whatever self-deprecating humour Schwartz intended with the 'self-appointment' of the laureate dissipates into a rather naked wish for self-aggrandisement. By contrast, Whitman in 'Song of Myself' matched his vatic posture with individual images of great sharpness and clarity. Too often the vagueness of thought in Schwartz's poems comes with a vagueness of language in tow.

These problems can be traced back as far as his first book. Indeed, it is hard to read *In Dreams Begin*

Responsibilities today with the enthusiasm that greeted it in 1938. Its half-hearted laments about urban life are rarely focused enough to sustain a coherent vision.

The past, a giant shadow like the twilight,
The moving street on which the autos slide,
The buildings' heights, like broken teeth,
Repeat necessity on every side,
The age requires death and is not denied

The poem repeatedly borders on images that are compelling and clear ('like broken teeth'), only to collapse back into abstraction. It is the 'buildings' heights', not the buildings themselves, that are compared to broken teeth, and the whole scene is framed as a vast allegory for 'the past'.

O son of man, the ignorant night, the travail
Of early morning, the mystery of beginning
Again and again,
    while History is unforgiven.

The final line does not so much give us a variety of possible meanings as bury the ending in a grandiose statement: 'History is unforgiven'. Schwartz, who up to this point in the poem had given us a series of descriptive details about the city, has done little to prepare us for the sudden turn to abstraction here. One gets the creeping sense that 'unforgiven' could just as easily have been 'excused'. At the very least that would fit with the grammatical contrast to the 'son of man', for whom the 'ignorant night', 'the travail', and 'the mystery' seem more of a curse than a blessing.

Schwartz produced far superior work in his short stories, where he was able to treat critically, and humorously, the very tendencies he was subject to in the poems. The best of the stories, 'The World is a Wedding,' describes the conversations of a literary clique. As portrayed by Schwartz, the talk is by turns witty and heated – and nearly always competitive.

'The contraceptive,' Edmund continued, 'has purified love by freeing it from the accident of children. Now everyone with any sense can find out whom he truly loves. Children can be chosen beings, and not the result of impetuous lust or impatient appetite. Now love is love and nothing else but love!'

'Yes,' said Rudyard, 'a mere material device has utterly transformed the relationships between men and women: a mere material thing!'

'On the other hand,' said Francis French, 'it also makes possible adultery, and promiscuity, not that I have anything against promiscuity.'

'I love my wife, but oh you id,' said Ferdinand, who had studied Freud and Tin Pan Alley.

Ferdinand means this as a joke, of course, and not a very good one. Yet the bit about his having 'studied Freud and Tin Pan Alley' cannily reminds us that his banter about Freud does enable him to show off his knowledge of Freud to his friends. This is less a story about ideas than a story about the way intellectuals use ideas among themselves; and as such it succeeds brilliantly.

It was suggested that some pathological feeling had compelled B. L. to marry Priscilla, either sexual feeling for his own sex, or a desire to possess an utterly passive wife. Francis French suggested that Priscilla might resemble B. L.'s mother when he was an infant at the breast. Rudyard thought it far more likely that Priscilla was seeking to escape from an incestuous desire for her father, since B. L. was truly as far away from her father as she could get. Rudyard also dismissed as banal, trite, obvious and hence untrue the view that B. L. might have married Priscilla because he wished to ascend in the social scale.

The final sentence is wonderfully double-edged, since the other ideas proposed were equally 'banal, trite, obvious', and what's more an obvious hypothesis can be true as well: one does not exclude the other. Schwartz captures, in one quick snapshot, the limits of this clique, where the veracity of each proposition gets judged according to its wit rather than its logic.

This interest in the way intellectuals talk lends the story a near-anthropological quality reflected, to some extent, in the tone. Schwartz coolly excises the various tensions motivating their banter, and recounts the disappointments of each character in the neutral form of a report.

Edmund Kish wanted to be a teacher of philosophy, but he was unable to get an appointment. Jacob Cohen, recognised by all as the conscience or judge of the circle, wanted to be a reporter, but there were few jobs for newcomers. Ferdinand Harrap tried to be an author, but none of his stories were accepted, and he supported himself by directing a business agency. Francis French and Marcus Gross were teachers in the public high school system, although this was far from their ambition.

Yet the list, by emphasizing the challenges each faced in his ambitions, takes on an elegiac air, as though we were hearing a catalogue of fallen heroes. The tone prevents us from taking this too far, of course, but the grandness is there in the background. Indeed, Schwartz's prose is at its most affecting when it is plain and unsentimental: 'The human beings of the circle and the circle as such existed for Jacob Cohen in a way private to him. The other boys of the circle often discussed each other, but seldom thought about each other when they were alone. They came together in order not to be alone, to escape from deviceless solitude.' There is real sadness to this passage, and more weight than its three sentences would seem to justify.

Schwartz's stories all have this eye for social comedy (and tragicomedy), even when they take place far from the literary milieu he was familiar with. His most famous story, 'In Dreams Begin Responsibilities', imagines his parents' first date as projected onto a movie screen:

My mother is holding my father's arm and telling him of the novel which she has been reading; and my father utters judgments of the characters as the plot is made clear to him. This is a habit which he very much enjoys, for he feels the utmost superiority and confidence when he approves and condemns the behaviour of other people. At times he feels moved to utter a brief 'Ugh' – whenever the story becomes what he would call sugary. This tribute is paid to his manliness. My mother feels satisfied by the interest which she has awakened; she is showing my father how intelligent she is, and how interesting.

Here, too, people perform for themselves and others in a way that leaves them deeply isolated. Remarkably, behaviours that in another writer's hands might easily have seemed pathetic are balanced out by pathos. One suspects this is how Schwartz felt all lives were lived.

The unevenness of Delmore Schwartz's writing does not detract from the quality of this edition, which does a handsome job selecting out a representative sample of his work. There are enough threads and echoes across genres here to make the book consistent in spite of the brevity of each section. So Schwartz's concerns about the decline of narrative and dramatic verse, put forth in 'The Isolation of Modern Poetry' essay, resurfaces thirty pages or so later in a 1938 letter to Ezra Pound, in much the same way that his professed desire (in the correspondence) to write an epic poem gets borne out by the selection of verse.

Indeed, Schwartz is one of the few writers of his generation I can think of who is best served by a multi-generic selection such as this. Though we remember him today primarily as a poet, 'writer' seems the more fitting title. Schwartz expressed a profound devotion to poetry in his essays, but in practice he was less wedded to poetic form – and to the musical possibilities of poetic language – than to the particular thoughts and feelings he wished to get across.

Ultimately, Craig Morgan Teicher succeeds in giving us a picture of Delmore Schwartz's mind, and it is here that the edition's principal interest lies. Schwartz emerges as an oddly quixotic figure – one who tried to give back to American verse the epic, narrative, and intellectual qualities he felt it lacked. If he was wrong on this last point, and if the intellectual stuff of American poetry was simply of a kind he did not recognise (not being so explicitly costumed as Marx and Freud), that does not quite take away from the value of his quest.

In the essay 'The Vocation of the Poet in the Modern World,' Schwartz argues that the poet is a 'creator, and metaphor-maker, and presiding bringer of unity', 'a kind of priest'. He laments the 'degradation' of contemporary English and mass culture, and offers the poet as the one who can restore dignity to the language: 'In the unpredictable and fearful future that awaits civilization, the poet must be prepared to be alienated and indestructible.' Schwartz could not help but buy into his own romance of the *poète maudit*. Yet is there not something a touch heroic about that, in the end?

Two Poems

DAVID YEZZI

Last Job

We finished school in May. I headed East.
She moved back home. We talked by phone. She
                                          came to
visit once and stayed in a hotel.
But the city wasn't going to work for her:
too tall, too many steam holes, too much noise.

Months before, we'd robbed a bookstore where she'd
been made manager. She had the keys.
With my blue Buick idling outside,
we helped ourselves to boxes full of books, walked
them right out the front door: poetry, a book on
flying, Kafka's stories, pulp.
Books were our thing. We loved them, and we felt they
should be ours, God knows why. So we took what we
                                          could
while it was ours to take.

Old Friends

They're bristly as a stand of winter wheat.
They slurp their soup and pinch your slice of bread and,
when you're in the can, softly repeat
the many sins they level at your head.

All for love. You're thinking of them now:
the bag of snakes that makes up their good graces, their
fellowship a roiled ebb and flow
of blood staining their hyper-tensioned faces.

Be glad for what you've got, for they are it –
the ones you've known for ages, who've known *you*, the
living record of the little shit
you've been at times, a virtual *Who's Who*

of who you've slept with, slights you've given, though their own
slight they just sweep behind the door.
But those tidbits are there for you to know, holding their
sins in trust, what friends are for.

Bink Noll

David R. Slavitt

THERE IS A SMALL, handsome book on my shelf called *Seven Princeton Poets* that my good friend the late George Garrett gave me, and the roster of its contributors is an impressive one: Louis Coxe, Garrett, Theodore Holmes, Galway Kinnell, William Meredith, W. S. Merwin, and Bink Noll.

The last of these names is remembered, if at all, by connoisseurs of catastrophe, because he was invited back to Princeton to give a reading and was deeply pleased to be returning to his alma mater to perform. But it didn't go well.

A graduate student had been charged with meeting him, taking him to dinner at one of the eating clubs, and then escorting him to the room where the reading was to be held. All very straightforward, or so one might expect. But the graduate student, having made strenuous apologies, explained to Mr Noll that he had learned just an hour or so before, that he could drive Albert Camus from his New York hotel to the airport for his plane back to Paris. This meant he would have an hour or so alone with Camus, the subject of his thesis. An opportunity of a lifetime. If it was all right with Mr Noll, then, the student would introduce him, leave him his cheque, and then leave to drive like a madman to New York. Would that be okay? Noll understood that this was important to the young man and said it would be perfectly fine for him to do that.

So they're in a lounge somewhere with a lectern and an array of green leather couches and easy chairs. On one of the couches there are a couple of undergraduates. The graduate student introduces Noll and dashes out, having of course forgotten to leave the cheque. Noll reads a poem. One of the undergraduates asks him if some kind of meeting is going on. They're studying for a chemistry exam. Noll apologises and leaves to go to the Nassau Inn and have a drink or three. The story circulates because, for the rest of us, no matter how minuscule we may fear our audiences may turn out to be, they are never so bad as a negative three.

All by itself, that disaster wouldn't have been enough to promote Noll to immortality, but it did qualify him as a minor divinity – like Oizys, the daimon daughter of Nyx (night), who presides over misery. Or, to speak more plainly, horror stories having to do with poets and poetry, of which there are too many, attached themselves to Noll. There is, for instance, an urban legend about a computer error that resulted in a book of poetry getting half its stock remaindered before publication date, at which point the publisher had no choice but to release the rest of it to buck-a-book tables. Did this happen? It has the dismal ring of truthiness. And it got attached to Noll and *Center of the Circle* because he was known as a likely repository of misery and bad luck.

As I think about it now, the problem with his luck was mostly his timing. I remember the excitement at Yale when Richard Wilbur's *Things of This World* appeared. Everyone, or at least everyone in the Elizabethan Club, was talking about it. I was of course too ignorant to understand how unusual this was, but I know now. The other book of poetry from about that same time to occasion that same buzz was Philip Larkin's *The Less Deceived* in 1955. By 1963, when *Center of the Circle* came out, the old order had collapsed. We had poems of protest, Beat poems, gay and Lesbian poems. The world was unfair and the youngsters thought they could and should fix it. The skewed tastes of the audience dictated which titles got onto the shelves of bookstores and sold well enough to be reordered. The audience for poetry is small enough that it can be terribly distorted by irrelevant enthusiasms of relatively few people. (On Wall Street they would refer to the situation as a 'thin float'.)

What was on offer from Noll? Mere excellence, a delicacy and accuracy of vision, a linguistic dexterity, and a celebration of ordinary things that is close to religious. He also had an uncanny ability to leap from some modest domestic detail to the great universe. Pindar and Bacchylides do this in their odes, soaring up from some sports victory to a larger myth and then gracefully modulating back down to the here and now. More recently, think of what Wilbur was able to do, turning sheets on a laundry line into 'Love Calls us to the Things of This World'.

There came a moment in the 1960s when devotees of protest and defiance became impatient with what they dismissed as elitist and, almost as damning, aesthetic. In only a few years the weather had changed – or even the climate. There was a plague of sincerity, and campuses got serious, about civil rights, about Vietnam, about the injustices of the world. Anger is easier than art, and when earnestness takes the stage, the old-fashioned, more refined practitioners are lucky to survive as buskers outside the theatre. Leaving aside literature for a moment, let me adduce the bizarre and poignant information that the Yale riot in my senior year was not about any deplorable injustices but merely whether the Good Humour man or the Humpty-Dumpty man should have the preferred spot as ice cream vendors at the corner of College and Wall Streets, just outside the post office. Absurd? Not at all! (Back then, the only emperor was the emperor of ice cream.) Such playfulness is just what *Studentenleben* is supposed to be. Eisenhower was president, and we had no worries, no causes, nothing with which to occupy ourselves except our studies and our fun. (No undergraduates since my day have had it so good.)

So there's Noll in 1962 at Princeton, his alma mater, with his elegant poems, and the undergraduates asking whether there is some kind of meeting going on.

•

No one knows what poem he read. We are, therefore, at liberty to pick whichever one strikes our fancy for Noll to have chosen for the edification and entertainment of the lectern, the couches, and the easy chairs. Arbitrarily, then, we may suppose it to have been

'Woman on the Verge of Plethora', a piece that is, in many ways, representative of his work. It begins:

Decades, she has used April to set plants
And so set down her idea of a garden.
Now she emerges in soiled gloves, smudged
And warm from the work of pulling weeds.
She admires the ranks of colour, the clean order
And shades her mind against the hot cause: Summer—
How it thickens in the stem of time,
A threat of fecund weeds against her plan.

So, it is a perfectly ordinary woman, weeding, made a little more vivid, perhaps, by Noll's mention of the warmth of her gloves. But of course, she is out there in a larger landscape of garden poems and their green thoughts in a green shade, and we are cognizant of the many possibilities for elaboration. It is not, actually, the garden she is working in but 'her idea of a garden'. All gardens are ideas, though, cultivated spaces, clearings in the jungle or oases in the desert. We are pleased to see the efficient exposition of dramatic tension between her plan and the habit, or necessity, of nature to reject any such imposition. Summer, against which she must shade her mind as well as her eyes, 'thickens in the stem of time'. The stanza concludes with the dexterous 'threat of fecund weeds against her plan', and, clearly, their stems are as much as what time thickens as her planned flowers or vegetables. The poem's concern then deepens and broadens out so that it is about the uneasy coexistence of 'The agent Life who kisses any seed / Even while she spends herself seizing weeds, Who would load the planet ten times over' and 'the agent Death, / Who soon must dry brave notions from her head / And drop wisdom back into its grotto'. The poet is willing to concede immediately that the woman in the garden 'dare not notice' either of these agents, 'naked giants locked'. Their antinomy hangs in the air high over the heads of the two students with their chemistry text to dissolve into the Princetonian atmosphere over which the ghost of F. Scott Fitzgerald still presides.

It is not a particularly demanding or difficult poem but it does require that the reader pay attention to small details and read closely enough not just to see but to feel the delicate balances of its machinery. Noll is given to these significant oppositions, which can sometimes pop up and bluntly declare themselves. In 'All My Pretty Ones? Did You Say All?' for example, he laments without any linguistic embellishment at all 'how the law is waste / And glories, waste and glories, waste and glories'.

The conclusion, or resolution, of 'Woman on the Verge of Plethora' is inevitable, but the acuity of Noll's perceptions manages to keep it from being predictable:

She feels how thin, how dangerous has been
The sack that holds her mortal fluids in.
She feels the blind fibrils of oak reach out
To use the mouldering she must leave.

•

Noll's three books are *Center of the Circle* (Harcourt, Brace, and World, 1962), *The Feast* (Harcourt, Brace,

and World, 1967), and *The House* (Louisiana State University Press, 1984), which is not so much a collection of poems as a single, long poem. A suite, really – or, say, poems that agglomerate to something larger with its own integrity. Auden's *About the House* has a suite, 'Thanksgiving for a Habitat', which operates in much the same way, celebrating various rooms, but the other part of his book, 'In and Out', ventures farther afield. Noll continues all the way through in the same vein, which is rich enough for him to maintain our interest (and, of course, his).

There is a line in one of his poems, 'Wedlock', in which Noll suggests that 'our *pas de deux*' might be named '"Taking the Usual for All It's Worth"' – which could well be the his motto. It is an ingenious poem because the marriage it describes turns out not to be that of the speaker to his wife but rather the speaker's to his dog. Only metaphorically, and all the more powerfully, does it refer back to his actual marriage. He says of the dog:

Now after four years he's like a wife
the way he sleeps with one eye open,
reads my mind, learns how not to annoy,
and thinks in the first person plural,
creature of habit all set to please
but also be pleased [...]

If there is a passage by some poet or other, male or female, that comes close to this felicitous accuracy describing the married state, I can't think of it. It would be mawkish, maybe, if the speaker were referring directly to his spouse, but we give ourselves greater latitude when we talk about pets. We are indulgent then to these descriptions of intimacy, while at the same time understanding perfectly well what he is 'really' talking about. The conclusion of the poem maintains that doubleness, making it even more basic:

our archaic hearts are lifted up:
hound and hunter, hunter and hound.
We act as we're bound to, partners that
dance out the words *meat* and *fire* and *house*.

There are some poems in the suite in which he turns to prose, perhaps for its nakedness. Or as if to say that some things are too important to be fussed with. (That may not be true, but it is generally the pretense behind prose-poems, which are, or should be, as carefully crafted as stanzas of verse.) Here is a random sample, a different instrumentation of some of the Noll's themes:

The house breathes in and out, and where I sit is the rib cage. For a while I am its breath. Beyond my ears, today's conflicts start and take place loudly and vanish, and already reporters are out gathering that news, but the worst news is always the constant underlying mess which we can't understand, no less do anything about and be free from.

Noll is surely one of those poets who deserves a second look – or he would be if he had ever had a real first look. His obscurity in the po' business isn't his misfortune but ours.

Five Poems

BINK NOLL

Nightlight

A noise I may have heard but am not sure
I've heard pries me from the bottom of sleep.
I rise against my will, a dark body
levitating and used to night – climbing –
and my eyes, not wishing to, open wide.
They hear the god breathing outside the door,
focus the way my head lies, on details
in the wallpaper and a round molding.
By the mopboard the nightlight congeals weight
and casts shadows that make me upside down.

That noise – if there was one – does not repeat
but I'm warned now anyhow and need to stalk
and do, and what I feel is nude and brave
to be a hero inventing a house,
a champion prowling down phantom stairs
into a cave where the man-eater stops
gnawing a skull and watches for my scent.
However, streetlight's there ahead of me
and reveals that he's gone leaving no trace.
Dwindled, I wonder at the lack of roar.

What I hear next is the house stretch and turn
after this nightmare it's had about me.
From danger I float back up the stairway
as a man will when bad news doesn't come,
light as pleasure. I lower into bed.
Without sound the house and I draw our knees
to our chests and then, before you know it,
the cardinal in his tree whistles and chugs
"Pretty. Pretty." for the first time today.
The house and dog are waiting to be fed.

Essences

I.

A gentleman near me in the plane
wears a lavender cologne that brings
a child's comfort, holding a big hand,
and my grandfather back to my side.

Ten, twenty years since I thought about
this scent, even in a barber shop,
yet now so accurate it implies
the stale cigar smoke in his wool coat.

II.

Steadily our house exhales clear haze
from its elements and honest age.
after she had flown a thousand miles
my grown child stopped, put what she carried

down, stopped inside the front door, shut it,
shut her eyes, leaned there and breathed in like
a small beast remembering it's safe.
She let her breath go: 'I know I'm home now.'

Lunch on Omaha Beach

The killers are killed, their violent rinds
Conveyed, and the beach is back to summer.
I eat sausage with bread. Full of ease, the sea
Makes the sound of cows chewing through high grass.

They're deposited in government lawn
Set with nine thousand decencies of stone
To wet the eye, shake the heart, and lose
Each name in a catalog of graven names.

They are wasted in the blank of herohood.
They are dead to fondness and paradox.
They're all the same. In the field of lawn
Above the beach, they're put away the same.

They should be left exactly here below where
Death's great bronze mares shook earth and bloodied
them,
Where violence of noise isolated each boy
In the body of his scream, and dropped him.

No worn Norman hill should be scarred and smoothed
To suit officials' tidy thoughts for graveyards
But the wreckage left, shrinking in rust and rags
And carrion to dust or tumuli.

To honor my thoughts against shrines, to find
The beast who naked wakes in us and walks
In flags, to watch the color of his day
I spill my last Bordeaux into the sand.

Watching, I wonder at the white quiet,
The fields of butter cows, my countrymen
Come to study battle maps, blue peasants
Still moving back and forth, the day's soft sea.

The Picador Bit

Inside that figure rides opaque malice
who by drilling makes the great heart lift
its fountain and waste the lake of blood.
His lance strikes, holds. Longer, the don's full weight.

Men for this circumstance of sport have made
laws that order place, gear, conduct, and four tries
but the bull learns rage instead. He erupts
through headlong pain and strikes wrath back again.

Today's malice, part horse saved by blindfold
and morphine from panic at horns, stands,
its legal right side out, and standing so
temps this, the next enlargement of the hole

– and part brawny don, mechanic who finds
and fits his point to drain the immense will.
Again the spot. The centaur shocks sideward
till the hole is important, like a whale's spout.

The crowd feels the lance in its own ripe hole,
in its hump knows the monster with two heads,
the blackness of its law, this letting of force
and the pump emptying the tongue of red.

Blood foams down. The head is dropped forever now.
Justice is satisfied. Its constable trots
darkly off. Left to his killers, the bull –
danger's substance, lure, huge, hates itself –

thrills every male groin while he swings there
and, helpless, spills the fire of his urine.

....

*Lou B. 'Bink' Noll was born in Orange, New Jersey,
on April 15, 1927. He graduated from Princeton
University in 1948, after having served in the
Merchant Marine from August 1945 to January
1947. He earned his MA degree from Johns
Hopkins University in 1950 and his PhD in English
Literature from the University of Colorado in
1956. After teaching at Beloit College in 1953–54,
he taught for six years at Dartmouth. In 1960–61
he lectured on American language and literature
at Zaragoza, Spain, on a Fulbright Fellowship. He
returned to Beloit College in 1961 where he was
promoted to full professor in 1969. He received a
National Endowment for the Arts (NEA) grant in
1974. He died on November 9, 1986. Bink Noll:
Selected Poems, edited with an introduction by
David R. Slavitt, will be published in October by
Little Island Press in their Memento Series at £25.*

The Words the Sirens Used

O Worriers! Quit and touch my shore.
I promise back original dark
where you were made. Come and endure.
With me be cave-quiet, closed and stark
as night occupying solid rock.

With or without you sons will thrive
and be harmed, with you wife and friend
will break faith – or without. O Lost! Arrive
where no man engenders or is ended.
All that breathes is the wind.

O Sleepers! Sleep beside me. Hide
from what the dragon gods prepare
outside you and what fatal appetite
excites within. Come touch my place where
flesh ends save and senses clear.

I sing. I am disembodied song,
the stone-dry and endless voice of wind
sounding across clean air-shaped stone.
I sing of the serene you want a friend
to cure you with. Come! Land!

The fool next to you won't consider how
you'll both die and rot anyhow after long pain
in a soiled place – not like this – if you don't quit now,
a man still more tired than now whose one chance
will have caused in the world no change

but dark-mooded you will choose
the ease of beaching where you can
outsmart the gods who chew men in their jaws
by turning dense a stone against
their trying you again.

O Worriers! Quit and touch my shore.
I promise back original dark
where you were made. Come and endure.
With me be cave-quiet, closed and stark
as night occupying solid rock.

Four Poems

JACK THACKER

High Wind

for Adam Crothers

My father ploughing
on the hill:
a ground beetle
trailing a flight wing.

The cattle sound off
in the barn;
soon they will learn
the grass. The sound of

the flight of swallows
overhead
is overheard
chatter caught mid-flow.

A gust blows the trees
wide open –
they hiss like rain
on fire. The eye sees

one thing the heart reads
another;
in such weather
the mind is emptied.

Hamlet

Three farms and a church
arranged a mile apart

form a constellation
of country lanes and hearths

and at the focal centre
an abandoned timber steeple

which is, in fact, for sale.
My Grandfather's burial

is to be the last
and now the parish offspring

sense a shift in gravity,
the pull of larger stars.

Hove

Streets like white cliffs
open out onto stony beaches,
where people stare at the surf

in silence from their deckchairs;
the view is an endless wedge
dissolving in foamy splashes.

Tiptoes skirting the edge,
a boy is skimming stones
but the water swallows each

and every one in one
gulp. Footsteps on the shingle.
A gull hiccups and is gone –

then recovers. It's simple:
tread lightly on your words
they whisper to me in pencil.

Epilogue

Flocks of swifts passed over our heads –
we heard the squeal of brakes.

Now, crane flies part at my tread.
I scale the field and cross the brook

to gain another perspective, sit
on the hillside and reflect for a while.

Remember how the sun would bite
down on each evening, recall

the turning of mill water, cattle in the centre
of the city and an open door

to a choir, the hush of a garden theatre
beneath a great maple, where

dragonflies danced at eye level?
All things unknown. I wait for your call.

Chatter & Donne

MARK DOW

THE BRIGHT-ORANGE-plastic-covered, vest-pocket-sized New King James Version given to me on Flatbush Avenue was published by the Gideons International of Nashville, Tennessee. 'THIS BOOK NOT TO BE SOLD' is printed on the inside front cover. The preface begins opposite an image of the American flag, and it includes a sentence with problematic syntax that seems to say that the Bible itself 'will condemn all who trifle with its sacred contents' – despite which the edition includes the complete New Testament but only Psalms and Proverbs from the Old. Another note says that John 3:16 has been translated into 'over 1100 languages' and 'is here recorded in 26 of the important' ones. These follow alphabetically, from Afrikaans to Icelandic to Vietnamese.

Some scholars think the King James translators didn't understand the Biblical Hebrew technique of parallelism. This is from is the vest-pocket NKJV's Psalm 102:7:

I lie awake, and am like a sparrow alone on the housetop.

Here's the 1970 Anchor Bible version:

I stay awake and have become like a sparrow,
　　　　like a chatterer on the roof all day long.

Anchor translator Mitchell Dahood restores the parallel structure. He argues that the Hebrew *bōdēd*, usually read as an adjective meaning 'alone', is actually a noun apposite to 'sparrow', and he renders it as 'chatterer'. Dahood, a Jesuit philologist, explains: 'That *bōdēd*, "chatterer," aptly describes a bird is sustained by the analogy of English "chatterer," any of several passerine birds having a chattering cry, as certain waxwings and cotingas. Whether this [Hebrew] root *bdd* relates to [the Ugaritic root] "to sing," is uncertain.'[1] Oddly, Dahood says nothing about going along with so many translators since Wycliffe in rendering the common Hebrew word for 'bird' as 'sparrow' in the first part of the verse.

On the subway, I looked up from Dahood's notes to listen to a teenage couple sitting to my right. They were speaking Dominican Spanish, which is fast. Then I became aware of the men standing in front of me, speaking Chinese (I'm not sure which dialect). Two women to my left, from Mali, were speaking French and perhaps Bambara (I asked, but there was some confusion). Words, in my imagination, floated in the space of a loose circle we all formed. The words were physical, if intangible, objects. I probably experienced the talk around me in this way because I didn't understand it, or, in the case of the fast Spanish, experienced it as foreign.

Some three hundred years before the birth of Christ, rabbis had the Hebrew Bible translated into Greek to keep it accessible to the shifting vernacular of the Jews. One rabbinic criticism of the Septuagint invokes the ultimate falsification: 'Seventy elders wrote the whole Torah in Greek for King Ptolemy, and that day was as ominous for Israel as the day whereon the Israelites made the Golden Calf, for the Torah could not be adequately translated.' On the other hand, 'according to an ancient rabbinic interpretation, Joshua had the Torah engraved upon the stones of the altar (Joshua 8:32) not in the original Hebrew alone, but in all the languages of mankind.'[3] Sixteen hundred years post-Christ, John Donne told congregants at Lincoln's Inn that the Psalms were his favorite part of the Old Testament because they are poems: 'such a form as is both curious, and requires diligence in the making, and then when it is made, can have nothing, no syllable taken from it, nor added to it.' That seems to be a strong case against translation, but not for Donne: 'Therefore is God's will delivered to us in Psalms, that we might have it the more cheerfully, and that we might have it the more certainly [...] The whole work is the lesse subject to falsification, either by subtraction or addition' (Sermon No. 1).

The linguist Alvin Liberman (from whom I was lucky enough to take a class at Yale in 1983) used to tell the story of a professional Russian-English interpreter who, on a job, began repeating Russian sentences in Russian instead of translating them. The interpreter didn't realise what he or she was doing. Liberman and his colleagues at New Haven's Haskins Laboratories had been studying the biological basis of speech perception and production. The point of his interpreter anecdote was that the brain could be fooled into this mistake because the principal task of language was still taking place. Recently, former United Nations interpreter Lynn Visson wrote in the *LRB* ('Diary', 7 November 2013) about an episode strikingly similar to the one Liberman had recounted: 'On one occasion I had to interpret for more than two and a half hours at a round of high-level negotiations. While absolutely convinced I was interpreting into English, I had in fact been repeating in Russian every word the speaker said, blissfully unaware of this because I was mentally interpreting into English – to an audience of one, myself.' I wrote Visson to ask if she was the interpreter in Liberman's anecdote of thirty years earlier. She wasn't: 'But Liberman's citing such an incident proves my point – that the interpreter's brain short-circuits at some point, and Liberman is totally right re the major argument that language conveys meaning and thus allows the brain to "forget" its error. I would have sworn in court that I was interpreting into English, because I had the English interpretation in my mind. But that interpretation simply wasn't jumping to the final part of the circuit, of physically going from Russian into English. And this kind of thing has happened to several of my colleagues after too many hours of work interpreting in two directions.' The moral of the story, Liberman used to say, is that *meaning is paraphrase*. Over in the English and Literature Departments, meanwhile, Delmore Schwartz's comment in a 1938 essay on R. P. Blackmur was still on target: 'That form and content are inseparable is a dogma which all modern critics accept, contradict in practice, and never elucidate.'

•

Several years ago I was reading a Baudelaire prose poem aloud to a friend who doesn't read any poetry except Dylan lyrics. I had been comparing translations; this one was by Michael Hamburger. It was fluid, but its vernacular was from another time and place, namely, 1940s England. Two years before Hamburger died in 2007, I wrote to ask him whether 'easier' should read 'less easy' in this sentence: 'No doubt it will be easier for you to understand it than for me to explain it to you...' ('Il vous sera sans doute moins facile de le comprendre qu'à moi de vous l'expliquer...').[4] Hamburger wrote back from Suffolk: 'I've checked the French text and my first publication of the translation (1946), done when I was 20 and serving in the army as an infantryman. What is astonishing is that in all this time – more than 60 years – no one pointed out the error.' City Lights made the correction in its 2013 reprint. Hamburger mentioned his glaucoma and failing eyesight, and he asked me to contact composer John Adams, too, who was planning to set some of the translations to music – though he later wrote, 'I can't imagine how anything like an opera could be made out of prose poems by Baudelaire.' I must have addressed him as 'Professor Hamburger', because after his signature he added, 'I'm not a professor now, only a poet.'

As I read the Baudelaire to my friend outside a diner in Manhattan, I found I had to improvise certain small changes (adding contractions, for example) to make it sound as if I was talking – which I was. Donne preaches that we need new sermons because the 'custome and formality' of the ones we already have are an impediment (Sermon No. 1). Only God's words will do, says Donne, but the copies and translations are also God's. In a twist, it's the interpreters and copyists of God's words who create the two-way communication, by virtue of having to translate God's metaphors. God, says Donne (to God), is 'direct' and 'literal' and 'plain' – and also 'figurative' and 'metaphorical'.

How often, how much more often, doth thy Son call himself a way, and a light, and a gate, and a vine, and bread, than the Son of God, or of man? How much oftener doth he exhibit a metaphorical Christ, than a real, a literal? This hath occasioned thine ancient servants, whose delight it was to write after thy copy, to proceed the same way in their expositions of the Scriptures [...] to make their accesses to thee in such a kind of language as thou wast pleased to speak to them, in a figurative, in a metaphorical language [...] (Expostulation XIX).

Sir Philip Sidney translated the first forty-three of the 150 Psalms. After he died, his sister Mary, Countess of Pembroke, revised his work and translated the remainder between 1593 and 1600.[5] Her title page stakes its claim: 'Psalmes of David, translated into divers and sundry kinds of verse, more rare and excellent for the method and varietie than ever yet hath been done in English.' What Donne tagged the 'Sidneian Psalmes' were well-known among contemporary poets, according to Rathmell, and 'were probably sung occasionally in private devotions.'[6] They were not printed, however, until 1823, and in an edition of two hundred copies; the 'Advertisement' to that edition reports that one handwritten manuscript of the poems was preserved when it was 'bought [...] among other broken books to putt up Coffee pouder.'[7]

In 'Upon the Translation of the Psalms by Sir Philip Sidney and the Countess of Pembroke, His Sister', as Donne maps out the transmission process, layers of metaphor yield a flow-chart of bifurcations.

[...] as thy blessed spirit fell upon
These Psalms' first author in a cloven tongue;
(For 'twas a double power by which he sung
The highest matter in the noblest form;)
So thou hast cleft that spirit, to perform
That work again, and shed it, here, upon
Two, by their bloods, and by thy spirit one;
A brother and a sister, made by thee
The organ, where thou art the harmony.

Next, Heaven's music flows to David, David gives it to the Jews, his successors 're-reveal' with new clothing: the Psalms are 'well-attired abroad' but not 'here', not until now. Donne was extending the clothing image from the Countess's dedicatory poem; she writes that her own muse dared to 'combine' itself with her brother's, just as what is 'mortal' combines itself with what is 'divine', and her connection to Sir Philip, through this project, is a version of God's putting on the flesh in Christ. The earthly garments of the verse forms are 'superficial tire / by thee [her brother's spirit] put on'. Their goal is 'to praise, not to aspire / To, those high Tons, so in themselves adorned / which Angells sing in their celestial Quire, / and all of tongues with soule and voice admire [...]'

Clothing, in these images, does not hide naked bodies but lets us see what is otherwise invisible. The metaphor begins to seem inevitable, which might suggest something fundamental about human knowledge and perception. Emily Dickinson has a similar conception but a very different sense of what the clothing does. She warned her correspondent Thomas Higginson that she wasn't sure if the poems she was mailing to him were different from the ones she had already sent (or, she might have meant, different from each other). It's not that she couldn't remember. Rather, 'While my thought is undressed, I can make the distinction; but when I put them [the poems] in the gown, they look alike and numb.'[8] The thirteenth-century *Zohar*, principal work of Jewish mysticism, assumes the clothing metaphor to be implicit in an image from Psalms: 'Israel here below is balanced by the angels on high, of whom it [the Torah] says: "who makest thy angels into winds [or spirits]" (Ps. 104:4). For the angels in descending on earth put on themselves earthly garments, as otherwise they could not stay in this world, nor could the world endure them [...] Thus had the Torah not clothed herself in garments of this world the world could not endure it [...] Whoever looks upon that garment as being the Torah itself, woe to that man – such a one will have no portion in the next world.'[9]

In Donne's poem, the next world returns us to an *ur*-language, or to something prior to that, maybe music; we'll sing our parts in the harmonious whole until we get there.

So though some have, some may some psalms translate,
We thy Sidneian psalms shall celebrate,
And, till we come th' extemporal song to sing,
(Learned the first hour, that we see the King,
Who hath translated those translators) may
These their sweet learned labours, all the way
Be as our tuning [...]

Incredibly, this song will also be God's back-formation of the various translations we've been using down on earth. He will 'translate the translators', maybe not into language but back out of it again. The competing versions of the Psalms, says Donne, are time-bound. For now they will guide us and bridge the gap –

Be as our tuning, that when hence we part,
We may fall in with them, and sing our part.

In *Meditation* XVIII, a few sentences before the famous 'for whom the bell tolls' passage, Donne uses translation as a metaphor for the change from life to death. The resurrection he envisions is a permanent simultaneity, and his bookish parable is straight out of Borges: 'When one man dies, one chapter is not torn out of the book, but translated into a better language [...] God employs several translators; some pieces are translated by age, some by sickness; some by war, some by justice; but God's hand is in every translation, and his hand shall bind up all our scattered leaves again for that library where every book shall lie open to one another.'

In non-preacher mode, Donne seems less hopeful – and less driven to invention.

'An Elegy upon the Death of Mistress Boulstred' begins: 'Language thou art too narrow, and too weak / To ease us now; great sorrow cannot speak.' Some of his plainest and most affecting phrasings are in his secular responses to death. Several lines later he writes: 'She changed our world with hers; now she is gone.'

NOTES

This text is excerpted from a longer essay in *John Donne and Contemporary Poetry*, edited by Judith Herz (forthcoming from Palgrave).

1 *The Anchor Bible: Psalms III.* Introduction, translation and notes by Mitchell Dahood, S.J. (New York: The Anchor Bible, 1970), 13.
2 *Sefer Torah* 1:6. In *Seven Minor Treatises.* Trans. Michael Higger (New York: Bloch Publishing Company, 1930), 10.
3 Preface to Jewish Publication Society's 1917 edition of the Hebrew Bible in English. www.mechon-mamre.org/p/pt/jps1917.htm.
4 'The Eyes of the Poor' / 'Les Yeux des Pauvres' in Baudelaire, *Twenty Prose Poems.* Trans. Michael Hamburger. (San Francisco: City Lights Books, 1988.)
5 J. C. A. Rathmell, ed., *The Psalms of Sir Philip Sidney and The Countess of Pembroke.* (NYU Press: 1963), xi.
6 Ibid., xvii.
7 Sidney, Sir Philip, and the Countess of Pembroke. *The Psalmes of David.* (London: Chiswick Press, 1823), 7. https://archive.org/details/psalmesofdavidtr00sidnuoft.
8 Higginson, 'Emily Dickinson's Letters', October 1891. www.theatlantic.com.
9 *The Zohar.* Vol. 5. Trans. Harry Sperling and Maurice Simon (New York: The Soncino Press, 1984), 3:152a, 211.

Poets Post-War
G. S. Fraser and Edwin Morgan
James McGonigal

'What did your faither dae in the war?' was a boys' school-yard gambit I recall from 1950s Scotland. The same question could now be asked about father-figures, including poetic ones, perhaps with the conjecture – 'and what did the war do to him?'.

The centenary of G. S. Fraser (1915–1980) has been marked by a fine *Selected Poems* from Shoestring Press. The press is run by John Lucas, poet, critic, literary historian and biographer, and Fraser's friend over many years. Fraser was based in England for most of his working life – in literary London just before and after the War, and then in Leicester University, where he became Reader in Poetry. But he was born in Glasgow, moved to Aberdeen as a boy and was educated there and

at St Andrews University, and then trained as a journalist on the *Aberdeen Press and Journal* in the 1930s. John Lucas re-introduced the man and his work at events in Edinburgh and Aberdeen, the first of these in the delightfully extended Scottish Poetry Library, featuring readings or re-readings of Fraser by Scottish poets and editors.

Fraser is sometimes connected with the New Apocalyptics of the late 1930s, anthologised in *The New Apocalypse* (1939) by another Glaswegian, J. F. Hendry. This movement, or loose grouping, wrote in reaction to the political and intellectual emphasis of earlier 1930s poetry, preferring the surreal, the subconscious, the mythic. Scottish and Welsh writers were associated: Norman MacCaig (in his early work, later disowned) and Tom Scott, Dylan Thomas and Vernon Watkins. Yet Fraser's own poetic style is notably more Audenesque than apocalyptic. His poetry offers argument, formal confidence and clarity. Similar qualities mark his prose, whether in reviews, essays or the critical overview of *The Modern Writer and His World* (1953, 1964). His early training in journalism shaped a vigorous style and an ability to work to deadlines – perfect skills for the literary journalism he engaged in with distinction in post-war London.

That transition sounds too easy. Servicemen and women carried the war back home with them. We pay more attention to post-traumatic stress these days than was admitted then. Reflecting on his generation of Scottish poets, Edwin Morgan would later ask in 'North Africa': 'Why did the poets come to the desert?' (*Sonnets from Scotland*, 1984). The answer to this question, apart from learning fragments of Arabic and military jargon, is a listing of memories and sharp impressions, gleaned from their later poetry and prose:

We watched MacLean at the Ruweisat Ridge
giving a piercing look as he passed by
fly-buzzed grey-faced dead; swivelled our eye
west through tank-strewn dune and strafed-out village
with Henderson; and Hay saw Bizerta
burn; Garioch was taken at Tobruk,
parched *Kriegsgefangener*, calm, reading *Shweik*;
Morgan ate sand, slept sand at El Ballah
while gangrened limbs dropped in the pail; Farouk
fed Fraser memorandums like a shrike.

(*Collected Poems*: 446)

G.S. Fraser was in Army Signals, based mainly in Cairo, and not far from El Ballah hospital, which was Morgan's first posting as a twenty-year-old private in the Royal Army Medical Corps. Fraser was five years older, and thought to be 'officer material', had he ever been able to clean and assemble a rifle properly or appear smartly on parade. He was shunted into work on army publications, and eventually promoted to sergeant and then warrant officer as staff writer in the Ministry of Information. Hence his dealings with the problematic and pro-fascist King Farouk in Morgan's sonnet. His war poem 'Egypt' records ennui and a bitter sense of distance from the real action, as in these final stanzas:

The desert slays. But safe from Allah's justice
Where the broad river of His Mercy lies,
Where ground for labour, or where scope for lust is,
The crooked and tall and cunning cities rise.

The green Nile irrigates a barren region,
All the coarse palms are ankle-deep in sand:
No love roots deep, though easy loves are legion:
The heart's as hot and hungry as the hand.

In airless evenings, at the café table,
The soldier sips his thick sweet coffee up:
The dry grounds, like the moral to my fable,
Are bitter at the bottom of the cup.

(*Selected Poems*: 21)

This poem was first published in his collection *The Traveller Has Regrets* (1948), but he had earlier published a pamphlet of poems with *Poetry London* in 1943, and then *Home Town Elegy* (1944). While in Egypt he was involved with two literary groups each with an associated journal. The *Personal Landscape* and *Salamander* poets included (to name only those now best remembered) Laurence Durrell, Keith Douglas and Terence Tiller. Demobbed in late 1945, Fraser returned to London with a ready-made group of contacts and re-entered literary life as a reviewer and broadcaster. Contributing to *The New Statesman*, *Encounter* and *London Magazine*, and editing poetry for the *Times Literary Supplement* and the BBC Third Programme, he was soon recognised as an effective and influential critic. Kathleen Raine and William Empson were among his friends.

Edwin Morgan's wartime experience in Egypt and his return to civilian life as a student at Glasgow University were different. In particular, he had found it impossible during five years of military service to write about his encounters with death, sexuality and a Middle Eastern cultural landscape (he later served in Lebanon and Palestine) fraught with ancient ruins and even more deeply buried histories of vanished empires. He did not keep a journal, claimed not to have engaged in much if any intellectual reading, and generally lived an outdoor life as 'one of the boys', refusing invitations to apply for promotion to NCO. Despite a poetic silence, he felt confidence in his keen memory for sense impressions, which could be recalled.

But it was only thirty years later that he managed to address in poetry those wartime experiences that had been at once revelatory, exotic and disturbing. 'The New Divan' was composed in one hundred stanzas of between twelve and sixteen lines between December 1973 and July 1975. Here is an example of young Morgan's Cairo recalled, which is far from Fraser's ennui:

97.
Domes, shoeshines, jeeps, glaucomas, beads –
wartime Cairo gave the flesh a buzz,
pegged the young soul out full length,
made pharaohs in the quick electric
twilight, strutting brash as hawks. Underneath,
a million graves, a withered arm,
sarcophaguses red
with blood and ochre, smooth
boats on a dark sub-Nile
of slaves and captives, the
oldest way of gold
over the dead with gold
and no haul of good.

(*Collected Poems*: 329)

This is not a typical stanza from the poem, but no obvious pattern ever emerges across the one hundred stanzas, except perhaps that of an intricate and magical Persian carpet ready for flight. Apart from dealing with seemingly buried memories of war, the poem was also in some ways Morgan's response to the Language poetry movement of the 1970s, and to questions about the very possibility of 'the long poem' in the late twentieth century. David Kinloch in *The International Companion to Edwin Morgan*

(2015) cites his close attention to Rosemary Waldrop's study *Against Language?* (1971), and also sees Gilles Deleuze's philosophy – where substance is replaced by multiplicity and essence by event – as lying behind the puzzling and seemingly structure-less form of 'The New Divan'. This long war poem proceeds not through an epic journey or traditional quest but by multiple trajectories, vanishing plot-lines and mysterious characters until, in the final stanzas, Morgan's actual war experiences 'flare intensely into view'. It was also a 'coming out' poem, with homosexual experiences described more explicitly than he had dared to before: 'Not in King's Regulations to be in love'.

Morgan's immediate post-war career also differed from Fraser's. Instead of the latter's seemingly smooth transition into metropolitan life, the younger man returned to live with his parents in Rutherglen. He struggled emotionally with academic study, especially of Romantic poetry, before taking an outstanding degree. Then instead of pursuing research at Oxford University, which he found at interview to be hidebound and hierarchical, he accepted the post of Junior Lecturer in English at Glasgow University, and would teach there with distinction until 1980.

Where had his war gone? In his Preface to the Carcanet Press edition (2002) of *Beowulf*, Morgan suggests that this was his unwritten war poem, a way of handling themes of 'conflict and danger, voyaging and displacement, loyalty and loss'. He began this translation shortly after he came out of the Army in 1945. It was published in 1952 by Erica Marx's The Hand & Flower Press, and in a long-lived American edition ten years later. In those early years Morgan found it difficult to get poems published, and indeed his poetry of the 1940s and 1950s now seems constrained and willed. Translation offered a way forward, with French, Russian, Italian and Anglo-Saxon poets providing other voices to express pent-up emotions of love and suffering. Editors at this time would often return Morgan's own poems but keep the translations for publication. In 1953, G. S. Fraser and Ian Fletcher accepted his versions of the Anglo-Saxon 'The Wanderer' and Maurice Scève's *Délie*, a Renaissance French sequence of sonnet-like love dizains, for their *Springtime: An Anthology of Young Poets and Writers*. Ian Fletcher later arranged publication of Morgan's *Poems from Eugenio Montale* (1959) through his connections with the School of Art in the University of Reading.

Fraser's return from war to London life had certainly appeared successful, but all may not have been as smooth as the surface suggested. There was the strange incident of his breakdown in Japan and subsequent hospitalization there and in England. He had gone to Tokyo in 1950 as a Cultural Advisor to the British Liaison Mission, replacing the Georgian poet and literary critic Edmund Blunden. In 'G. S. Fraser: A Memoir' (*Jacket* 20, December 2002, available online at: http://jacketmagazine.com/20/fraser.html) his wife Paddy Fraser recounts the circumstances of a failed suicide attempt when he was travelling alone into the north of Japan on a lecture tour, and then throwing himself from the train to hide helplessly in the fields. He spoke no Japanese and missed her calming organisational presence, as she was pregnant and had remained in Tokyo. She wonders, however, whether the appearance of tough American Military Police on the train may have brought flashbacks of his harsh and unsuccessful early training in the Black Watch. The breakdown was complete, and he needed lengthy recuperation.

Nightmares and flashbacks were also part of the context of Morgan's true war poem, 'The New Divan'. The Yom Kippur conflict in October 1973 was widely broadcast, and televised imagery of desert warfare revived haunting memories of that landscape. He would begin his Divan (the Arabic term for a collection of poems that he recalled hearing in Egypt) two months later. I was perhaps an unwitting participant in this. In that month I began part-time study for a new Masters course that Morgan had devised: 'British Literature and Literary Theory post-1945'. We began with an overview of war literature, particularly the war poetry that had seemed at the time so problematic by its absence, compared with the First World War. 'Where are the war poets?' the journalists had demanded.

Of this war poetry, Morgan particularly admired Hamish Henderson's *Elegies for the Dead in Cyrenaica* (1948), for its modernist form and its humanity. I can't recall if G. S. Fraser's poetry was mentioned, but *The Modern Writer and His World* was on the booklist – a godsend to me, trying to complete the course as a beginning teacher with young children, a mortgage and an evening class. Such part-time study is not unusual nowadays, but certainly was then – and my reading was not distinguished by breadth or depth. I had undertaken it for a reason that was also connected with the Middle East – and one that possibly influenced Morgan's return to his desert war. Really, I wanted to explore the work of Basil Bunting (1900–1985), the Northumbrian modernist, disciple and then critic of Ezra Pound. As an undergraduate I had been captivated by *Briggflatts* (1966), the 'Sonata' which brought Bunting fame late in life, and I wanted to understand the causes of that poetic impact. So the broad Masters course gave some grounding in the context of Bunting's work – although in truth he wrote at a remove from much of British literary life – and the dissertation would also allow me to discover whether there was more to say about his poetry than the little that had been previously written. Fraser's introductory *Ezra Pound* (1960) was helpful, although I was not aware then of Morgan's somewhat dismissive view of it in *Review of English Studies* (1960), where he considered that Fraser had let Pound off the hook with regard to his fascism, anti-Semitism and crazed ideas of finance. In the 1930s Bunting had tried to shift his mentor from this mad path. The former conscientious objector of the First World War enlisted in the new war against fascism, was eventually posted to Persia on the strength of his understanding of the language (learned in Rapallo in order to translate poets such as Hafiz, the model for Morgan's Divan), and rose to squadron leader in RAF intelligence. His post-war Sonata 'The Spoils' is set in Persia and Mesopotamia but ends in a convoy journey across the war-strewn North African desert.

I did not then know, of course, how closely that movement from youthful pacifism to military life among Middle Eastern cultures mirrored Morgan's. But it did, and, although Bunting was not an absolute favourite of his, it is possible that dealing with my attempts to understand Bunting's structures had some impact on his own thinking about the form of a long poem. Despite Bunting's musical analogy, I was arguing for a mythopoetic quasi-narrative substratum to the mysteriously-varied surface of these Sonatas. In his shape-shifting Divan, Morgan multiplies and truncates many narratives, his war experiences among them, with hints of a journey towards self-knowledge.

Our discussions continued through the years from 1974 to 1978. I was school-teaching in Dumfries and Galloway and so doctoral supervision was at a distance, supplemented by visits to Morgan's home in Glasgow. I would post a chapter for comment, and then visit during school holidays for a response. On one of those visits he showed me the latest stanzas of the Divan, just to let me see what he was working on, now that teaching was over for a while. I was only one correspondent among hundreds, of course. Morgan was so widely-read and generous with advice that tutors in other universities would encourage their students to write with enquiries. Researching in the Edwin Morgan Papers in Glasgow University Library for *Beyond the Last Dragon: A Life of Edwin Morgan* (2010, 2012), I was astonished by the variety of letters. In the 1970s, two sets of correspondence stood out, both connected to G. S. Fraser.

The first of these was with Max Jacobs, whom Fraser was supervising towards a doctorate on Laura Riding, or Laura (Riding) Jackson as she now preferred. Morgan had always been impressed by her work, first encountered as a teenager in the *Faber Book of Modern Verse* (1936). It was through Max Jacobs' links with Laura Riding that Morgan became one of her correspondents too (one of the few she seemed really to trust: she was often touchy and combative), recommending her work to Michael Schmidt of Carcanet Press, who needed little persuasion to issue it in the UK. In time, G. S. Fraser asked Morgan to be external examiner for Jacobs' successful thesis.

The second shared correspondent was Veronica Forrest-Thomson (1947–1975), formidably intelligent and experimental both as a reader and a writer of poetry. She had written to Morgan while still at school and attended some of his readings in Glasgow, asking mature questions about poetry. She then went on to study at Liverpool University, followed by doctoral work on Science and Poetry with J. H. Prynne at Cambridge. She taught with G. S. Fraser at Leicester University and then at Birmingham, dying tragically early at twenty-eight of a drug overdose in possibly accidental circumstances.

Both poets wrote elegies for her. Morgan's 'Unfinished Poems' catch the qualities of the young poet to whom the sequence is dedicated, being quirky, sharp, vulnerable, emotional – and prematurely cut off, so that the reader strives constantly to catch and complete the last line of each poem. Fraser's elegy, 'A Napkin with Veronica's Face, not Christ's', is more formal and allusive, written in the knowledge that she would have been responsive to its artifice. In the *Selected Poems* it follows a longer and more experimental work, 'Two Letters from, and a Conversation with a Poet' (*Selected Poems*: 52–56). The poet's voice is clearly Veronica Forrest-Thomson's and the subject of her sharp scrutiny in Section 1 of the poem is Laura (Riding) Jackson: 'I feel her mind / Energizes in a void'. Fraser then counterpoints her voice with those of other anonymous poet-critics in different letters (internal reference suggests Donald Hall on Bunting and Pound in Section 2).

So lives and letters intersect. Mine did too, in a way that makes me grateful to G. S. Fraser. Just as I completed my thesis on Bunting in early September 1978 and posted it to Edwin Morgan for final assessment, he suffered the loss from cancer of two men of huge significance to him. Hugh MacDiarmid had been a father-figure, aggressive and insulting about Morgan's experimental poetry in the 1960s, yet much more reconciled in the 1970s with the realisation that the younger man appreciated, as few contemporaries could, the extent of his achievement in both Scots and English, including the later difficult poetry of scientific and linguistic fact. The second loss two days later was more serious. John Scott, the man whom Morgan had loved most deeply since the early 1960s, died estranged from him. After a holiday quarrel a year earlier, Morgan had hardened his heart and made no contact, and he could not forgive himself.

Distraught, he found himself unable continue with academic work, and took leave of absence. Time passed. I wrote eventually, tentatively, enquiring about progress towards a viva. He replied that there was a university regulation which said that if both the internal examiners (himself and Philip Hobsbaum) and the external examiner, G. S. Fraser, were satisfied that there were no concerns about quality, and no outstanding questions worth pursuing, no viva was necessary. I was happy to be spared the last hurdle, and also that three distinguished poet-critics had been so convinced by my thesis. Now I am not quite so sure – there is a small unfinished 'but'. But I remain grateful to G. S. Fraser for his confidence, which ultimately changed my life.

Shortly thereafter, Fraser and Morgan were both demobbed from teaching service into the other life of retirement. Fraser's was far too short. Morgan chose early retirement at sixty and extended his work of poetry, drama and translation for a further quarter of a century and more.

REVIEWS

Magical Mystery Tour

Gregory Woods
*Homintern: How Gay Culture
Liberated the Modern World*

Yale University Press, 2016 (£25)

Reviewed by NICOLAS TREDELL

Homintern is a fascinating excursion, a 'magical mystery tour' as Woods calls it, with an itinerary that is nonetheless solidly founded on scholarly research and empirical evidence. It is 'a poet's book', written with clarity, wit and precision, which often aims 'to cast an image, or sequence of images, on the reader's visual imagination, rather than persuade by linear argument'. Woods has 'no qualms about using literature as evidence', quoting copiously from prose and poetry by writers who felt they could only speak the name of their love indirectly, in fictional guise, and he knows how to select material that is both revealing and richly phrased.

The word 'Homintern' is derived from the abbreviation 'Comintern', used to refer to the Communist International (also called the Third International) that Lenin established in 1919 and that lasted until 1943. Cyril Connolly, Maurice Bowra, W. H. Auden, Jocelyn Brooke and Harold Norse have all been credited with coining the word but Woods suggests that 'it was the felicitous invention of many minds'. While Connolly, Auden and others jokingly applied it to 'the sprawling, informal network of friendships' among homosexuals, Cold War paranoia presented it with grim seriousness as 'the international homosexual conspiracy'. In fact, Woods argues, the Homintern, in this coherent and conspiratorial sense, did not exist. 'It was a joke, a nightmare, or a dream', depending on your viewpoint, but 'despite its lack of substance, it still occupied a solid and prominent site near the centre of modern life'. Networks of gay friendships did exist but the 'Homosexual International' they could seem to constitute 'was sometimes only superficially international and sometimes only half-heartedly homosexual: it was also a matter of surfaces, fashions and styles'. The term tended to denote male networks partly because women – and even more so lesbians – appeared to pose little threat and wield little influence; but, as Woods's study shows, women played an active and often culturally influential part in them. His working definition of the Homintern is 'the international presence of lesbians and gay men in modern life. Imagined as a single network, it is either one of the major creative forces in the cultural development of the past century, or a sinister conspiracy against the moral and material interests of nation states. You decide.'

Although Woods's tour is not strictly linear, it does have a clear chronological dimension. It starts with the trials of Wilde (1895), which cast its 'long shadow' down the twentieth century; of Eulenberg (1906–09), whose lasting effect, in and beyond Germany, was 'the naturalisation of the relatively new term "homosexual"'; and of Pemberton Billing (1918), where the word 'orgasm' went public for the first time. It ends, for Woods, with the appearance of the elderly Louis Aragon 'at Gay Pride parades in a pink convertible surrounded by ephebes'. In between, there are journeys to a range of places and encounters with a wide variety of writers and artists. The places exist in what William Burroughs, speaking of Tangier, called the 'interzone' between reality and fantasy, locale and libido – for example, Russia, Paris, Berlin (Sodom on Spree), Capri, Sicily, Tangier, Harlem, Hollywood, Havana and the Alexandria of Cavafy which, 'for all its modernity', 'sits on many layers of history, on the edge of a sea on which history and myth, far from being written on water, are lastingly inscribed as if on stone'. The people include figures such as Diaghilev, Dolly Wilde, Radclyffe Hall, Eisenstein, Lempicka, Nureyev, Hirschfeld, Mishima, Puig and Roger Peyrefitte, whose *L'Exilé de Capri* (*The Exile of Capri*, 1974) offers perhaps 'the best fictional celebration of the idea of the Homintern' (though not named as such).

As Woods points out, the 'modern history of homosexuality is also, perforce, a history of homophobic responses to homosexuality'. On the homophobic scale, George Orwell, a master-practitioner of prejudice posing as plain-man frankness, registers strongly, with his references to 'Nancy boys' and 'the Nancy poets'. Orwell was not alone; as Spender pointed out in 1930, Roy Campbell, Wyndham Lewis and Robert Graves were 'carrying on a great campaign against homosexuals'. It would be wrong, however, to imply that Woods displays a homophobe-hunting zeal. He can be combative but his attitude is less one of anger than of amusement at the absurdity of anti-gay attitudes.

Woods's focus on writers and artists, often privileged through their background and/or literary and artistic ability, raises questions, of course. At one point, he observes that the 'two fragmentary glimpses of gay life' in Alfred Döblin's *Berlin Alexanderplatz* (1929) make the 'important point' that 'the lives of homosexual people take shape [...] in the attempts by ordinary individuals to establish their own private lives'. But this emphasis on the ordinary is rare in *Homintern*, which, perhaps necessarily, focuses on the extraordinary and thus consigns vast swathes of same-sex experience to the enormous condescension of posterity. There is also an issue around Woods's term 'individuals'. Discussing Vasily Vasilievich Rozanov's *People of the Moonlight* (1911; revd 1913), 'his main statement on homosexuality' and 'one of very few volumes on the topic published in Russia for many decades', Woods finds that it exemplifies the 'same reluctance to countenance a collective, political existence' which 'characterises most of the twentieth century's approaches to homosexual law reform as, more or less reluctantly, espoused by heterosexual people'. Near the end of *Homintern*, Woods contends that real change in the legal, social and cultural status of homosexuals needed, not merely coming out – since, as he has shown, 'many men and women had been out for decades, and could not have gone back in again' – but 'an openness that was more than individual', indeed 'mutual identification on a grand scale'. It was such 'subcultural solidarity' that enabled gay communities and movements to mount a response to the AIDS crisis when politicians, journalists and medical establishments initially reacted with hostility and inertia. But so much of his book has focused on 'individuals' – most of whom, it must be said, look unlikely candidates for collective action, whatever their networking skills – that its assertion of the importance of being collectively urnist (to derive an adjective from Karl-Heinrich Ulrichs's term for homosexuals, 'urnings') is not fully assimilated into an overall argument.

This is an index of a more general problem with *Homintern*: while Woods is excellent on the empirical level, he is casual on the conceptual plane; in this respect, our poet-prestidigitator relies too much on sleight of hand, so that key terms like 'individual', 'network' and indeed 'homophobia' itself whisk past us like misdirecting veils. But there are potentially fruitful suggestions for further research in which the empirical and conceptual could work together, as when, discussing the reluctance of some gay men and women to come out after the Sexual Offences Act of 1967, he observes: 'We do not yet have a cultural history of homosexual "discretion", yet we need one: for "discretion" is absolutely central to the formulation of homosexuality as a socially acceptable condition of life'. This is one of *Homintern*'s many fingerposts pointing out new directions to those who embark on its exhilarating, if sometimes conceptually corner-cutting, magical mystery tour.

Boiled Cabbage Cut into Sections

C.D. Blanton, *Epic Negation: The Dialectical Poetics of Late Modernism*

Oxford University Press, 2015
(£41.99)

Reviewed by ANDREW LATIMER

The jacket copy to J.H. Prynne's 1968 collection, *Kitchen Poems,* opens with an abridged quotation from Eliot's wool-gatherings on culture: 'Culture, as Eliot observes, "includes all the characteristic activities of a people: dog races, the pin table, Gothic churches, and the music of Elgar."' Compare this to the full unabridged piece, which appeared in book form as *Notes Towards a Definition of Culture* in 1948. Culture is 'all the characteristics and interests of a people,' Eliot writes, including:

Derby Day, Henley Regatta, Cowes, the twelfth of August, a cup final, the dog races, the pin table, the dart board, Wensleydale cheese, boiled cabbage cut into sections, beetroot in vinegar, nineteenth-century Gothic churches and the music of Elgar.

With limited space, cuts of this kind are inevitable. But where exactly these amnesic excisions were made is telling; lost are the references to the days out – 'Derby day', 'Henley Regatta', 'Cowes' and the 'cup final' – neatly segmented between commas that serve to reinforce the class distinctions they uphold. Gone as well are the portable foodstuffs that help to sustain the mirage of an archaic England that, by 1948, had been all but destroyed by the war.

The jacket copy to Prynne's volume betrays this fact. It reads like a bombed-out city, where the destruction goes unmentioned – not even alluded to in the form of editorial ellipses. This is late modernism: a city undergoing repair, but healthy in its own right.

Berkley's associate professor of English, C.D. Blanton, in his latest academic work, *Epic Negation*, discards the well-established conception of late modernism associated with the likes of J.H. Prynne, Charles Olson, Andrew Crozier and Louis Zukofsky, and replaces it with a late modernism that arrives 'not as a sequent term in a larger historical series (modern, late modern, postmodern)', but as 'a dialectical fold *within* the logic of modernism as such'. Late modernism, argues Blanton, is 'the completion of its [modernism's] thought'.

Without so much as a nod to the perspicacious poets and critics who have sweated over exactly what distinguished British and American poetry after the Second World War from that which came before it, Blanton swoops in to claim the label 'late modernism' and spits outs the meaning, bloody context and all. The content of *his* book, then: late Eliot, Auden, MacNeice and the very late H.D. (from *Trilogy* onwards). For followers of modernism the list is oddly familiar. For the tardy followers of late modernism, however, one-third of Blanton's title is basically incorrect. If we must categorise our literature, which we must, then historical periods seem as good a way as any – broad, serendipitous and often internally contradictory. But to delineate periodically with any success we must be precise and consistent; when we depart from the status quo we should be clear in justifying our audacity.

To be modestly reductive, then, modernism as a 'live tradition' (in Pound's words) ends conveniently but convincingly with Hitler's invasion of Poland on 1 September 1939. There are persuasive arguments that would refute or refine that statement but they are not to be found in *Epic Negation.* Eliot's *The Waste Land* and *The Criterion* were published before the beginning of the Second World War, so periodically speaking this is modernism. As with Louis MacNeice's 1939 *Autumn Journal.* Similarly, Auden's collection *Another Time*, published in 1940, can hardly be said to have far escaped the confines of modernism. In Blanton's book, it is only H. D., then, with her *Trilogy,* including *The Walls Do Not Fall* (1944), who fits Blanton's profile for any kind of a 'late modernism' as 'the completion of its [modernism's] thought'. Even H. D., however, is not such an easy captive, her later poetry making such a defiant break from the earlier *imagiste* stuff. Not a completion, then, but a fracture. A new start.

The copywriter to Prynne's 1968 *Kitchen Poems* book jacket provides a more rigorous argument as to what late modernism actually was than does Blanton. In late modernism, Eliot is there, perhaps even Pound is there as well, but they are not themselves. They appear as quotations, allusions, as apparitions in the way Virgil came to Dante. Furthermore, they are cut up, excised and expunged of the many unwanted cultural connotations: they are both included and excluded. Rather than late modernism being 'a fold within' modernism, as it is in *Epic Negation,* the reality is quite the opposite. In late modernism, modernism becomes the victim of another of Blanton's curiously applied *bon mots*: negation.

Before we move to closing statements, the most excitingly absurd argument of this book begs a mention. I quote, for fear of being incarcerated

myself: 'Once recognised as a dislocated epic in itself, *The Criterion* draws to the surface a set of connections that a poem can frame but not press into language.' Yes, it is a fascinating supposition, that Eliot's *Criterion* might be momentarily conceived as a kind of epic poem, perhaps *the* epic poem of the first half of the twentieth century (over *The Cantos*). But only metaphorically. *The Criterion* is *like* an epic poem but surely, one would hope, nobody with a tenure worth their salt would argue that it is *actually* an epic poem in and of itself. Astoundingly, Blanton sees it through.

For all the obvious differences in tone and topic, *Epic Negation* is reminiscent of Harold Bloom's 1973 *The Anxiety of Influence,* where an interesting theory repeatedly founders as it is brought into practice. In both works, rather than the critical application of theory to text, we instead find ourselves slipping into the hellish lair of the academic's subconscious, where Pidgin-Freudian is the *lingua franca* and in order to survive we must find our way to the end of sentences with demonic syntax like 'the juxtaposition enacts the problem of order in dialectical form, testing the figurative method through which poetry comes to intend culture as such.'

Going over the Ground

Edmund Blunden's Undertones of War
Edited by John Greening
Oxford University Press, 2015 (£30)

Reviewed by ROBYN MARSACK

Edmund Blunden's *Undertones of War,* one of the crop of books that appeared around the tenth anniversary of the end of the First World War, has never been out of print since. The war indeed remained Blunden's constant theme; in his long and prolific writing life he went over and over that contested ground, in sorrow and pride, in bewilderment and suppressed fury.

The rich hinterland of the text is mapped with care and sensitivity in this excellent scholarly edition by the poet and critic John Greening. Most readers now will probably be familiar with the Penguin Classic, which reprints the 1930 text, in fact the ninth impression or 'third edition'. Greening reprints the 1928 edition – written in Japan with only some notes and three old maps as aid – with textual variations from subsequent editions, and explains various references – Blunden is a naturally allusive writer – as well as drawing on associated writing, early and late. An example of textual variation a few pages into the book is Blunden's 1928 remark that in a black ditch of drying mud 'were to be seen a variety of old grenades brown with rust.' Later editions add, 'tumbled in with tin cans and broken harness.' The substantial variations are always of this detailed sort, as though re-reading enabled Blunden to recall more precisely. There are

a myriad minor variations – 'a' for 'the' and so forth – which the editor no doubt had to include, having decided to make a complete record of the texts, but which make a reader dutifully flipping between text and notes a little impatient. The medal for patience must go to the editor's wife, duly acknowledged, who apparently read the text aloud twice to enable the most accurate comparison between editions.

Supporting material includes excerpts from his own notes for a war diary, and from the Battalion War Diary, kept immaculately by Blunden for various periods, detailing for instance the kind of trench-work that could be done in a quiet week: 'Day spent in cleaning tunnels, building latrines, rearranging accommodation and burying dead' (this recorded by Blunden as Field Works Officer, shortly before his twentieth birthday). 'Cleaning tunnels' does not begin to suggest what might be found there in the way of body parts. Greening is able to take advantage not only of Barry Webb's comprehensive biography, but also of two collections of correspondence that have been published since: one with a master at Christ's Hospital, and the three-volume correspondence with Siegfried Sassoon; letters to his family from papers at Texas are also quoted. Blunden complains to his mother that his siblings do not write often enough to him; whereas he, of course, is intent on writing, under scarcely conceivable circumstances: 'Write that letter or get that hour's sleep? It's a nasty dilemma.'

Anyone who has had the pleasure of looking at books owned by Blunden will have seen how extensively he wrote in them, in his distinctively elegant hand (also reproduced here), and how he continued to annotate works he had edited himself with later discoveries or thoughts. In this volume, Greening has used copies of *Undertones* that Blunden annotated: for Aki Hayashi, his Japanese mistress; for James Cassels, with whom he served; and for his friend and publisher Richard Cobden-Sanderson. Some of these annotations found their way into subsequent editions; some were simply reminders to friends of the shared experience of the Western Front, which – as both writers and critics have acknowledged – was in some sense incommunicable to those who had not shared it. The novelist H. M. Tomlinson, when he reviewed *Undertones* on its first publication, described it as a book 'by a ghost for other ghosts'; Blunden wished he could evoke – as well as Tomlinson himself had – 'the sunny terror which dwelt in every dust-grain on the road [...] the clatter of guns, the co-existent extraordinary silence, the summer ripeness, the futility of it [...]' which they had experienced, a year apart, in haunted Richebourg St Vaast.

Greening endeavours to anchor Blunden's evocations in fact by – for instance – providing running heads with the place and date of the activities described (following Martin Chown's detailed chronology). This does not intrude on the reader's experience but provides useful information if wanted. It underlines the fact that this account covers the period April 1916 to February 1918; one is tempted to say, a 'mere' two years. Not even half the war, it was a very small proportion of Blunden's life (he died in 1974, aged 77), although he was probably the writer who saw the longest period of continuous service, astonishingly without being wounded. Yet it is striking, on re-reading this book in the year of the Somme centenary, how his accounts of those two years differ in tone and temper, how the memory of '16 ghosts '17 and beyond, how a pervasive depression sets in as one by one friends are lost, and no territory gained.

Blunden begins to recognise the signs of earlier years – not only the distant past, which he also comments on, but the marks of '15 which suggest that the war is fought over and over again on the same ground. Port Arthur in July 1916 'seemed to be remembering the war of a year ago'; a secret passage leading into a communications tunnel turned out to be 'the work of our enemy in days gone by'; there was a heap of tins of bully beef in a dugout – no one thought this unusual but 'such heaps would not be found in 1917'. In late July, in a quiet interval, Blunden notes that the 'ugly useful discomfort' of steel helmets, 'curious green mushrooms', had supplanted the soldiers' 'friendly' soft caps, and with this signalled the change in the war from 'personal crusade' to 'a vast machine of violence'. The complete rout of the battalion in early September 1916 is clear enough in *Undertones*, but intensified by the notes supplied to the paragraph: Blunden's reflecting in an article a year later, 'The Somme had pulled us under once, and we emerged just gasping'; and thirty years later, as Greening says, still appalled and trying to make sense of that action – 'So we were "a complete failure", and there were miles of that [...]'

Returning to Hamel in October 1916, Blunden stumbles upon a huge quantity of rations – marmalade, 'soup squares', tins in their thousands – the one bright occasion in a landscape of powerful reminders that the German positions were supposed to have been taken by the British on 3 September. Worse still, there were coils of British barbed wire beyond the German defences, 'the simple evidence of a still greater and more melancholy date, July 1.' Later editions, Greening notes, sharpen the word 'evidence' to 'trophy'. In August 1917 the company was taken out of the front line for a few days, except even in the 'rest' area German planes flew overhead: 'Out of the line was out of the line in 1916, but we are older now', writes Blunden of himself, not yet twenty-one.

By summer 1917, with the preparations for Third Ypres, there is a desperate sense that all is visible to the Germans and thus already a futile campaign. Their airmen were active. Even a small detail, for example about the laying of new wooden tracks 'through the crowded, airless shadows', is suffused with melancholy foreboding. And yet, as ever, nature provided 'a gorgeous and careless multitude of poppies and sorrels and bull-daisies' in the grounds of Vlamertinghe Château, 'not much hurt, but looking very dismal in the pitiless perfect sun.'

A note at this point directs us, quite rightly, to Blunden's sonnet on passing the château, included in the extended section of poems. The additional poems are clearly signalled: they underline Blunden's life-long engagement with the subject. As his daughter Margi wrote, they suggest 'the battle to find a present in the face of such an obstructive past'. Greening's commentary on the poems usefully brings in comparisons with other war poets as well as annotations made by Blunden later in life, and all this material is illuminating. The decision that I would take issue with in this edition is the placing of relevant poem titles at the head of the chapters. These prompts seem out of place: either we are reading the 1928 text (which has been annotated so scrupulously) or we are reading Greening's version of the 1928 text, which slightly muddies the idea that we have the original and that all editorial matter is confined to the notes. The same confusion occurs with the placing of Blunden's dedication to Philip Tomlinson – a new reader could mistake this for Greening's dedication.

The form of the book is defended within the text by the author. Walking towards Hooge in spring 1917, Blunden saw

a sentry crouching and peering one way and another like a birdboy in an October storm. He spoke, grinned and shivered; we passed; and duly the sentry was hit by a shell. So that in this vicinity a peculiar difficulty would exist for the artist to select the sights, faces, words, incidents, which characterised the time. The art is rather to collect them, in their original form of incoherence.

There cannot be a narrative of progress in *Undertones of War*. Greening's very welcome edition, with its collection of texts, and photographs too (lovingly compiled by Blunden), gives us the range of materials out of which Blunden constructed his account and shows us how he went over and over it – in the interests of accuracy, of making the experience a little clearer to those he loved, of doing justice to those he had served with and lost. The 'incoherent' original emerges as eloquent and moving as it ever was; perhaps, as Greening suggests, Blunden's 'greatest poem'.

The Scattered Treasure

René Char
Hypnos: Notes from the French Resistance (1943–44)
translated by Mark Hutchinson
Seagull Books, 2014 (£14.50)

René Char
The Inventors and Other Poems
translated by Mark Hutchinson
Seagull Books, 2015 (£14.50)

Reviewed by JOHN NAUGHTON

Often remembered as 'the poet of the Resistance', René Char was in fact a significant poetic figure well before and well after the period of the Nazi occupation of France. It is a virtue of these small, elegant volumes published by Seagull Books and masterfully translated by Mark Hutchinson that, in addition to the wartime writings of the first, the second offers important texts from other periods, both early and late, of Char's career.

It is nonetheless the journal Char kept during his time as head of a resistance network that has received the most attention. Titled *Hypnos,* the work is made up of 237 fragments or feuillets, and it communicates an acutely visceral sense of what a poetic sensibility such as Char's observed and endured. The work is published in English translation only and does not include the French texts. The translations, made in response to what Hutchinson calls the 'ungainliness' of previous Char translations, do in fact read as English texts in their own right.

The fragments are sometimes described as aphoristic or lapidary, although neither term does justice to the diversity of the entries, for included among them are longer narrative pieces that vividly describe events associated with Char's activities when he was in charge of landing operations and parachute drops in his region of Provence. In a short preface to this work, Char himself maintains that the notes 'owe nothing to self-love, the short story, the maxim or the novel'. They were written, he maintains, 'under stain, in anger, fear, rivalry, disgust, cunning, furtive reflection, the illusion of a future, friendship, love'. One of the striking features of these fragments is the association implicitly drawn between Char's duties as head of a resistance group and his conception of what poetry should be. He asks that his men be taught to be 'workmanlike'; they should learn 'to be attentive, to give an exact report, to set down the arithmetic of a given situation.' If the 'impossible' and the 'inaccessible' daunt the human mind, it is only because 'poetry [...] is not everywhere sovereign'. The poet, otherwise 'inclined to exaggerate, thinks clearly under duress', and the Resistance means coming 'face to face with death at its most violent and life at its most clearly defined'. The resplendence that resides in the impossible and the unforeseen

is 'the poet's escort' and also what 'girds the man of action'. Of his own writing Char says, 'I keep my writing short. I can hardly be away for long.' One of the most arresting passages in this respect is in fragment 97, which describes a nocturnal drop.

The plane flies low. The invisible pilots jettison their night garden, then activate a brief light tucked in under the wing of the plane to notify us that it's over. All that remains is to gather up the scattered treasure. So it is with the poet [...]

Char's notes register unmistakably a kind of cynicism ('an intellectual heritage') that never manages to completely overwhelm a precarious hopefulness. 'Resistance is nothing but hope.' This hopefulness is buoyed up by 'undying friendships' and the kind of comradeship that at certain moments compels the poet to love 'his fellow creatures fiercely' and 'far beyond the call of sacrifice'. Together, Char and his comrades are struggling with an 'unformulated far horizon' in their hearts, and as Char writes most movingly, 'at every meal taken together, we invite liberty to sit down. The seat remains empty but the place is laid.'

Hutchinson manages to bring all these fragments to life in an admirably successful way. Even one very familiar with the French text will have a fresh encounter with the vision of this poet and man of action, seeking, as he says, to be 'the most useful and least conspicuous' part of things.

•

Shortly after the publication of Hutchinson's English translation of *Hypnos*, Seagull Books brought out a companion volume by the same translator, titled *The Inventors and Other Poems.* In Hutchinson's view, the two volumes 'form the heart of Char's work – or that part of it, at least, that is patient of English translation'. In the forest of Char's manifold writings, the texts chosen by Hutchinson are what the translator calls 'the clearings', although many of these are resistant to any easy interpretation.

Some forty poems make up *The Inventors and Other Poems,* and Hutchinson has chosen poems of differing kinds and from periods both early and late. He has included Char's poems inspired by the Lascaux cave paintings, as well as by some of the most celebrated paintings of Georges de la Tour. There are short lyrics and longer poems that register the pessimism that seemed to haunt Char after the war. 'When I was young,' he writes in the prose poem 'Lombes' ('Loins'), 'the world was a blank white wilderness where glaciers rose up in rebellion. Today it's a bruised and swollen wilderness where even the most gifted soul is master of nothing but his own self-importance.'

Surely the most powerful of the poems translated by Hutchinson are 'The School Girl's Companion', written shortly after the bombing of Guernica in 1937 and dedicated to 'the children of Spain', and 'The Inventors' (1949). Through simple narrative, both poems evoke impending disaster unforgettably.

Char once said of himself that he was 'obsessed with the death of man'. And in *Hypnos*, fragment 127, he notes: 'Like a sleepwalker, man advances towards the murderous minefields, led on by the song of the inventors'. Many readers have observed, Hutchinson among them, that as a boy Char was profoundly marked by what he observed during the First World War. His father, who was mayor of Char's village at the time of the war, took upon himself the duty of personally informing every family of a death, and 220 lives were lost during the conflict. The father was ill during the entire duration of the war and died in 1918. It would have been natural for the young boy to associate personal pain with general warfare. After the death of the father, Char was routinely beaten by a much older brother. These two forces seem to have created in the poet the ability to feel the wounds of war in his own body and allowed him to experience political and social discord at the most personal level. Again and again, he will lament moral obtuseness and 'mankind ruined by political perversion' (*Hypnos*, fragment 69), setting what he calls the 'inventor'

('who adds nothing to the world, brings nothing to his fellow men but masks and middlings, iron gruel') against the 'discoverer' in search of 'new life dawning.'

It may be that the strain of pessimism that runs through so much of Char's work, as well as the rhetorically harsh judgments that pervade it, have alienated some readers. Hopefully, these new translations by Mark Hutchinson will bring renewed attention to the poet, since they are superbly done. Together they bring a major poet and a figure of commanding moral stature to readers familiar with Char's work, as well as to a new generation of English-language readers less acquainted with it. Both books contain brief but effective introductions, as well as useful and scholarly notes. The translations are the fruit of many years of thoughtful reflection by the translator, and the product of a patient and meticulous craftsmanship.

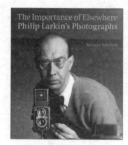

Nutritious Images

Richard Bradford
The Importance of Elsewhere: Philip Larkin's Photographs

Francis Lincoln, 2015 (£25)

Reviewed by NICOLAS TREDELL

Philip Larkin's 'Lines on a Young Lady's Photograph Album' is an essential, perhaps the quintessential, poem about photography and it also offers a penetrating poetic analysis of regret. But the speaker of that poem (this slightly awkward phrase is used to offset the crass conflation of poet and persona that bedevils Richard Bradford's text) is a voyeur who might contemplate stealing a photo but never admits to taking one – in this differing from Larkin who, as this volume shows, was a committed photographer, prepared to invest money and time in the process. The striking cover image, a self-portrait with camera, both anticipates and undermines the emergence of the photographer as a glamorous icon of male sexuality in the 1960s Britain (think of David Bailey, Terence Donovan, Patrick Lichfield, Lord Snowdon) which found its cinematic epitome in the figure of Thomas in Antonioni's *Blow-Up*. In this selfie, Larkin looks tense, concentrated, slightly sinister: put a cine-camera rather than a Rolleiflex Automat in his hands and he might be a forerunner of Mark in Michael Powell's film *Peeping Tom*, bearing more than a passing resemblance to the 10 Rillington Place serial killer, John Reginald Christie.

Photography and sexuality were profoundly interwoven for Larkin: the most arresting picture inside the book is of a bespectacled Monica, the most enduring woman in Larkin's life after his mother Eva, sitting in an armchair wearing the vivid striped tights

that Eva had given her (in a photograph of Eva and Monica together, they look like mother and daughter). Bradford observes that, since the early 1950s, Monica 'had sent Larkin photographs of herself, often semi-clad, and included commentaries on what they might be doing if the photographic image were real'. In the photos in this book, Monica, however *déshabillé*, is never shown without her spectacles and one wonders whether she and perhaps Larkin himself could have said, like Tim Irwin in Alan Bennett's *The History Boys:* 'Taking off my glasses is the last thing I do.'

Richard Bradford's text has the same qualities as his full-length biographies of Larkin, Kingsley Amis and Martin Amis: it is highly readable, gossipy and uncommonly obtuse in its analyses of both life and work. (Symptomatically, he even manages, on page 97, to misquote 'Lines on a Young Lady's Photograph Album', substituting 'here' for 'hard' in 'however hard we yowl'.) Often, for Bradford, it is not so much that Larkin's life has a hole in it as that Larkin's texts have large holes in them through which we supposedly see his life. He claims, for instance, that 'Larkin's letters during this period show that the poem ['Love'] was transparently autobiographical'; that the opening stanza of 'Annus Mirabilis' is 'sardonically autobiographical'; that the novel *Jill* is 'a fictionalised version of what we now call a misery memoir' (the crude generic classification also typifies Bradford's blunt-instrument approach). It is as if all those attempts to distinguish the writer and his work in the interests of finer analysis, from Eliot through Wimsatt to Barthes, had never happened and we had reverted (apart from the sexual frankness) to the mode of an Edwardian man-of-letters. But Bradford's conversions of Larkin's texts into gaping apertures giving on to his life can distort his judgements, not only of the texts, but of the life: he declares that 'Larkin had never felt exhilarated by anything', but his poems suggest otherwise since they evoke moments of exhilaration which are enhanced rather than subdued by their contrast with the black backdrop of death and the grey-on-grey of slow dying: the 'attics cleared of me' of 'Absences'; the 'unfenced existence' of 'Here'; the 'million-petalled flower' of 'The Old Fools'; the 'Regenerate union' of 'Show Saturday'.

Bradford also fails to maintain a focus on Larkin's photographs. He occasionally makes interesting comments on these, for example when he remarks that a 1948 photo of the bombed-out Coventry Cathedral taken from the then-unsafe tower is 'an early example of [Larkin's] taste for scenes captured from a considerable height'. But most of the time he offers a potted biography with photos loosely attached. There is also some fanciful caption writing: 'His face, pensive, seems directed towards something to the left of the camera yet his eyes betray an almost guilty interest in the capturing of his own image'. The most impressive account of Larkin as photographer in the book occurs in the introduction by Mark Haworth-Booth, former Victoria and Albert Museum curator who helped create its rich photographic collection. He tells us about the cameras and accessories (colour filters, close-up lenses) Larkin used; his expertise, in the predigital era, in marking up contact prints for enlargement and in cropping (the latter skill exemplified in his well-known portrait with an 'ENGLAND' sign, presumably taken by Monica); and the magazines (*Lilliput* and *Picture Post*) which might have influenced him. But despite the drawbacks of Bradford's text, this is a fascinating book full of, in the memorable phrase from 'Lines on a Young Lady's Photograph Album', 'nutritious images'.

Come Into The Open

J. H. Prynne, *The White Stones*
New York Review Books, 2016

Reviewed by IAN BRINTON

In Volume 12 of *Grosseteste Review,* published in 1979, Nigel Wheale began his substantial study of Prynne's *The White Stones* by quoting from *The Philosophy of Money* by Georg Simmel. Referring to the use of metal coins as a method of exchange Simmel asserts that the lives of many people 'are absorbed by such evaluating, weighing, calculating and reducing of qualitative values to quantitative ones'. The appropriateness of this reference relates not only to Prynne's own 'A Note on Metal' (1968) but also to the hand-written inclusion of a Simmel quotation to the twenty-six lettered copies of *Aristeas* which Andrew Crozier's Ferry Press had published in that year. Wheale also referred to the visual presentation of the poems highlighting that those in the first half of the book, a series of poems rather than a collection, are frequently indented at the left hand margin giving the appearance of dressed stone quoins at the angle of a building of some pretension, 'as of a temple or bank, Barclays or Jerusalem'.

This new edition of *The White Stones* contains not only the poems from the Grosseteste first edition of 1969 but also the short prose piece 'A Note on Metal', which had first appeared in Series 2 of *The English Intelligencer,* and the privately-printed *Day Light Songs* (1968). Peter Gizzi, editor of this welcome new edition of one of the landmark publications from the end of the 1960s, suggests that there is a metamorphic language at play in these poems and that naming is the prerogative for knowing since 'In Prynne's conception, both court systems and glaciers are players in a larger formation, they endure now in their afterlife as a lyric poem.' 'A Note on Metal' focuses upon this metamorphosis as Prynne asserts that the 'early Bronze Age would, I suppose, locate the beginnings of Western alchemy, the theory of quality as *essential*'. The poet focuses upon these alchemical changes which inform our lives in the ninth poem of the series, 'In the Long Run, to be Stranded':

Finally it's trade that the deep changes
work with, so that the lives are heavier,
less to be moved from or blunted. The city
is the language of transfer
    to the human account. Here
    the phrases shift, the years
    are an acquiescence.

The connection between movement (tread) and the exchange of commodities associated with 'trade' is held in the word's derivation: a path, course of action, borrowed from Middle Dutch or Middle Low German *trade*, track; Old Saxon *trada*, footstep. In Prynne's poem words, our exchange of thoughts rather than objects, thicken over the years 'as the coins themselves wear thin'; as readers we are held in a tension between two opposite meanings of 'stranded' as the shore, or beach, may be where we find ourselves in the long run whilst the individual fibres of a rope are both broken and formed in the verb 'to strand'. Prynne's poetry plays with multiple meanings as puns jostle shoulder-to-shoulder with the dictionary of etymology. Our sense of who we *are* is intimately bound to our sense of who we were, and to the geographer 'the Pleistocene is our current sense' in 'The Glacial Question, Unsolved'. With a sense of shared humanity the opening lines of 'First Notes on Daylight' are central to this powerful series of poems which appeared one year before Ted Hughes's *Crow*:

Patience is truly my device, as we wait
for the past to happen, which is to come into
the open.

True to Imperfection

Carole Coates, *Jacob*
Shoestring Press, 2016 (£10)

Martin Stannard
Poems for the Young at Heart
Leafe Press, 2016 (£10)

Reviewed by IAN SEED

Carole Coates's *Jacob* is a long narrative poem, the bulk of which tells us the story of a boy growing up in suburban England during the years following the Second World War. We also see him as a young man in the late 1960s and in the final section as an older man in the early part of the twenty-first century. Much of the drama revolves around his troubled relationship with an unstable mother and its effects in later life. A series of other important family relationships is woven into the story and plays a crucial part in the formation of Jacob. The connections are not immediately clear, and indeed the situations and scenes themselves can take some time to come into the kind of focus we would expect from a conventional novel. Coates (in a manner sometimes reminiscent of Toni Morrison) uses the language of poetry to take us into the subjective world of her main character so that we experience his curiosity, disorientation, anguish, pain, love, terror, disgust or delight from inside his head and body. She eschews punctuation and capitalisation, save for two brief monologues by Jacob's grandparents. The book opens with Jacob as a toddler in his back garden, and because of Coates's use of the senses we are there with him and perhaps also thinking of our own earliest memories:

the snail is so light   not stone-like at all
he licks the shell   following the curve   (p. 4)

We see the mother through Jacob's eyes when she tells him she loves him and in the same breath says (in a kind of Laingian double-speak) that he is making her 'ill':

she jumps her blouse out of her skirt
she jumps her face shiny and red
she jumps three birds from a tree
and they crackle and flap   (p. 3)

Jacob's father returns from military service in 1948. There is little understanding between father and son, or between husband and wife, and Jacob is often used in the tug of war between them. Jacob does however develop nourishing relationships with his illegitimate female cousin Teddy (or the 'Devils Spawn', as his mother calls her) and his pacifist grandfather, who has a love for literature. Indeed, it is Jacob's own love of learning and literature which enable him in his teenage years to construct his own world of freedom, however claustrophobically family life impinges on him:

and his father's bare feet slap slap on the lino and the

lavatory seat
clack and the hiss of the pee and ping of a fart [...]

Jake Jake make me a cup of tea, Jake
that's her ill voice he'll have to go into their room   (p. 63)

This short review cannot do justice to the complex web of relationships portrayed in this narrative poem, nor to the eras that come so vividly to life as Jacob grows up in the 1960s. The central relationship, however, remains that between Jacob and his mother. He is still trying to understand her and come to terms with the past when he goes to sort out her belongings after her death in 2003.

•

Martin Stannard has clearly been influenced by the New York School poets (above all Kenneth Koch) and the English Romantics (with a special fondness for Coleridge). He shares with Carole Coates a sense of failed quest, an ethic of being true to imperfection, and a refusal of closure. His work is celebratory and achingly funny, usually parodic, but there is an ever-present undertow of melancholy and loss, combined with philosophical exploration. It works through the adoption and abrupt juxtaposition of different narrative voices, though these are cleverly joined together, united around a theme, motif or particular form, for example the epistle:

Dear Emptiness,

I have heard it said
when you pay a call it's impossible to know
if your stay will be brief or stretch
to the end of one's days. My home is
a humble one, and the rooms are already filled with
solitude, so perhaps you could stay with
my sister instead. She is more deserving,
and has a bigger house.

('Letters from the Light to the Darkness', p. 49)

Stannard exploits cliché and sendup underpinned by a fairy-tale surrealism reminiscent of Kenneth Patchen's. The result can be at once comical and poignant:

I would try to spend Summer in my head
then discover I have a head of Winter. I must
have a head of Winter because snow
covers my hair, or my hair is snow, and ice forms
where a smile should be, or people
toboggan down my face and clamber up the back of
my neck in their heavy boots. Birds
who used to nest behind my ears appear
to have abandoned me for sunnier climes.

('How I Watch a Year Go By', p. 38)

Some poems take the form of outright satire, for example 'Appendix 2: A Test for Poets', others of affectionate parody, of the pastoral in 'Chronicles (3)'. Yet there is ever present a sense of elegy, which occasionally comes more directly to the surface, in poems like 'Things My Father Never Said' and 'To Nigel Pickard', though these too never lose a comical edge. Stannard's poetry is 'charming', a charm this reviewer finds hard to resist.

This is My Letter to the World

Katy Evans-Bush
Forgive the Language
Penned in the Margins, 2015

VALERIE DUFF-STRAUTMANN

The key to good blog readership is continual publication of work that reads conversationally to a general reader, and when Katy Evans-Bush blogs about 'poetry, arts & culture' (routinely on *Baroque in Hackney* since 2006), she works in that world of direct transfer. In the ether, her material is largely unedited, in the sense of having a disinterested third party who shapes it for publication. This puts *Forgive the Language*, her new book of essays, in a category that feels somewhat new (the way collecting private letters for publication at one time was new). These are not essays in the formal sense, nor are they book reviews, nor are they letters in a formal sense, either, but posts that seem to sense their limitless freedom.

But when the expanding and ever-shifting interests of blog writings coalesce into a unit (book), there's a certain disjunction. On the page, one wants to tease out threads from the vast picking and choosing and stumbling upon that happens in the web's endless continuum. The package in hand begins to resemble an anthology of an era's greatest hits with the inevitable sorting through and asking what it culminates into.

Evans-Bush's advantage is her consistently engaging voice, which never flags as the conversation twists and turns. In her essay about Dylan Thomas, she remembers her adolescent attraction to Thomas's writing, but when considering his staying power, she writes of the nuances of his Welsh background:

You don't need to speak a language to be influenced by it, if you are part of a culture that was formed out of the language and hear it all around you [...] In his 2003 Arena programme about Dylan Thomas, Nigel Williams talked about this rhetorical style, too, saying Thomas clearly picked it up from everywhere: from the preachers in

Swansea, from the air. Though this style of preaching has almost died out, he described Thomas as having the very Welsh (i.e. untranslatable) quality of *hwyl*.

That sort of stretch is made possible by the blog-osphere, and Evans-Bush plays it as a personal strength – the seamless movement from the general relatable pop response to a poet to an understated, individual, absorbing commentary on the man. Similarly, in 'Men's Troubles: Seidel, Ashbery, Elliott' (consider the range in the subtitle grouping alone), she chooses to include and examine the work of the polarizing Frederick Seidel:

Seidel is, in fact, a poet who wears his heart on his sleeve, and he gives himself the same treatment he metes out to others.

In the poem quoted above, the poet almost immediately adds, 'Don't be a ghoul. Don't be a fool, / You fool.' The frailty, fear, visceral physicality in the poems are always, at bottom, his.

And an essay that begins with Philippe Petit's *On the High Wire* transforms into an exploration of the tensions of the poetic line, with an examination of Sharon Olds among others as high-wire artist: 'Putting the stress on the first word of the line below [...] creates a sense of urgency as well as hesitancy, and disorients the reader, who then grabs for the emotional content as for a lifeline.' Evans-Bush's insights are unpredictable and the paths these essays travel are often their own reward.

My main criticism is not of the writer and the breadth of her writing, although at times I found myself looking for a place to rest in the midst of it. I do take the publisher to task for leaving it without design; if design is here, I don't find it intuitive. And I would have felt less wary of the project's guiding hand if I hadn't run across many typos – 'Virginia Woof', 'Wilfred Own' – which seem a spoof but ultimately detract from Evans-Bush's singular voice. These concerns put into question the project as a whole, and the no small undertaking to move from unedited to edited writing, from the expansive and ever-changing web to paper.

Home

Warsan Shire, *Her Blue Body*,
Flat Pamphlet Series (No. 14)

Laura Scott, *What I Saw*,
The Rialto, £5.50

Emily Wills, *Unmapped*,
The Rialto, £6.25

Martina Evans, *Watch*,
Rack Press, £5.00

Reviewed by
ALISON BRACKENBURY

'I brought the war with me': Warsan Shire was London's first Young Poet Laureate, part of the Olympic 'legacy'. Her pamphlet's cover describes her as 'a Kenyan-born Somali writer [...] raised in London'. Her poems reveal migrants' hidden pain: 'the war' ever present. 'I hear its damp breath'.

New British poetry does not often have such terrible subject matter as the legacy Shire confronts: genital mutilation. Her lines build quietly to a final, devastating word. A recovering girl is a 'mermaid with new legs / soft knees buckling'. 'Two girls lie in bed [...] comparing wounds.' But Shire also records a range of reactions, equally shocking – and involving. A boy, Hussein, explains (at school?) how it feels to have sex with a girl who has been sewn up. 'The girl beside me shudders'.

'At parties I point to my body and say *This is where love comes to die. Welcome, come in, make yourself at home*' ('The House'). In 'Her Blue Body Full of Light' cancer's terrible energy is poured into one long sentence, 'her throat a lava lamp, sparklers beneath breastbone –'. Shire's descriptive 'fireworks' are indeed brilliant, but selfless, dedicated to a loved body 'glowing and glowing, / lit from the inside'.

Her Blue Body is already out of print. I have reviewed it because of the wise strength of poems by a young writer ('working' her cover tells us, 'on her first full collection of poetry'). Displacement, disease and deliberate injury haunt Shire's work. Yet her poems make their home in love.

·

The poems in Laura Scott's fine first pamphlet are unusually at home with time:

How did you get here, old rose, were you smuggled
through a chink in the years on to the walls of my garden?

Scott's light syllables are as numerous as the rose petals: 'so many crinkled together'. Her lines illuminate many folds, in clothes, 'the pleats of her bodice', in time, 'the folds of her years'. Her rich, restrained work does not exclude intricacies of wealth and class. Her godmother's flat contains a 'damp maid's kitchen'.

As her title, *What I Saw*, suggests, Scott's poems are confident, with a rare 'gift to be simple'. But her view of the familiar is never static. A painter sees an egg near a candle: 'the heart beating right up against the shell'. *What I Saw* includes memories, from childhood, of adult conflict: 'To go to that house [...] 'his face still angry, hers, / harder to read'. There is humour and tenderness in her re-telling of *The Wizard of Oz*: 'even Toto gets clipped'. Then Scott's quiet 'and' leads to a plunging line division, of unexpected pain:

          and our voices aren't breaking yet
with that cry of home rushing up our throats.

Yet

                    I loved that
place, a pearl hanging on a necklace somewhere [...]

Art and imagination can enfold Scott and her reader: a momentary home. But her poems also embrace life's continued energy, in a daughter 'fizzing like sherbert'. She celebrates 'the air's joy'. Her own work is airily abundant: a delight.

·

Boldly and ruefully, Emily Wills' opening lines confront the 'manly poem' which offers no home for

          the usual mess of grief and bodily fluids
which have to be dealt with, of course,
in another kind of poem.

Skilled and strong-minded, Wills offers many kinds of poem in her compelling third collection, *Unmapped*. She is entirely at home with science: 'bits of double helix'. Her botanical precision is admirable: 'marram and thrift'. Yet she is also a chronicler of the dark side of domesticity. With unromanticised and rejected food, 'potatoes, sullen as damp towels', anorexia, Wills states bleakly, 'begins on washday'. Nor does her Girl Guide speaker duck teenage fury, when asked to tie knots: 'what was the fucking point?' I relished the bitter humour, in a prose poem, of late-night sewing of nametapes: 'just to prove you're not the sort of mother who uses the iron-on kind'.

Yet the dangerous 'Long Lane' leads to intense lyricism whose half rhymes link like generations:

          through treacherous bends,
and the scent of violets, to a son, and so on to my mother
calling into the lane, dusk fallen, the cows already home.

One of Wills' greatest gifts as a poet is her final surge of phrases, a grace like a lifting wave. Playing with nephews, her speaker recalls being 'the last to be chosen' for teams. Yet 'the last ball [...] through forty years, applauds / into my stunned and waiting grasp'. How many sympathetic readers will feel that ball hit home?

·

Watch is, by my calculation, Martina Evans' sixth poetry publication: brief, excellent – and hard-hitting: 'The night before my wedding / I put my wristwatch through the machine cycle'. Evans' tales are carefully told, in a recognisable voice, with the nonchalant ease of a novelist. An account of a daughter's birth lightly damns an ex-husband, twisting the tail of myth:

          too late for the epidural
I'd been persuaded was a must for a nervous person
like myself who was writing a poem about Persephone
during the second stages of labour and Pluto was –

where else? – down below in the pub.

                    ('My Persephone')

The speaker's view of her London house is factual but slightly nightmarish: 'some strange yellow / cauliflowers are growing / inside the kitchen walls'. This may be more familiar to many of us than an Ideal Home. But though her home is 'warm and small', the ruthless speaker does not want to meet its former inhabitants 'with moist green teeth', 'like the Irish fairies' (another cultural legacy sharply reviewed!) She is, however, a perceptive observer of cats: 'Their pupils fill with black to allow / more light'.

Evans' poem 'London' offers a warm final twist: 'Feverishly, I return always running / from Ireland' to 'the babble on the 76 of 77 languages'. Here is Warsan Shire's city, sheltering, however inadequately, its migrants and refugees. Here, Evans' speaker, generous and keen-eyed, waiting for her London bus as 'in the black night', sees 'in a blaze / the lights of home'.

Calm Stars

Philip Gross
Love Songs of Carbon
Bloodaxe Books, 2015 (£9.95)

Reviewed by
EDMUND PRESTWICH

Love Songs of Carbon explores what it is to be a mind in an aging body, a self mysteriously and precariously alive in the physical world. As the title suggests, Gross combines lyrical subjectivity with science-based reflection.

Extended metaphors evoke the outer world's impact on the mind, as in this comparison of child-hood days to raindrops:

> each hung from the dark top lip of window,
>
> sometimes glittering, more often grey,
> with an upside-down world in it, tiny and shivering.

They often address the fraught relations both between the body and the mind, and within the body and mind themselves:

> **This body,**
>
> brute
> fact, given thing
>
> that winces sometimes
> from the mere jolt of itself

Time's pressure is keenly felt, in ways that bring together hard biological observation and the sugges-tiveness of the poetic image:

> **Translucence**
>
> : with time
> the skin thins; we become more see-through
> as if the drip
> of it, passing, was diluting us.

The last two quotations illustrate how Gross exper-iments with layout to control the way his poems are spoken. Such fine-tuning has a price. It can work brilliantly to capture movements of thought or movement in the visible world, but in weaker poems can seem fussy and restrictive. Even in strong ones, by limiting the reader's freedom to speak the words in different ways, it limits the poem's ability to layer tones and let them play against each other. For me, the most impressive formal achievement is 'Epstein's Adam', which combines a relatively conventional sonnet framework with the distinctive cadences that in other poems are visually defined by stepped free verse lines. Here, the reader seems to be taking in two quite different kinds of formal organization simultaneously. Moreover, by loosen-ing his control on how the poem is spoken Gross allows it to change and grow in our imaginations.

Though Gross's father was an intensely-felt presence in the poet's previous two collections, you don't get a strong sense of *people as individuals* in this one, except in 'A Love Song of Carbon' itself. This weakens the endings of several poems appar-ently addressed to Gross's wife. Their intimate note might ring true among family and friends, but an outsider needs a sense of the addressee to be created by the poem. 'Love in the Scanner' is an example. The last line falls flat. However, the rest of the poem achieves considerable power by rapid shifts of perspective, from the awkwardness of the modern young love-makers climbing into the MRI machine to the raw exposure of a bride in times when proofs of virginity and consummation were expected of the marriage night, then on to the mechanical obser-vation of the scanner, which records lovemaking as pure movement of matter. In the last stanza, Gross turns the whole description into a metaphor for what's left of life and love for the speaker and his partner in the last stretch of their lives, exposed to the inhuman gaze of time and the stars in lines that serenely accept the littleness of a human life within the vastness of the cosmic order:

> We're as still
> as those two must be
> yet do what they came for,
> here in the narrowing space
>
> of our lives, with years and calm stars
> turning round us...

SOME CONTRIBUTORS

Paul Batchelor was born in Northumberland and currently teaches at Durham University. He has published a book, *The Sinking Road* (Bloodaxe, 2008), and a chapbook, *The Love Darg* (Clutag, 2014), and has received various awards including the *Times* Stephen Spender Prize for Translation. www.paul-batchelor.co.uk. **Stephen Burt** is Professor of English at Harvard and the author of several books of poetry and literary criticism, among them *The Poem Is You: 60 Contemporary American Poems & How to Read Them*, due autumn 2016 from Harvard University Press. **Simon Collings** lives in Oxford, UK. He has published poetry, short stories, and reviews in a number of journals and eZines. https://simoncollings. wordpress.com/. **Patrick Cotter** lives in Cork, Ireland. Recent work has appeared or is about to appear in the *Financial Times*, *Poetry* and *Poetry Review*. **John Dennison** was born in Sydney in 1978 and grew up in Wellington. He is the author of *Otherwise* (Carcanet; Auckland University Press, 2015) and *Seamus Heaney and the Adequacy of Poetry* (OUP, 2015). He lives with his family in Wellington, where he is a university chaplain. **Mark Dow**'s e-chapbook 'Feedback' and Other *Conversation Poems* is online at *Mudlark: An Electronic Journal of Poetry and Poetics*. He was writer-in-res-idence for the 2016 International Conference on the Evolution of Language in New Orleans. **Valerie Duff-Strautmann** is poetry editor at *Salamander*. Her poems and reviews have appeared in *AGNI*, *The Boston Globe*, *The Critical Flame*, *Salamander*, *The San Francisco Chronicle*, *The Wolf*, and elsewhere. **Ken Edwards**'s most recent book is *Country Life* (Unthank Books, 2015). The sequence in this issue is excerpted from *a book with no name*, to be published shortly by Shearsman. **Jerzy Ficowski** (1924–2006) was a prolific poet, songwriter, and scholar on the Polish Roma population. Recent translations of Ficowski's work into English have appeared in *American Poetry Review*, *Poetry*, *The Nation*, *New York Review of Books*, *Ploughshares*, and elsewhere. **Roger Garfitt** has just recorded *In All My Holy Mountain*, a celebration in poetry and jazz of the life and work of Mary Webb, to a score by Nikki Iles. **Florian Gargaillo** is a PhD candidate at Boston University, working on modern poetry and public rhetoric. His essays have appeared, or are forthcoming, in the *Yale Review*, *Literary Imagination*, and the *Journal of Commonwealth Literature*. **John Greening**'s recent books include *Heath* (with Penelope Shuttle), and the music anthology *Accompanied Voices*. His collection *To the War Poets* was published by Carcanet in 2013. **Jennifer Grotz**'s third book of poems, *Window Left Open*, recently appeared from Graywolf Press. She is director of the Bread Loaf Translators' Conference. **S. A. Leavesley** edits V. Press and won the Overton Poetry Prize 2015. Her latest pamphlet is *Lampshades & Glass Rivers* (Loughborough University, 2016). A poetry-play, *The Magnetic Diaries*, tours the UK in 2016. **William Logan**'s new book of poetry, *Rift of Light*, will be published next summer by Penguin USA. **Duncan MacKay** is a Senior Research Fellow at the Centre for Astrophysics & Planetary Science, University of Kent, Canterbury; he is also engaged in research at the Centre for Modern Poetry in the School of English. **Maitreyabandhu** has won the Keats-Shelley Prize, the Basil Bunting Award, and the Geoffrey Dearmer Prize. His debut collection, *The Crumb Road* (Bloodaxe, 2013) is a PBS Recommendation. *Yarn* (also with Bloodaxe) was published in autumn 2015. **Robyn Marsack** edited *Fall In, Ghosts: Selected War Prose* by Edmund Blunden (Carcanet, 2014). She was Director of the Scottish Poetry Library 2000–2016. **James McGonigal** is Edwin Morgan's biographer and literary executor, and co-edited his *The Midnight Letterbox: Selected Correspondence 1950–2010* (Carcanet Press, 2015). **André Naffis-Sahely**'s *The Promised Land* will be published by Penguin in 2017. **Samira Negrouche** was born in Algeria in 1980. Trained as a doctor, she has for the past few years devoted herself to literary work – her own poetry, editing, translation, and literary collaboration. *Le Jazz des oliviers* was published by Les Editions du Till (Algeria) in 2010. **Mary Noonan** lectures in French literature at University College Cork. *The Fado House* (Dedalus Press, 2012) was shortlisted for the Seamus Heaney Centre Prize and the Strong/Shine Award. *Father* was published in a limited edition by Bonnefant Press in 2015. For his translations from the Italian **Todd Portnowitz** received fellowships from the Academy of American Poets (Raiziss/de Palchi, 2015) and the Bread Loaf Translators Conference. His poems, translations and essays have appeared in *Asymptote*, *Guernica*, *Poetry*, *Modern Poetry in Translation*, *Agni* and elsewhere. He lives and works in New York. **Ian Seed**'s most recent collection of poetry is *Identity Papers* (Shearsman, 2016). His translation of Pierre Reverdy's *Le Voleur de Talan* will be published by Wakefield Press in autumn 2016. **Piotr Sommer** is the author of *Continued* (Wesleyan University Press) and *Overdoing It* (Hobart and William Smith Colleges Press). His collected poems, *Po Ciemku Też* (*Also in the Dark*) appeared in Poland in 2013. **Jack Thacker** grew up on a farm in Herefordshire. He is currently a PhD student in English at the Universities of Bristol and Exeter. **John Welch**'s *Collected Poems* were published by Shearsman in 2008. There have been two further collections from the same publisher since then, most recently *Its Halting Measure* in 2012. **Peter Zervos** is from Athens, Greece. He holds a M.A., a M.F.A. and a Ph.D. from Indiana University Bloomington. He teaches academic writing, creative writing, and literature at The American College of Greece.

--- COLOPHON ---

Editors
Michael Schmidt (General)
Luke Allan (Deputy)

Cover
Hannah Devereux
2016

Design
Set in Arnhem (Fred Smeijers) and
Freight (Joshua Darden) by LA.

Editorial address
The Editors at the address on
the right. Manuscripts cannot be
returned unless accompanied by a
stamped self-addressed envelope
or international reply coupon.

Subscriptions (6 issues)
individuals: £39/$86
institutions: £49/$105
to: PN Review, Alliance House
30 Cross Street, Manchester
M2 7AQ, UK

Represented by
Compass Independent Publishing
    Services Ltd
Great West House, Great West Road
Brentford TW8 9DF, UK
sales@compass-ips.london

Trade distributors
NBN International
10 Thornbury Road
Plymouth PL6 7PP, UK
orders@nbninternational.com

Copyright
© 2016 Poetry Nation Review
All rights reserved
ISBN 978-1-78410-141-1
ISSN 0144-7076

Supported by